BOATING
SKILLS &
SEAMANSHIP

U.S. COAST GUARD AUXILIARY

FOREWORD

It has long been recognized that knowledge is the route to greater boating safety and increased boating pleasure. With this conviction the Coast Guard Auxiliary strives to reach and teach as many of the boating public as possible. The rapid growth of recreational boating makes this no easy task, but one well worth the effort in terms of problems avoided and lives saved.

This text, prepared by the Auxiliary, is a comprehensive course, expanded to include new areas in the realm of boating activity. The Boating Skills and Seamanship course is designed to awaken new safety awareness and provide for greater proficiency that will make the boating experience more safe and trouble free.

As Commandant of the United States Coast Guard, I strongly commend the Auxiliary for its concern for safe boating and for the development of this course, which I heartily recommend to all boatmen as a step toward safer recreational boating on America's waters.

O. W. SILER
Admiral, U. S. Coast Guard
Commandant

Preface

You are about to enter into an adventure in reading that will not only add to your pleasure but will enrich your knowledge. BOATING SKILLS AND SEAMANSHIP, used in connection with the United States Coast Guard Auxiliary Public Education Program, will give you the answer to those problems encountered in the fastest growing sport in the world, pleasure boating.

The United States Coast Guard Auxiliary has drawn upon the experiences of its over 47,000 members to enrich the knowledge of not only America's pleasure boating enthusiasts but also of thousands of other boaters around the world.

The BOATING SKILLS AND SEAMANSHIP Education Course presented by qualified Auxiliary Instructors will give you a broad boating education. The completion of these lessons ensures the knowledge and understanding necessary to cope with almost any situation in which you find yourself during the enjoyment of this great water adventure.

This course has been prepared by our Department of Education with the guidance, assistance and cooperation of the United States Coast Guard. We are greatly indebted to them for their outstanding efforts in the preparation of this textbook.

J. Kevin Mitchell
National Commodore
United States Coast Guard Auxiliary

April, 1977

Contents

CHAPTER 1

The Safe Way to Boating Enjoyment

Introduction

Pleasure boating as a family sport is growing in popularity with each passing day. Our modern industrial technology has given us more leisure time than ever before in our history. As a result, American families in ever-increasing numbers are turning to the water for their recreation. They are finding that boating is one of the few outdoor sports that can be enjoyed as a family—it's as much fun for mom and dad as it is for the youngsters.

However, with any outdoor sport, certain hazards may be encountered and pleasure boating is no exception. Knowledge of potential hazards and reasons why accidents occur should be a part of every boatman's education. Chapter 1 outlines this information. Detailed information contained in the remaining chapters will enable the conscientious boatman to operate a vessel in the safest manner. To fully enjoy the pleasures of boating, every effort should be expended toward becoming well informed.

In recent years, refinements in hull design and modern production methods have placed safe, well-designed pleasure craft of every description within the reach of a vast multitude of Americans. It is safe to say that if the present trend continues we will soon become a nation of boat owners.

In order to serve the needs and comforts of our expanding boating population, marinas and marine facilities can now be found on every body of navigable water in the country. These marinas offer a variety of products and services to help make it pleasant and convenient for families to enjoy the sport of pleasure boating. Reputable manufacturers and dealers of marine products offer an endless array of equipment and accessories to make our boating safer and more trouble free. In addition, several boating-safety oriented organizations now make it possible to learn the rudiments of safe boating in an organized manner in classes designed especially for the beginner boatman. The United States Coast Guard Auxiliary is among the leaders in this endeavor. The purpose of these courses is to introduce to all owners and operators of pleasure craft, safety requirements and safe practices in the operation and navigation of their boats. The secret of boating safety is *KEEPING OUT* of trouble rather than *GETTING OUT* of trouble after you get into it.

Boating Accidents

Unfortunately it is a fact that some of our pleasure boatmen do manage to get into trouble afloat and, in some cases, end up as "statistics" in the local press.

Every year the United States Coast Guard publishes a BOATING STATISTICS REPORT. This report is called Coast Guard Publication CG-357, and copies of this report are available to the public on request to Commandant (G-BP), U.S. Coast Guard, Washington, D.C. 20590. This report covers accident reports from all fifty states and also includes the Virgin Islands and Puerto Rico.

From a five year study, the following statistics were obtained: There were 4,917 boating accidents involving 6,230 vessels. These accidents resulted in 1,537 fatalities, 1,291 personal injuries and over 9.4 million dollars in property damage. A lot of lives, injuries and money! Can this be prevented? The answer is an emphatic YES! Most boating accidents are the result of a lack of knowledge on the part of the boatman. Let's look briefly at the record in each category.

Fatalities

The record shows that year after year more lives are lost as the result of vessels capsizing than any other type of casualty. Why do vessels capsize? In most cases the operator is at fault. Standing in the boat and improper loading are the principal reasons, and ignoring weather warnings ranks next. Unfavorable weather and sea conditions which exceed the capabilities of the craft and the operator's training or experience cause many boats to capsize. Even under the best of conditions, if a boat is improperly loaded, it can (and all too often does) capsize without warning. Large steamships have capsized when all passengers rushed to one side. The load must be distributed properly if the boat is to handle well.

Weight Carrying Capability

When loading your boat, weight should be evenly distributed from bow (front) to stern (back) and athwartships (from side to side). The more weight you put into a boat, the deeper it sinks into the water, thus reducing the amount of freeboard. Freeboard is the vertical distance from the gunwale (pronounced gun'l), or top edge of the hull, to the water. The more you reduce the freeboard, the greater the tendency to swamp (fill with water) or capsize. An overloaded or improperly loaded boat is unstable and dangerous. Many boats today have a capacity plate, generally on the instrument panel where it can be easily seen, which indicates its weight-carrying capacity. Remember, this is the recommended maximum weight. Whether you should carry this amount of weight depends on several factors.

The first factor to consider is the anticipated sea-state, or water condition. It is important to realize that if rough water is expected, less weight should be carried. A heavily laden boat will ship water more easily than one which is riding higher in the water. Watch your freeboard. Many small boats have swamped or capsized when they were loaded to the point where they had insufficient freeboard.

The second factor to consider would be the activity in which you expect to engage while under way. For instance, if you want to do some fishing it's possible that persons will stand up occasionally in the boat. Standing up in a small boat is extremely

1-1 Overpowering and Improper Loading Resulted in this Swamping.

dangerous, especially if it is done in choppy water conditions or if the boat is too heavily laden. By standing up you will change the center of gravity of the boat and, if the hull is being buffeted about appreciably, it could cause the boat to capsize, or for you to fall overboard.

Other factors would be the weight of the equipment, fuel, tools, food and other gear which will be carried. The more gear that is loaded aboard, the less passenger-carrying capacity you will have left. Under Federal regulations, all monohull boats less than 20 feet in length whose construction began on or after 1 November 1972 must display capacity information by means of a capacity plate. The exceptions to the rule are sailboats, canoes, kayaks and inflatable boats.

In the absence of a capacity plate, a rough guide for weight-carrying would be as follows:

Boat Length	Number of Persons	OR Maximum Weight Load
10 feet	2	410 lbs
12 feet	3	575 lbs
14 feet	4	740 lbs
16 feet	5	975 lbs

Know your boat. Know what it can do and what it cannot do, and how it will handle in all kinds of weather. Don't load more weight aboard than recommended by the capacity plate. The ideal boat should have positive buoyancy. This means that it should float even if filled with water or capsized.

If your boat has level flotation, stay in the boat, because it will most likely remain afloat. You should see to it that nobody attempts to swim for shore. Remember, the chance of being located by a search plane or boat is far greater if all hands stay with the boat and hang on.

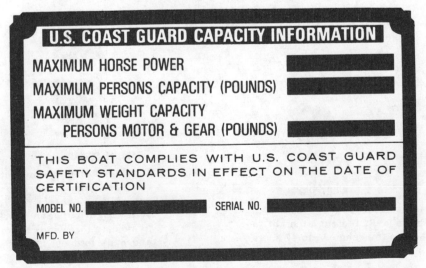

1-2 Capacity Plate for Outboards

1-3 Capacity Plate for Inboards, etc.

1-4 Certificate of Compliance

1-5 Combination Capacity Plate and Certificate of Compliance

For rough weather conditions it is important to carry considerably less than the maximum allowable weight. If rough water is expected, one should give serious consideration to whether the boat should be used at all. This is particularly true for boats under 16 feet in length which may be suitable for calm conditions only.

Weather Conditions

At selected locations in and near boating areas, storm warnings are displayed by flag hoists or lights. Display points may be Coast Guard stations, marinas, lighthouses or municipal piers. Boatmen should become familiar with the display points in their area and the meanings of the signals displayed. The small craft advisory is a red triangular pennant by day and a red light over a white light by night. The display of this signal means that conditions are expected to be unsafe for small craft. Don't ignore this warning.

As an aid to boatmen in getting weather information, the U. S. Weather Bureau publishes *COASTAL WARNING FACILITIES CHARTS* for local areas on the Atlantic, Pacific and Gulf Coasts as

SMALL CRAFT

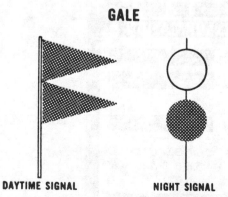

DAYTIME SIGNAL   **NIGHT SIGNAL**

One RED pennant displayed by day and a RED light over a WHITE light at night to indicate winds as high as 33 knots (38 m.p.h.) and/or sea conditions considered dangerous to small craft operations are forecast for the area.

STORM

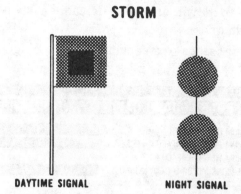

DAYTIME SIGNAL   **NIGHT SIGNAL**

A single square RED flag with a BLACK center displayed during daytime and two RED lights at night to indicate that winds 48 knots (55 m.p.h.) and above are forecast for the area. If the winds are associated with a tropical cyclone (hurricane), the "Storm Warning" display indicates winds 48 to 63 knots (55 to 73 m.p.h.) are forecast.

HURRICANE

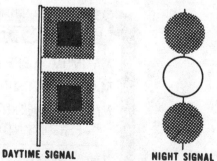

DAYTIME SIGNAL   **NIGHT SIGNAL**

Displayed only in connection with a tropical cyclone (hurricane). Two square RED flags with BLACK centers displayed by day and a WHITE light between two RED lights at night to indicate that winds 64 knots (74 m.p.h.) and above are forecast for the area.

GALE

DAYTIME SIGNAL   **NIGHT SIGNAL**

Two RED pennants displayed by day and a WHITE light above a RED light at night to indicate winds within the range 34 to 47 knots (39 to 54 m.p.h.) are forecast for the area.

1-6   Warning Display Signals

well as the Great Lakes, Puerto Rico and Hawaii. These charts give the locations and telephone numbers of all Weather Bureau offices and the location and time schedules of all AM, FM and TV stations that broadcast marine weather information. Also included are the weather broadcast schedules of marine radiotelephone stations and air navigation radio stations. Additionally, the location of all storm warning display stations are also shown, with an explanation of their meanings. These charts can be obtained by writing to the Superintendent of Documents, Government Printing Office, Washington, D.C., 20401, and stating the local area desired.

Marine Weather Forecasts

Weather sense begins before leaving your slip. Many centers of boating activity have a nearby National Weather Service office that provides marine weather forecasts by phone 24 hours a day — look under *United States Government — Department of Commerce* in your directory. A marine weather forecast should be part of every boatman's routine preparations before casting off. If your FM radio receives bands as high on the scale as 162 MHz, you can probably get the Weather Radio Service of the National Oceanic and Atmospheric Administration (NOAA). These continuous broadcasts consist of taped weather messages repeated every four to six minutes and revised four or more times every 24 hours. Special warnings concerning fast-developing weather conditions of potential danger to the mariner are put on the air immediately.

NOAA Weather Radio stations are located at key points around the coasts and inland. Their effective range is 25 to 50 miles and there are three frequencies in use — 162.40, 162.55 and 162.475 MHz. Nearly all marine VHF-FM transceivers offer receive-only channels for at least two of these stations; your local weather service office can tell you the frequencies of the Weather Radio station nearest you.

Also available are inexpensive VHF-FM receivers that have only the Weather Service channels. Some of these sets are equipped with an audible alarm, triggered when the Weather Service broadcasts a special signal that indicates a weather warning will follow: Thus, the set may be left on at minimum volume, but you're sure of being alerted to any storm warning.

1-7 Speed and Inattention

1-5

Falls Overboard

Falls overboard and vessel sinkings were the second and third major types of casualties resulting in boating fatalities. As a boat operator, you must recognize these dangers and learn how to avoid them. High Speed turns are the principal causes of falls overboard and vessel capsizings.

Collisions

Of 1291 personal injury cases, about half were attributed to collisions. The principal cause of a vessel colliding with another vessel or with a fixed object is failure of the operator to maintain an efficient forward lookout. Water skiing has contributed significantly to this problem. It's impossible to watch the skier and the area ahead of the boat at the same time. Some states have enacted laws which require a wide-angle rear view mirror, or a second person in the boat to watch the skier. Some states also limit the number of skiers that may be towed at one time.

If your boat is equipped with an automatic pilot, don't set it and forget it. An automatic pilot is an ingenious instrument but it will not steer around obstructions nor take over for you in a potential collision stiuation with another boat. There is no mechanical replacement for the operator.

Fires and Explosions

Fires and explosions resulted in the second largest number of personal injuries. A number of things can cause a fire aboard your boat. Among these are careless smoking, spontaneous combustion caused by oil or gasoline soaked rags or paper left aboard instead of being disposed of on shore, an electrical short, a flame-up of the galley stove or ignition of gasoline that has not been contained properly. Explosions occur when there is the correct mixture of gasoline and air, and this explosive vapor is ignited by a spark. A gas tank could leak at any time and, if the engine is running, ignition is introduced to the situation. Remove any one of these ingredients and you will not have an explosion. Perhaps the best way to prevent an explosion is to keep the gaso-

line and air mixture from reaching the explosive point. This is accomplished by thoroughly ventilating the areas where explosive mixtures are most likely to form. Gasoline vapors are heavier than air and will seek the lowest parts of the bilge spaces. Consequently, these areas are the ones that must be well ventilated.

Be defensive against causes of fires and explosions. Three steps are necessary to reduce the chance of flammable vapors collecting in your boat: (a) have a safe fuel system aboard and maintain it in good condition; (b) observe all safety precautions in handling volatile fuels; and (c) have a good ventilation system to conduct fresh air into each fuel tank and engine compartment to remove vapors from the bilges to the open atmosphere. Three of the federal requirements for motor boats (flame arresters, fire extinguishers and adequate ventilation) are intended to minimize the danger of fire and explosion. This is sufficient evidence of the seriousness of the fire and explosion hazards in engine and fuel tank compartments. The galley is another potential fire hazard. Electric, alcohol, kerosene, butane, coal and wood burning cooking appliances are recommended types for use on boats. Gasoline stoves should never be used. The stove should be fastened securely in place. The counter top and bulkheads (vertical partitions) around the stove should be protected with a fire-proof material. Curtains and draperies which are near the stove should be of flame retardant material and should be tied back before lighting the stove. Do not place a fire extinguisher on a bulkhead in such a position that you must reach through a fire to get to it. Mount it nearby where it can be easily grasped. Fire extinguishers should be checked and serviced regularly, and as soon as possible after use.

Correct Fueling Procedures

In spite of the fact that regulations concerning ventilation of engine and fuel tank spaces are now being clarified and widely enforced, many boats explode every year. Most explosions in inboard powered boats occur shortly after refueling. Refueling is dangerous. But, if certain precautions are carefully observed, many of the potential hazards of refueling can be controlled.

1-8 A Fractured
Fuel Line and
A Loose Battery
Cable Connection.

1. Be sure that the boat is moored securely to the fuel float or wharf.

2. Extinguish all fires aboard the boat. This means cigarettes, cigars, pipes, galley stoves and other appliances which have an open flame. Also, turn off all electric motors which may be running.

3. Close all doors, windows, portlights, hatches or other openings which may allow fumes to enter the bilge spaces of the boat.

4. Remove the gas filler cap and secure it so that it will not fall overboard. Estimate the approximate number of gallons the tank will take. This is a precaution against taking on more gas than your tank should hold. If this should happen, lift a hatch and inspect the bilges immediately to see where the gas is going! Gasoline flowing through the fill pipe could create static electricity. While fueling, it is imperative that you do not allow static electricity to build up and discharge. This can be controlled by grounding the hose nozzle firmly against the fuel pipe intake fitting. A fuel hose should never be left

unattended while fuel is flowing through the hose. Even though some nozzles are equipped with shut-off devices which shut off the flow when the tank is full, if the nozzle were to slip out of the fill pipe it could be pouring gasoline over the side or into your boat. While fueling, it is good practice to watch for gasoline fumes which should be coming out of the fuel tank vent pipe. This vent pipe should vent overboard. If you do not see fumes the vent may be plugged and should be cleaned. When the tank is nearly full, gasoline may discharge from the vent, which is not unusual. This gasoline may discolor your paint in addition to being a fire hazard, so it should be washed down as soon as possible.

5. When the tank is full, replace the filler cap and wipe up any gasoline that may have spilled. Then wash down the area thoroughly. Place gasoline soaked rags in a tightly sealed metal container and dispose of them later on shore.

6. Open all portlights, hatches, doors and windows. This should allow any fumes which may have

entered the closed areas to escape. If you have a bilge blower, turn it on. Allow the boat to ventilate for at least five minutes. Then check the bilge areas for fumes. Remember, gasoline vapors are heavier than air and will seek the lowest point in the boat. Even though it may appear undignified, stick your nose down in the bilge and check for vapors. Expensive bilge-sniffing devices are fine, but they are not infallible.

7. After you have done all of the above and are satisfied that there are no fumes present, you may start the engine.

Outboard powered boats with portable fuel tanks should not be fueled with the tanks in the boat. Portable fuel tanks should be lifted out of the boat and placed on the wharf to be fueled. Do not attempt to do the job alone. Pass the tank to the attendant on the wharf and, after fueling, have it passed back to you. Don't forget to secure the tank and wipe up and wash down any fuel which may have spilled. If there are any decked-over areas on the boat be certain to ventilate thoroughly for at least five minutes before starting the engine.

To review briefly the safe fueling practices:

1. Boat moored securely.
2. All flames extinguished.
3. All openings closed.
4. Hose nozzle grounded.
5. Wipe up and wash down.
6. Ventilate thoroughly, check for fumes.
7. Start engine.

Unsafe fueling practices, lack of experience, faulty fuel tank installations, and improper wiring of engines and equipment accounted for more than 60% of vessel explosions and fires in cases where the cause of the accident could be determined.

Personal Flotation Devices (PFD)

All federal, state and local laws require at least one Coast Guard approved personal flotation device (PFD) aboard and readily available for every person on board the boat.

An average of 1,396 persons drown each year in boating accidents. In a recent study of personal flotation device usage in boating accidents, it was noted that 74.8% of the persons involved in an accident had personal flotation devices available at the time of the accident. Only 26.6% of these people actually used the PFDs. A PFD is a device which when properly used will support a person in the water.

Most boatmen comply with the law which requires them to have an adequate number of Coast Guard approved personal flotation devices aboard. However, in all too many cases these devices were stowed in places where they could not be grabbed quickly when needed. In numerous other instances nobody knew how to use them. Personal flotation devices are effective only when available and properly used. These devices should be treated as though your life may well depend on them.

Be sure to provide personal flotation devices for all hands aboard. These must be Coast Guard

1-9 Type I
(Life Preserver)

1-10 Type II
(Life Vest)

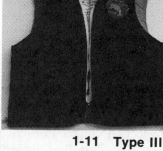

1-11 Type III
(Ski Jacket)

1-12
Type IV (Throwable)

PERSONAL FLOTATION DEVICES (PFD)

approved, kept readily available, in good condition and of appropriate sizes. This applies to all boats, regardless of size. Prudent boatmen generally carry more personal flotation devices than they expect to need. It is better to have a few extra devices aboard and not need them than to need them and not have them. PFDs should be worn by all hands when inclement conditions are expected, and by children and non-swimmers at all times.

How to Enjoy Your Boat Safely

Cruising

Cruising is the most popular form of pleasure boating. Places to go, sights to see, fresh air, relaxation and family fun; these are the ingredients of pleasure cruising. You may cruise along a shore or you may strike out across open waters. Carefree days afloat should not end in tragedy. You can insure this by taking a few simple precautions. Avoid becoming a "statistic" by paying attention to some common-sense rules for safe cruising:

Before shoving off, study your chart for places of shelter in case of bad weather. Familiarize yourself with all aids to navigation and tides and currents that may be encountered. Be sure that you have enough fuel to get where you intend to go. It's a good idea to have twice as much as you will need, to allow for water conditions which may cause you to use more fuel than anticipated. Be sure that your compass is operating properly and don't place metal objects nearby which could deflect the compass and give you a false heading. Learn to trust your compass. If properly maintained it's a very reliable instrument.

Have plenty of line on board so that you may properly secure the boat wherever your journey may take you. If your boat is wired for 110-volt shore power be sure to have extra extension cords aboard, as you may be required to tie up some distance from a power outlet. It is also advisable to carry a double outlet and spare fuses. If a number of boats are using the same outlet, the voltage to your boat may be low and, as a result, cooking on an electric stove may take longer than expected. If you have an electric refrigerator, low voltage could cause the unit to overheat. Also, be certain that no electric cords are allowed to hang down into the water.

1-13   Forward Lookout.

If you cannot find space along a wharf, it may become necessary to anchor overnight. It is best not to attempt this unless weather conditions are good. Carry two anchors with plenty of line. If possible, put down a bow anchor and a stern anchor. This will keep your boat from swinging around with changes in the wind or current, and possibly colliding with another boat. When anchoring, lower the anchor over the side hand over hand — don't throw it. Anchor well clear of navigable channels and don't forget to light your anchor light at night. Anchor lights will be discussed in the chapter on Rules of the Road and the art of anchoring is discussed in some detail in Chapter Three, Boat Handling.

If it is impossible or undesirable to anchor, you may consider asking a fellow boatman whose boat is tied to a wharf if you can tie up to his boat. This is the nautical version of "double parking" and is known as rafting. Several boats can be rafted together.

What are the hazards of cruising? The most common type of accident while cruising is collision with another vessel. Failure to maintain an efficient forward lookout, or careless and negligent operation on the part of the operator, are the major causes of most collisions. The second most common type is collision with a fixed object. There is little excuse for this type of accident but each year an average of 2,700 vessels collide with other vessels and 535 vessels collide with fixed objects resulting in an average of 608 lives lost in cruising accidents.

Keep a good lookout. Your primary consideration should be the area ahead and on the right side of your boat. Vessels approaching from the right (starboard) side have the right of way over your boat and you should keep clear of them. This will be discussed in the chapter on RULES OF THE ROAD. It's a good idea to look all around the horizon occasionally to see what is going on around you.

Hunting and Fishing

Hunters and fishermen often use their boats as a form of conveyance rather than for boating enjoyment. Many of them are not aware of the potential dangers of boating and, as a result, it is estimated that in the last few years hunters and fishermen have been involved in approximately 24% of all boating fatalities. Hunters and fishermen often become so engrossed in their sport that they forget all about the weather. If they happen to notice the weather, they may think they can beat the weather and make it back safely to shore. Many times they find themselves on the sheltered side of an island or in a sheltered cove. When they start their journey back they are surprised by the water conditions on the unsheltered side which must be contended with in order to get back to port. Hunters and fishermen would be well advised to wait in sheltered waters until sea conditions improve before attempting to return home. It could save their lives!

Fishermen may get fishing lines tangled around the propeller, rudder, outboard engine or anchor line. In attempting to disengage these lines they often lean too far over the side, with the result that falls overboard are commonplace. To compound this even further, fishing lines sometimes get tangled around a fisherman who has fallen in the water, thus seriously impairing his ability to swim. Most hunters and fishermen carry a sharp sheath knife. This knife should be kept in the sheath at all times when it is not actually being used. This knife could be used to cut the lines and possibly save his life.

A hunter should never stand up in a small boat to shoot. The recoil could knock him overboard. Most high-powered rifles and shotguns recoil considerably and should be fired from a sitting position in a small boat. By using common sense most tragedies might be averted, with the result that more hunting and fishing trips could have a happy ending.

Swimming

Some boatmen use their boats as swimming and diving platforms. A secluded cove with deep, clear water can be most attractive. Swimming and diving are a lot of fun but common sense should not be overlooked. It is usually best to anchor the boat before the swimming party begins. If yours is a shallow draft boat (one which can float in very shallow water), the wind could cause the boat to drift away at a good rate of speed. One person should remain aboard to act as a life guard and to see that the anchor doesn't drag. It is good practice to tie a long line to a life ring and secure the other end to the boat. This should be allowed to drift in the area of the swimmers. Before anyone dives in, the best swimmer aboard should enter the water cautiously to determine the depth as well as inspect the bottom for underwater obstructions. Swimming and sun bathing are as synonymous as sun bathing and sunburn. The sun's rays reflecting off the water, as well as its direct rays, can result in a serious sunburn in a very short time. Keep sunbathing periods shorter than usual and make sure the first aid kit contains ointments for use in such cases.

Water Skiing

Water skiing is increasing in popularity in all parts of the country. Skiers skim over the water at speeds of 25 knots and upwards. Two skis, slalom, backwards, no hands—real fun! How safe? It can be very safe if the skier wears a Coast Guard approved personal flotation device and the boat operator knows what he is doing. Here are a few pointers which will insure your safety without spoiling your fun:

1. Install a wide-angle, rear-view mirror or take along a second person in the boat to watch the skier. In this way an efficient watch can be maintained both fore and aft. Some states require the mirror or an observer as a matter of law.

FASTER

SLOWER

SPEED O.K.

RIGHT TURN

LEFT TURN

BACK TO DROP-OFF AREA

CUT MOTOR

STOP

SKIER O.K. AFTER FALL

PICK ME UP OR
FALLEN SKIER — WATCH OUT

1-14   Water Ski Hand Signals

2. Don't tow a skier in heavily traveled or restricted waters such as anchorages, swimming or fishing areas, narrow winding channels or around piers, floats or buoys.

3. Make sure that the skier is wearing a Coast Guard approved personal flotation device. If he tumbles, the boat should come about and approach him from the lee side.

4. Stop the engine before taking the skier on board.

5. While taking the skier on board be careful not to swamp the boat. In smaller craft it is usually safer to take a person aboard over the stern.

The following set of hand signals is recommended by the American Water Ski Association:

FASTER — Palm pointing upward.

SLOWER — Palm pointing downward.

SPEED O. K. — Arm upraised with thumb and forefinger forming a circle.

RIGHT TURN — Arm outstretched pointing to the right.

LEFT TURN — Arm outstretched pointing to the left.

BACK TO DROP-OFF AREA — Arm at 45 degree angle from body pointing down to water and swinging.

CUT MOTOR — Finger drawn across the throat.

STOP — Hand up, palm forward, policeman style.

SKIER O. K. AFTER FALL — Hands clenched overhead.

PICK ME UP, OR FALLEN SKIER — WATCH OUT — One ski extended vertically out of the water.

(See page 1-11 for Illustration)

Skin Diving

A relatively new flag is appearing on our waters. It has a red-orange background with a white diagonal stripe from corner to corner. This is the divers' flag. When you see it flying from a boat, or from a float, do not approach too closely or attempt to pass between the flag and the nearby shore. This flag indicates that there are divers down in the area and it requests you to keep clear. If you have ever seen a person who has been cut by a boat's propeller, you will not easily forget it. The International Code Flag B (BRAVO) A (ALFA) may also be used with the same meaning.

Cold Water Survival

The loss of body heat is probably the greatest hazard to the survival of a human being immersed in cool water, be it a pond or the ocean. The body's core must be maintained at a temperature close to

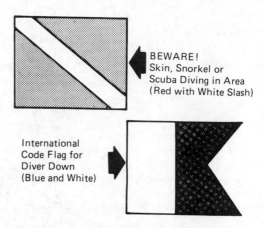

1-15 Beware — Diving in Area

98.6° F, and when the body's surroundings are considerably colder than that, as they nearly always would be when one is in the water, the body gives off its heat at a rate dependent on a number of factors, including water temperature, the kind of protective clothing that may be worn, and the manner in which the swimmer conducts himself. While staying aboard your boat, dry and warmly dressed, is the best course of action in cold weather, should you fall in — *or should you run any risk of falling in* — here are some important considerations to bear in mind:

Locate and put on a PFD as quickly as possible;

Do not remove your clothing — though soaked, it will still conserve body heat;

Protect the key areas of body-heat loss — head, neck, groin and armpits;

If you must abandon your boat, try to get directly into a raft; if you must get wet, enter the water gradually to minimize shock;

While afloat, stay as still as possible — unnecessary swimming motions only dissipate body heat;

Assume a doubled-up position in the water with your knees drawn up to your chest and your arms tight against your sides;

Get out of the water and into shelter as quickly as possible.

Safety Considerations Applicable to Any Type of Boating Activity

Keep in mind at all times that everything that is done and everything that is used on a boat affects the safety, not only of those aboard, but also those nearby.

If your boat is small, remember that you must board it by stepping into the center of the bottom, not onto a gunwale or seat. Never jump into a boat. Don't stand up in a small boat without hanging on, and don't rock the boat just to show off. Use a safety chain or cable on the outboard engine. Engines have been known to come loose occasionally.

Be familiar with emergency procedures and distress signals. Familiarize your crew with them. Without frightening them, you could conduct a personal flotation device drill. Show them how to adjust the devices so that they will be effective if needed. Calmly explain to them exactly what they should do in case of a capsizing. This information could avert unnecessary panic if the unlikely situation arises.

In addition to the equipment required by law you should also have a good first aid kit, a good local chart, a flash light, distress flares, a paddle or oars, extra shear pins, a bailer or bucket, an extra anchor and plenty of anchor line, mooring lines, fenders, a good tool kit, a compass, reserve fuel and extra spark plugs, emergency water and emergency food rations, and a transistor radio capable of receiving on the marine band. These would be considered the minimum requirements and, if you give the matter some thought, you will think of many more items you would want to have along.

It is most important that you practice mooring and docking your vessel. A crowded marina or anchorage is no place for learning.

Know and obey state and federal boating laws. Nautical traffic laws are known as RULES OF THE ROAD. These rules differ according to where you do your boating. You should become conversant with the set of rules which applies to your local waters and you should abide by them.

Leave a float plan with a friend or relative before departing on a boating outing. Don't simply hand it to a bystander on the wharf. Be sure that you leave it with someone who will miss you if you do not return on time. A float plan should include the following information: (a) where you intend to cruise; (b) a description of your boat and your state registration number; (c) communication equipment aboard and radio call sign if you have one; (d) the names of all persons on board; (e) safety equipment carried; (f) the estimated time of arrival at your destination or return; and (g) your alternate plans in the event of an emergency or in case of bad weather. After returning to home port, your float plan should be cancelled.

Pay attention to your boat handling. High speed and sharp turns are frequent causes of accidents on water as well as on shore. Keep an eye on your wake. Even the wake of a small outboard boat can cause damage to others. You could be held legally liable for any damage caused by your wake. Keep away from swimmers and divers. Slow down when passing fishing boats. When passing sailboats, don't pass between the sailboat and the wind. Pass to leeward (the downwind side). Keep well clear of large vessels and tows. Their wakes are dangerous to small craft. Do not allow passengers to ride on the bow deck or on the gunwales. Any sudden motion of the boat could cause them to fall overboard.

Keep clear of fixed obstructions. When passing under a bridge keep well away from the piers. Portions of caissons and pilings used in the construction of the bridge may be just under the surface of the water. Also, on large rivers, the water around bridges can be turbulent and dangerous. Keep clear of breakwaters and jetties. If your engine should fail while near these obstructions your boat could drift into them before you could get an anchor down.

Watch out for overhead power lines. Fire aboard, serious injury and even death can suddenly strike if the mast or radio antenna of your boat touches an overhead electric wire. Always keep a sharp lookout for aerial power lines. Watch for them across shorelines, coves, rivers and inlets — at marinas and launching ramps.

If you are involved in an accident, be sure and submit an accident report. Legally, you are required to submit one under certain circumstances. Chapter 4 details these instances.

Keep the boat in good condition. Make necessary repairs as required and check all safety equipment regularly.

And finally, don't operate a boat while intoxicated. An intoxicated boat operator is just as deadly as an intoxicated motorist. Save the libations for the time when the anchors are down and securely set, or after you have returned safely to your slip. If you must drive home, save them until you get there. Don't become another statistic.

Proper Selection of a Boat

The key to boating enjoyment is to have a boat that is exactly right for you and your family, and the kind of boating you intend to do. Another thing to consider is the water conditions in your boating area. A boat that is adequate for a small inland lake might not be safe on an unsheltered body of water. A boat that does not have sleeping or cooking facilities would not make a good cruising boat. A boat designed for a top speed of 18 knots will not be a good ski boat. A family of eight is not very safe in a 14-foot boat.

A boat should be purchased because it fits your needs and not because it is offered at a bargain price. Be sure that it is large enough to accommodate your family and guests. Many boats are equipped with a capacity plate which will indicate the recommended size of the engine and the number of pounds the craft is designed to carry safely. To exceed the recommendations of the capacity plate is to be asking for trouble. Overpowering an outboard boat with an engine that is obviously too large and too heavy will have the effect of reducing freeboard at the engine well and your boat could be swamped by taking water over the stern if stopped quickly. The stern wave could roll right in. If you are in doubt concerning the condition of a boat that you are thinking of buying, the best thing to do is to employ the services of a qualified marine surveyor. The surveyor will give you a complete report on the condition of the boat. He will look for things like rot, cracked or broken frames, split planking and mechanical defects. A good survey could save many dollars in the long run.

Trailering

Selection and care of your boat trailer is just as important as that of your boat. The size of your boat determines the size of your trailer. There must be adequate support to prevent warping of the hull. The load placed on the trailer should not exceed the maximum load capacity as stated on the data plate attached to the trailer.

When trailering your boat, periodic checks should be made to ascertain that all tie-downs are secure and that the load carried in the boat has not shifted. Gear loosely stowed and allowed to move freely with the motion of the trailer can damage the hull of the boat.

Make sure the tires on the trailer are in good condition with sufficient pressure. Test your brakes, check the hitch and safety chain and all lights. Replace any frayed lines. Care of your trailer begins at home, not at the side of the road where you may be forced to go simply because you neglected to provide routine maintenance.

Get a Courtesy Examination

To be doubly sure that your boat and equipment meet the minimum safety requirements, ask for a free Coast Guard Auxiliary Courtesy Examination. The Auxiliarist will examine your boat for compliance with federal regulations and certain additional recommendations which the Auxiliary considers desirable for your safety. If your boat passes the Courtesy Examination, a current Courtesy Examination Decal will be placed on the boat. Unless you are obviously violating the law, Coast Guard Boating Safety Detachments will not normally board any vessel displaying a current decal. If your boat does not pass, a report will be given to you indicating the areas in which your boat or equipment was found to be deficient. No record of this examination is made nor kept by the Auxiliarist and no report is made to any law enforcement agency including the Coast Guard.

UNITED STATES COAST GUARD AUXILIARY
COURTESY
U.S. COAST GUARD AUXILIARY
EXAMINATION
No.
CG-2902 (Rev. 11-68)

1-16 Seal of Safety

Boating Safety is a State of Mind

To the safe boatman, safety is the first consideration. Think and practice safety all the time and soon it will become second nature to you. The peace of mind that comes from owning a safe, well equipped boat, and knowing the proper way to operate it safely, will make your boating experiences pleasant and relaxing. Only then will you join the vast majority of boating enthusiasts who say with conviction, "SAFE BOATING IS FUN."

CHAPTER 2

Boater's Language & Trailering

Introduction

The language of seafaring has been developed over the years to the extent that it should be understood if one is to fully enjoy the sport of pleasure boating. You will soon discover that a word or phrase means one thing to a "landlubber," and quite another thing to a boatman. For example, most of us would agree that descending from one level to another is going downstairs, and is accomplished by means of stairs or steps. To a boatman, it is *going below* using a *ladder*.

The terms defined in this chapter should gradually become a part of your boating vocabulary. As your boating knowledge increases, you will find yourself using many of these terms to describe parts of your boat and its equipment. These terms may also be used when giving instructions to others aboard your boat. The first few times you use a nautical term, explain it carefully so that your crew members will know what it means.

Basic Terminology

Listed below are some of the nautical terms that you should learn now so that you may fully understand this chapter and those to follow. They are common, everyday terms as far as boating is concerned. Each has a specific meaning that will be understood by other boatmen.

The following terms describe parts of a vessel:

HULL—The body of a vessel exclusive of superstructure such as the cabin, flying bridge, masts, etc.

Bow—The forward part of a vessel.

STERN—The after part of a vessel.

TRANSOM—The stern of a vessel, when it is cut off flat, at right angles to the boat's centerline.

BOTTOM—The surface of the hull below the waterline.

CHINE—On a flat or vee-bottom boat, the fore-and-aft line formed by the intersection of the side and the bottom.

KEEL—The principal framing member of a vessel, running the entire length fore-and-aft and supporting the frames.

FRAMES (Ribs)—The curved framing members attached to the keel of a wooden boat.

DECK—The floor of a vessel, resting upon the beams.

GUNWALE—The top edge of the hull.

TOPSIDES—The outer surface of the hull from the waterline to the gunwale.

BILGES—The lowest internal spaces within a vessel's hull.

BULKHEAD—A vertical partition aboard a vessel.

COCKPIT—A space or well, sunken below the gunwale line, usually in the after portion of the vessel.

PORTSIDE— The left hand side of a vessel facing forward.

STARBOARD SIDE—The right hand side of a vessel facing forward.

PORTHOLES OR PORTS—Openings in the vessel's sides for admission of light and air.

SCUPPERS—Overboard drain holes on the deck.

HATCH—An opening in the deck to afford entry to spaces below.

HEAD—The vessel's toilet compartment.

GALLEY—The area aboard a vessel where cooking is done.

LADDER—Stairs or steps aboard a vessel.

WINDWARD SIDE—The side of the vessel exposed to the wind.

LEEWARD SIDE—The side of the vessel sheltered from the wind.

Terms that describe fittings and other equipment are:

LINE—Rope that has been put to use aboard a vessel.

CLEAT—An anvil-shaped deck fitting to which lines are secured.

CHOCK—A deck fitting through which lines are passed.

RUDDER—An underwater vertical blade which can be pivoted to steer the vessel.

HELM—The mechanism by which the vessel is steered, including the rudder, wheel, etc.

FENDERS—Padded bumpers hung over the side of the vessel to protect it from chafing.

Some of the fittings and equipment found on sailboats should be of interest. A few are mentioned here. Chapter 10, which is about sailboats, goes into much more detail.

MAST—A spar set upright from the deck to support rigging and sails.

SHROUDS—Wire lines on each side of a vessel, reaching from the masthead to the vessel's sides, to support the mast.

STAYS—Wire lines used to support masts, leading from the head of one mast to another, or to the deck. Those which lead forward are called forestays. Those which lead aft are called backstays.

HALYARDS—Lines used for hoisting and lowering sails.

BOOM—A spar used to extend the foot of a sail.

BOWSPIRIT—A spar extending forward from the bow of a vessel.

JIB—A triangular sail set on a stay, forward.

MAIN SAIL—The principal sail.

The dimensions of a vessel are:

BEAM—The breadth of a boat at its widest point.

DRAFT—The vertical distance from the waterline to the lowest part of the vessel beneath the water.

FREEBOARD—The minimum vertical distance from the waterline to the gunwale.

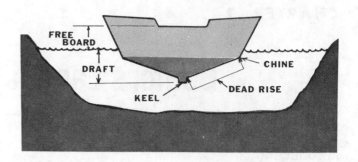

2-2 Parts of a Boat

LENGTH—The distance from the bow to the stern, measured along the vessel's center line, exclusive of bowsprits and other projections.

SHEER—The longitudinal upward or downward curve of the deck fore-and-aft.

The following terms describe directions or locations of items aboard the vessel or closely alongside:

ABAFT—Toward the stern.

AFT—Near the stern.

ALOFT—Above the deck.

AMIDSHIPS—the center of the boat—with reference to her length or to her breadth.

AHEAD—In the direction of the bow.

ASTERN—In the direction of the stern.

ATHWARTSHIPS—Across the line of the vessel's keel.

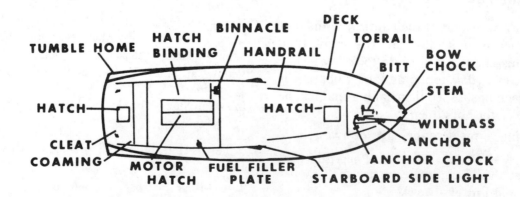

2-1 Topside Nomenclature

BELOW—Beneath or under the deck.

FORE-AND-AFT—Lengthwise with the vessel's keel. The opposite to athwartships.

CLOSE ABOARD—Alongside, close to the hull.

FORWARD—Near the bow.

INBOARD—Toward the centerline of a vessel.

OUTBOARD—Away from the centerline of a vessel.

WINDWARD—Toward the wind.

LEEWARD—The direction opposite that from which the wind blows; downwind.

The following terms describe relative directions as viewed *from* a vessel *toward* an object which is *not aboard* the vessel:

AHEAD (Dead Ahead)—In the direction of the vessel's fore-and-aft center line, forward of the bow.

ABEAM—In a direction at right angles to the vessel's keel, on either side.

BROAD ON THE BOW—In a direction half-way from ahead to abeam of the vessel, on either side.

ASTERN (Dead Astern)—In the direction of the vessel's fore-and-aft center line, behind the stern.

BROAD ON THE QUARTER—In a direction half-way from abeam to astern of the vessel, on either side.

Types of Motorboats

If you are shopping for your first boat, you will find that there is an infinite number of models and sizes on the market. Each has been developed over the years to meet a specific need. Some are adapted to suit specific boating activities and are not suitable for others. So when you select a boat, be sure that it will suit your purposes.

Skiffs are utility boats. They are popular because of their simplicity and durability. Skiffs are flat-bottomed with either straight or slightly flared sides. A skiff is easy to row and may be fitted with a small outboard engine. Because it is flat-bottomed, a skiff is ideal for a hunter or fisherman to operate on protected shallow water.

Prams and Dinghies are small boats with wide beams for their short length. They are intended for rowing but may be fitted with small outboard engines and are used principally as tenders carried aboard larger craft.

Utility outboards are favored by boatmen who rely on outboard engines for power. They are specifically designed for outboard propulsion and consequently are difficult to row. Most utilities are completely open, though some have decked-over bows.

2-4 Utility Outboard

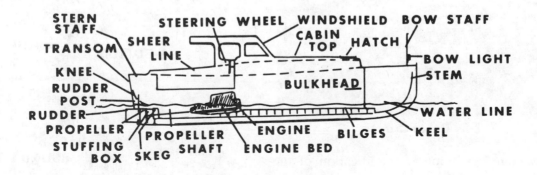

2-3 Sectional Nomenclature.

Runabouts are more sporty craft than utility outboards. Most runabouts have decked-over bows and are intended for general use such as cruising, water skiing and fishing. Most are powered by outboard engines although some runabouts have inboard engines.

2-5 Outboard Runabout

Cruisers are built in a wide variety of shapes and sizes depending on their intended use. Small cruisers are designed for occasional overnight use; large cruisers are used by some as houseboats. The cruiser "type" is described by the configuration of the hull and super-structure—raised deck, flush deck, trunk cabin, sedan or flying bridge. Power can be inboard or outboard, depending on the size of the boat.

2-6 Cabin Cruiser

A *houseboat* is a popular modification of the cruiser. Until the early sixties the houseboat lacked dash and appeal. Today's modern houseboat offers all the conveniences of home. Some have sufficient power and speed to tow water skiers.

Hull Design

There are two basic types of boat hulls — displacement and planing. The displacement hull displaces a volume of water equal to the weight of the boat regardless of the boat's speed through the water. A displacement boat is limited by its design in its top speed. In a displacement hull, there is a direct relationship between the shape of the hull, the length of the boat's waterline and hull speed. A displacement hull vessel should not be forced to attain a speed greater than that for which it was designed. Adding more horsepower to increase speed usually results in reducing the handling characteristics of the boat. Displacement hulls are found on most larger sailboats and ocean-going powerboats, as well as rowboats, canoes, dinghies and prams.

At slow speeds the planing-type hull displaces water in the same manner as a displacement hull. As speed is increased, the hull design imparts a lifting effect. When sufficient speed is attained, the hull comes up "onto the plane." This planing effect decreases the displacement and makes practically unlimited speeds possible, dependent on horsepower only. To help a planing boat achieve a greater speed, light, strong materials are used in its construction.

While there are no hard and fast rules, displacement boats are constructed usually with round bottoms or deep vees, while planing boats are built mostly with shallow vees, flat or channel bottoms. But it should be pointed out that marine architects will adapt all types of construction to obtain the desired results in any particular boat design.

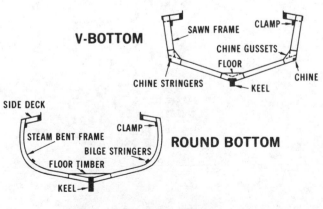

2-7 Boat Construction

Construction of Boats

The types of materials used in the construction of boats have changed considerably in the past few years. Until quite recently, most pleasure craft were constructed of wood only. Now, most boats are built of fiberglass or aluminum. Even wood construction has changed in some instances. Wooden vessels used to be planked; now they are made also of plywood and laminated wood strips.

Wooden Construction

Whenever wood is used for construction, it should be treated thoroughly with a decay resistant compound. Fastenings used on wood hulls should be of non-corrosive material. Closed compartments should be kept clean, dry and well ventilated to prevent dry rot. Periodic bottom painting is required to resist the action of marine borers.

The use of marine-grade sheet plywood has become popular for moderate sized hulls of hard-chine construction. Also, one-piece moulded plywood or laminated construction is often found in smaller hulls.

There are several types of wood plank hull construction. The planks, or strakes, of a carvel-built hull lie alongside each other without overlapping. Each strake is fastened directly to the frames, which may be either bent or sawed.

In lapstrake or clinker construction, the planks overlap at the edges like clapboarding on a house. Rivets are generally used for fastenings. These rivets pass through the upper overlapping strake, the lower overlapped strake and then the frame. In this type of

construction the frames are usually of the bent type. Seams are left unfilled, or various compounds are used between the strakes. The lapstrake hull makes a very light, strong boat.

Diagonal-built hulls have two layers of planking. The first is laid tending forward at a 45 degree angle to the keel. The second layer is laid tending aft at right angles to the first. This type of construction requires little framing and still makes a very strong hull.

Fiberglass Construction

Fiberglass-reinforced plastic, known simply as "fiberglass," has become probably the most important building material for pleasure craft of all sizes and types. In the 30-odd years since it was commercially introduced, it has proven itself strong, impact- and chafe-resistant and watertight. Its apparent drawback of being difficult to repair has proven to be an illusion, now that more and more boatyard workers and skippers have become proficient in fiberglass repair and maintenance, and as resins have become easier and more reliable to work with.

The major of fiberglass boats today and in the foreseeable future are molded. The basic construction materials consist of liquid plastic resin and fiberglass cloth. The cloth is wetted thoroughly with resin, and when the resin hardens a smooth, flexible shell of considerable strength is formed. The fiberglass cloth thus acts as a reinforcement for the resin, just as steel rods are employed to reinforce concrete.

The glass filaments employed appear in one of three basic forms -- "woven roving" is a coarse, criss-cross fabric of great strength that leaves a waffle-textured surface which is rough and difficult to smooth off; "mat" consists of loose fibers chopped into strands and compressed with a binder, and is used for smoothing over the roving; fiberglass cloth is a compromise material, offering reasonable smoothness and good strength. In some inexpensive, mass-produced boats, much of the construction is with so-called "choppedstrand," which is pre-mixed with resin, and fired into the mold with a chopper gun.

To build a fiberglass hull, a *plug* is made, often of wood, as a first step. The plug is the exact shape of

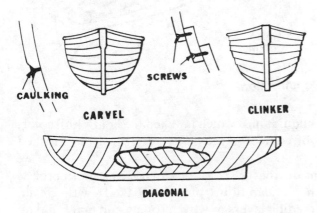

CAULKING

SCREWS

CARVEL   CLINKER

DIAGONAL

2-8 Basic Wood Plank Construction

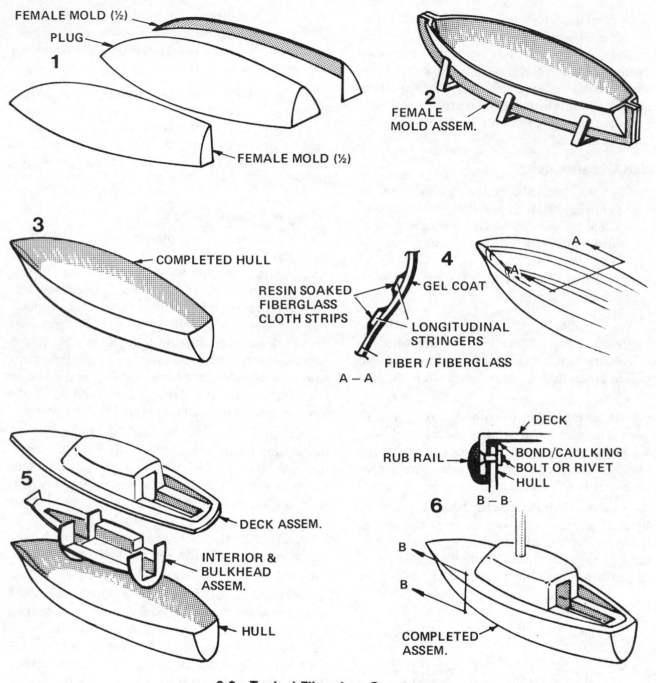

2-9 Typical Fiberglass Construction

the hull, and is sanded, polished and buffed to near-perfection. From this plug a *female mold* is made, often in two parts for easy removal of the finished hull. In *hand-layup* construction, the preferred process today, the inside of the mold is first painted with a waxy *mold release agent,* to keep the plastic of the mold from adhering to the plastic of the newly-molded boat. Next, a layer of *gel coat* is sprayed on.

This liquid, into which is mixed the boat's hull color, will of course be the shiny surface of the finished hull.

Inside the gel coat, the first layer of fiberglass cloth is carefully placed, soaked with resin. Succeeding layers of woven roving and mat build up the hull thickness to the architect's specification. It's easy to see that this thickness can be varied as required -- beefed up at the keel and thinned at points where little stress is expected.

The hull and deck are sometimes one piece, but more often are separate units, joined along the gunwale and sealed with a caulking compound, then riveted or otherwise secured. Interior components, which may be plastic or wood, are usually built outside the hull, then lowered into place and fiberglassed to hull and deck with strips of fiberglass cloth and resin. The bulkheads generally form what few thwartships reinforcements are necessary, and a few longitudinal stringers, either wood or fiberglass, may be added to support machinery as well as strengthen the hull in a lengthwise direction. But the traditional backbone-and-ribcage construction of keel and frames isn't necessary.

Now that fiberglass has been around for three decades, variants on the basic construction method have developed. Because bare fiberglass hulls resonate like drumheads, sound-deadening cores are frequently molded in between the inner and outer layers -- especially in decks of larger boats. These cores also help prevent condensation inside the boat. Methods for mechanical molding of smaller hulls, without expensive hand-layup, are now common, and a new type of fiberglass planking (in which glass rods are incorporated in the fiberglass cloth) allows for building larger hulls without a mold. There are

even processes that combine resin and wood -- saturating the latter material under pressure with resin.

In spite of long-term uncertainties about the source of petrochemicals from which most fiberglass-reinforced plastics are derived, it seems likely that there will be continued development of this essentially satisfactory material for building pleasure boats.

Aluminum Construction

Aluminum is widely used for hulls and also for superstructures. It is light, strong, fashioned with greater ease than steel, and (when anodized) is corrosion resistant. Aluminum hulls are built in one of two ways. Sheets are bent to the desired shape or they are pressed into shape by hydraulic presses. The resulting plates are welded together or, if riveted, the seams are filled with synthetic caulking compound. "5000" series marine aluminum alloy is extremely corrosion resistant, even in salt water. However, salt water will attack the surface of other aluminums, so it helps to give the hull a coat of paint. Aluminum causes the greatest amount of trouble when it comes in contact with other metals under water. When used adjoining a dissimilar metal, aluminum must be insulated from it in order to prevent galvanic action or electrolysis.

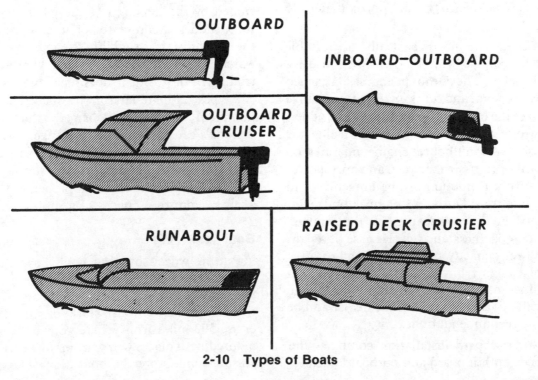

2-10 Types of Boats

Propulsion

There are various types of marine engines on the market today. Most engine systems are designed for a particular type of craft. Matching the wrong engine to a boat might be disastrous. When you buy an engine, the recommendations of the manufacturer concerning propulsion requirements should be followed. Keep in mind that if the horsepower of the engine is doubled, it does not necessarily follow that the speed of the boat will be doubled. The increased weight of the larger engine, plus the weight of the extra fuel and accessories that will be required to accommodate the larger engine, may cancel out much of the anticipated extra speed. Also, it may destroy the trim of the boat.

Inboard marine engines manufactured today are either gasoline or diesel piston types. Most operate on the four-stroke cycle. A diesel engine usually weighs more than a comparable gasoline engine, but its economy of operation and comparative safety are appealing to many boatmen. An inboard engine is mounted within the hull on an engine bed, and transmits power to the propeller by way of a shaft extending through the hull. The water forced back from the propeller impinges on the movable rudder and tends to force the stern of the boat to one side or the other giving steering control. Horsepower ratings for these engines begin at approximately 15 hp.

The outboard engine is basically a portable gasoline fueled engine with its own integral drive shaft and propeller. The outboard engine is attached to the boat's transom, and turns on a pivot to change the direction of the boat. These units have no rudder, the steering effect being obtained by turning the propeller itself. An outboard engine operates on either the two- or four-stroke cycle, and horsepower ratings vary from a fraction of one horsepower to well over a hundred. Outboard engines find favor among many boatmen because of the engines' portability, compactness and relative ease of repair. The horsepower capacity plate should indicate the recommended engine horsepower for the boat. If your boat does not have one of these plates, you would be well advised to consult the dealer and be guided by his recommendations.

The inboard-outboard installation combines the best features of both inboard and outboard engines.

The engine is mounted inside the hull and connects through the transom to the propeller assembly. This assembly has all the characteristics of the lower portion of an outboard engine shaft. It is also known as a stern drive, outdrive or I/O.

The tunnel drive has recently reappeared on the boating scene in small boats, although the idea of enclosing the propeller in a tunnel has been developed for many years. The boat hull has a tunnel formed in the bottom toward the stern. The engine is set low in the hull and practically horizontal in a position forward of the tunnel, with the shaft projecting through the hull and out into the tunnel. The advantages of such an installation are worthy of mention. The propeller is protected by the tunnel so that it is possible to beach the boat as easily as an outboard or in-out propelled boat. The tunnel arrangement permits the boat to be operated safely in very shallow water. It has a conventional installation — engine, transmission, shaft and propeller. The cost of such a conventional installation is considerably less than that of a normal stern drive installation.

The jet drive is another system of propulsion. It is an inboard engine coupled to a high-speed water pump. The water being pumped out at the stern propels the boat. The direction of travel is controlled by the direction of the jet, hence the need for a rudder is eliminated. The chief advantage of the jet drive is its ability to operate in shallow water. The bottom of the hull has nothing protruding from it. But it does have one disadvantage. All types of material can be sucked into the jet pump. Most can be discharged safely but certain materials can cause a total blockage, and the pump will have to be taken apart to be cleared. Clearing a jet drive water pump is not as simple as cutting a piece of rope from a fouled propeller. It will most likely require the services of a professional.

Boat Trailering

Putting wheels on your boat, power or sail, can vastly increase her horizon, but only if you know what you're doing. By fitting your boat with an over-the-road trailer, you can start your annual vacation cruise 500 miles from where your boat is normally moored, visit places you'd normally never see and, at season's end, store the boat alongside your house where you can work on her through the winter months, as the weather allows.

Boat trailering, which has taken such a quantum leap in the last few years that figures have yet to catch up, is firmly based on the development of lightweight, well-balanced modern trailers. Your first requirement, however, is a suitable boat. As many people know, the maximum width for general highway trailering without a special permit is eight feet. Many states have additional laws regulating the total length of boat plus towing vehicle, and a common combined length is 50 feet. Since the maximum length of most trailerable boats is around 25 feet, there should be no problem for most skippers.

Obviously, your boat must have a fairly flat bottom, if you're going to haul and launch her at a municipal ramp or off a beach. Even the small, stub keel of certain sailboats can pose considerable problems when selecting a stock trailer: The rollers of the trailer are often designed for the flat conformation of a standard utility outboard hull, and it may not be possible to adjust them enough to support your boat properly. If in doubt, call the boat manufacturer or his dealer, and ask for names of trailers designed to handle that particular hull. Chances are that there was a standard brand of trailer in mind when the boat was designed.

Certain legal requirements apply to highway trailers, as they do to any vehicle intended for over-the-road service. There are, in addition, other important things to consider besides the law. Legal requirements are still in the course of development in many areas, as more and more states turn their official attention to the dangers inherent in trailering. For up-to-the-minute information, consult your state police and your motor vehicle bureau.

In addition to vehicle size mentioned above, the law will probably require license plates and lights. If possible, try to locate your rig's rear lights and license plate on a demountable fitting — one you can remove before backing the trailer into the water. No lighting system yet devised can shrug off repeated immersions, despite what a builder may claim. You'll also have to have turn indicator lights and, if your trailer is near the eight-foot maximum width, side lights as well.

Other regulations commonly pertain to brakes.

While state standards vary enormously, the American Boat & Yacht Council recommends that trailer manufacturers offer brakes for all wheels of trailers designed for a gross weight (trailer plus load) of 1,500 lb. or more.

Brake requirements in many states can still be met by any one of the three common brake systems — *electrical, hydraulic* or *surge*. The first two types are universally acceptable, but the surge brake, which is activated by the trailer's momentum and is not under the driver's direct control, is outlawed in an increasing number of states. Make sure that your trailer's brake system operates automatically when the towing vehicle's service brakes are applied, and continues to operate even if the trailer separates from the tow car.

Like brakes, there are three kinds of towing hitch attachments. In ascending order of capacity, they are the *bumper hitch* (which fastens directly to the tow vehicle's bumper, and which is illegal in many states); the *frame hitch,* which bolts to at least two of the towing vehicle's structural members — frame or unitized body/bumper; and the *weight-distributing hitch*, a complicated mechanical device that uses leverage on both car and trailer to distribute the load evenly and keep the towing vehicle even with the ground. A frame hitch can be used on gross weights up to 3,500 lb. or so, beyond which a weight-distributing hitch is virtually mandatory.

The key point in the hitch itself is the ball and socket connection between towing vehicle and trailer. There are two common sizes of towing ball — 2″ in diameter and 1 7/8″ — *and they are not interchangeable.* They are also close enough in size

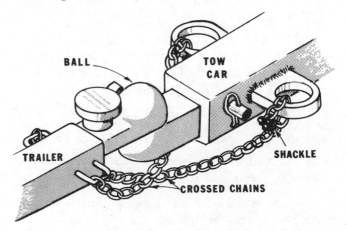

2-11 Trailer Hook-Up

so that you can't expect to eyeball the difference. But too large a ball won't fit the socket; and a too-small ball can spring free from the socket's automatic clamp. The American Boat & Yacht Council recommends use of the 1 7/8″ ball for gross loads up to 2,000 lb. and the larger ball for heavier weights. Among your spares you should carry an extra ball, in case turning-stresses or wear force yours out of true roundness. Like all trailer connections, the ball should have a lock nut to hold it in place.

The final requirement under law (in most states) is a set of safety chains. These consist simply of a pair of chains with S-hooks, running from the tongue of the trailer to the towing hitch, crossed under the hitch in such a manner that if the ball and socket fail, the trailer tongue won't hit the ground, dig in and cause a somersault. The chains should be just long enough to permit free turning of the rig.

The chains themselves should be welded steel, with a breaking test load equivalent to the trailer's recommended gross weight. Although a single length of safety chain, looped through the eyes on the trailer tongue, may be used, individually-attached chains provide an extra safety factor. In no case should the chains be attached to a fastener common with the ball, for obvious reasons.

But the most important thing of all is that the trailer should properly support the boat. Partly this is a question of handling the weight of the load, and you must be sure that the recommended maximum load for your trailer is well above the weight of your boat, her engine, full fuel and water tanks, anchor and line, battery, and other major weights carried aboard.

Partly it's a matter of bracing the boat where the maximum loads occur -- even sturdy fiberglass hulls can be badly wrenched out of shape if they're not braced at critical points. The problem is that no roller system can act wholly correctly on a hull that was designed to be supported evenly at all underwater points by a liquid. You have to do the best you can with what's available, and there are a few things to watch out for.

For most hulls, vital support points are the forefoot, just under the bow; the line of the keel and the planking at each side; the turn of the bilge (especially where interior weights are concentrated);

and the transom. Any other spot where a specially heavy downward force is exerted on the hull should also be braced from below when the hull is fully seated on the trailer. Some major weights were mentioned above; for a sailboat, a retractable keel is an overriding weight, as is an inboard engine or sterndrive.

On most trailers, the rollers and bolsters are adjustable, both up and down and fore and aft, and the winch column and wheel assemblies can also be moved along the frame. Given a trailer of adequate length, therefore, it should be possible to adjust the various elements of the frame and the supports to match the individual boat. Remember to be extra careful when adjusting any part that has a matching component on the trailer's other side: An inch or so of fore-and-aft difference between the wheels can make a serious riding problem for the whole rig.

A trailer's tires and wheels undergo far more strain than do the ones on your car. Not only are a trailer's wheels subject to immersion, often in corrosive salt water, but they are smaller to begin with, and must therefore turn at far higher speeds. Tire pressures for various standard loads are usually indicated on a decal on the trailer frame. They are considerably higher than the pressures of standard auto tires. You should carry a pressure gauge and check the air in the tires frequently. If you err, it should be on the side of too much air in the tires, not too little: Low air pressure in a small, high-speed tire causes it to heat up faster and fail sooner.

Under way on the open road, a trailed boat is subject to a type of rapid motion that it will never encounter on the water. Not only should every unattached piece of gear in the boat be firmly secured, but also the boat itself should be securely lashed in place. The first point of attachment is forward, at the winch used to retrieve the boat from the water and pull it back on the trailer. If you plan to do your own launching and recovery, your trailer's winch is an especially important piece of equipment, usually an extra-cost option.

The winch should have an anti-reverse gear, so the boat can't escape, and unless the boat is very light, the standard rope on the winch drum should be replaced with wire cable. For larger cruisers, geared winches and electrical winches running off the car's battery are available. The winch drum should, if possible, be approximately on a line with the towing eye (if any) on your boat's bow. If there's no eye fitting, the angle of pull from the bow cleat through the chocks to the winch should be only slightly downward.

But don't expect the winch to hold the bow in place. An extra wire cable, preferably with a turnbuckle for tensioning, should connect the boat's stem to the winch pillar. In addition, there should be a non-stretching strap across the after part of the hull — three — or four-inch webbing will do nicely — and perhaps a pair of lines running from the foredeck cleat aft on either side, made fast to the frame about level with the trailer wheels.

Useful extra equipment, in addition to winch and brakes, includes the following items: spare trailer wheel; bearing grease and a complete set of wheel bearings; bulbs for the trailer lights (they won't burn out, they'll be vibrated to death); a jack — probably different from your car's jack, because a flat trailer is usually too low for the standard bumper jack; a set of long-handled wrenches for tightening the various bolts periodically; outside mirrors for your towing car, if necessary; flares, trouble flag and trouble light, just in case; perhaps, if your rig is extra heavy, you'll want to consider booster brakes and heavy-duty shock absorbers for the towing vehicle.

Balancing the load on the trailer is an important aspect of successful towing. What it amounts to is adjusting the boat's gross weight -- that's the boat and her contents -- so that the load on the trailer tongue is somewhere between five and seven percent of the *total* gross weight of the tow — boat + contents + trailer. For the average passenger car, the weight at the tongue shouldn't be much more than 100 lb. Working backward, that indicates a gross weight of 2,000 lb. as the maximum that the family car should be asked to pull.

To ascertain tongue weight, stack two or three cinder blocks under a set of bathroom scales and ease the trailer tongue down on the improvised weighting platform. If the weight is over 75 lb. (and within the five-to-seven-percent rule), consider fixing a retractable dolly wheel on the tongue as a safety factor.

If weight at the tongue is much higher than the recommended maximum, the car will have too much load behind and be hard to handle at speed. If the tongue weight is too little, on the other hand, the trailer will be likely to fishtail. What you need is a happy medium. And if you're pulling a load over about 4,000 lb., by the way, you'd best consider a *tandem* — four-wheel — trailer, as well as a beefed-up tow car.

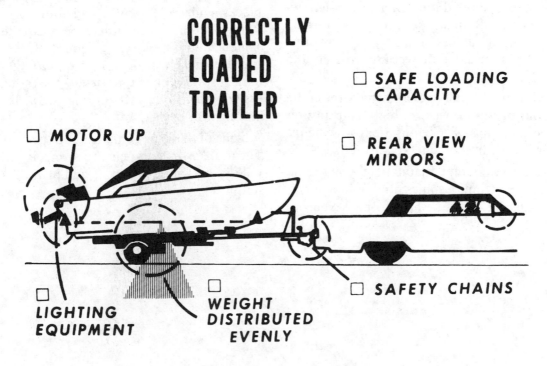

CORRECTLY LOADED TRAILER

☐ SAFE LOADING CAPACITY

☐ MOTOR UP

☐ REAR VIEW MIRRORS

☐ LIGHTING EQUIPMENT

☐ WEIGHT DISTRIBUTED EVENLY

☐ SAFETY CHAINS

2-12 Correctly Loaded Trailer

Before setting out, you should check the weights in the trailer to make sure they're securely set in place. Be certain also that no one's tossed in last-minute items that will crash about or significantly alter the trailer's balance. Check also that the trailer's frame bolts are all tight — they can work loose slowly without anyone's noticing. Now check the boat tie-downs. Be sure the outboard engine is locked up or down — opinions vary as to the best position. Check that the lights and brakes work: Connections between the car and its trailer are always more fragile than the heavy-duty couplings would indicate.

If yours is a sailboat, be certain the mast and rigging are securely lashed down — shock cord ties will hold the rig in place. If the mast protrudes over the stern, it should have a red rag at the end. Exposed moving parts, like winches and sheet track and goosenecks should be covered to protect them from road grit.

Under way, never forget you have a boat behind you. This sounds foolish, but when you're wheeling along at highway speeds, it's all too easy to lose a feel for the tow — until you have to pass, turn or brake. Always start slowly, in low gear, and take the car up through the gears gently.

Think twice about passing other vehicles — but if you decide to pass, don't dither. Be alert for signs restricting trailers. Remain sensitive to unusual sounds or handling factors, and if there's anything that seems at all unusual, pull over immediately and check.

In fact, you should pull over and check the entire rig every hour or so — check for high temperatures in the wheel bearings, slackening tiedowns, lights, tire pressure and car engine temperature.

Before you ever attempt a launching, you should put in a couple of hours some Sunday in a supermarket parking lot, learning how to back your rig easily. It's a lot simpler than docking your boat, but it does take practice. If you have an exceptionally heavy or unwieldy trailer, you may want to get an auxiliary front bumper hitch, which will make close-quarters maneuvering much simpler.

When launching, try to avoid getting the trailer hubs in the water. If you can't avoid dunking them, at least let them cool off first. If you don't the heat will simply suck the bearing full of water. One way to pass the time, if you're a sailor, is to step the mast right in the parking lot. Before you do this, make sure there are no low power lines or other overhead obstructions between you and the launching ramp: A few boaters get electrocuted every year by touching a live wire with rigging wire or metal mast.

Once the trailer wheels do get soaked, repack the bearings with grease. It doesn't take long, and it's a lot easier than changing a burnt-out bearing on the road home.

When launching or recovering, never turn the car's engine off. If you have an automatic transmission, leave it on in "low," with the brake set, while you work the boat on or off the trailer. And make sure you never cast off *all* the lines from the boat before launching.

When your boat is on her trailer at home for any length of time, get the weight off the wheels. Cinder blocks under the tongue and four corners of the frame of the trailer should be adequate support, shimmed up if necessary by boards. Once the trailer frame is jacked up, check to be sure that the boat itself is still evenly supported — the frame itself can easily be bent out of its normal shape by excessive jacking at a corner.

None of this is as complicated as perhaps it seems. The trick, as in so much of boating, is simply to envision what might go wrong and plan ahead to forestall it.

CHAPTER 3

Boat Handling

Introduction

Handling a boat is an interesting and sometimes exciting experience. Often, a first-time boat owner may find it is so exciting as to be frightening. His boat may respond in ways that he does not expect. He may well feel that he does not have control over the situation.

Handling a boat, like driving an automobile or flying a plane, is a skill which is acquired as the result of study and practice. Basic boat handling skills require, as a first step, a knowledge of how and why boats behave as they do. This can be obtained by trial and error—but errors on the water can be dangerous to the boatman and to others nearby. A certain amount of basic knowledge can be learned in the classroom at much less risk and in a more efficient manner.

Once the basic principles are learned, they should be applied on the water. The boatman should learn about *his* boat. This understanding must include everything about the vessel; its hull, with its characteristics and limitations, its machinery and rigging, its underwater gear and all equipment aboard. Once this understanding is achieved, it is reinforced by constant practice. How does the vessel behave in turns? How much way is required for effective rudder control? How does she behave in varying sea conditions? If left to her own resources, will she wallow in the trough or turn her stern into the wind? How responsive is she in close quarters? How well does she carry her way? What are her backing characteristics? In a seaway, is the hull tender or stiff? How much power is available for emergencies? What is her fuel consumption? How much fuel does she carry? What are the effects of a beam wind, and what allowances must be made in these circumstances? These questions, and many more, must be answered by the boatman; and their answers must be thoroughly understood. He must practice to improve his skills and develop a solid feeling of confidence in himself and his equipment. This cannot be done ashore but a good knowledge of what is actually happening when he turns the wheel or opens the throttle can make the learning process quicker and easier.

The propeller and the rudder are the two principal devices which control the boat. They both act in complex ways—but by looking at a simplified picture of their actions we can understand more about their practical effects on the handling characteristics of the boat.

The Propeller

Almost all pleasure boats are propeller driven. Propellers are designed to rotate in either a clockwise or counter-clockwise direction. When the propeller is viewed from aft (looking forward) and it is seen to turn in a clockwise direction to propel the vessel forward, it is called a right-handed propeller.

3-1 Left Hand Propeller   Right Hand Propeller

If it is seen to turn in a counter-clockwise direction it is called a left-handed propeller.

Propellers may be easily identified as right-handed or left-handed by inspection. Also, most propellers are stamped "RH" or "LH" on the hub. Other markings which may appear on the hub are the diameter and pitch. The diameter is generally measured in inches and represents the diameter of the circle described by the outer tips of the rotating blades. Pitch is also measured in inches, and represents the *theoretical* distance that the hub would travel forward with one complete rotation of the propeller. Pitch is easiest to visualize if one thinks of the propeller as moving through a solid mass. The pitch would be the distance in inches that the screw would penetrate the mass in one complete revolution. One point to keep in mind concerning the pitch dimension is that this is a theoretical value only, since the propeller is working in a liquid and not a solid.

Surprisingly, not too many people know how a propeller works. Because a propeller is made up of twisted surfaces resembling a screw (technically a helicoid) it is often called a screw. But it doesn't simply work its way through the water like a screw in wood. If this were so the best blade shape would be sharp at the leading edge to "bite" the water easier. If you look closely at a propeller blade you will see that, in section, it is shaped about like an airplane wing.

It is in reality a lifting surface, just like an airplane's wing. As it rotates, water passes over the blade's section. There are a lot of high-powered mathematical formulas about the effects of this— but basically the water going over the "fat" side which faces forward relative to the boat has farther to travel than that which goes by the "thin" side which faces aft. This results in a reduction in pressure on the fat side and the propeller tends to move in that direction.

A marine propeller is *not a pump!* It is not a reaction machine pulling in water from ahead and pushing it astern. Because it does not operate in ideal conditions some of this does happen, and it can be of use to the boatman—maneuvering at low speeds. But, to understand a propeller's operation one must consider it as being like a spiral shaped air foil.

Boat propellers, unlike airplane propellers or wings, operate in water. This means that because of the high density of water we can use a smaller propeller for a boat than for an airplane of the same horsepower. But we are faced with a serious practical limitation called cavitation. On the extreme, cavitation can reduce propeller efficiency and can seriously damage the propeller and even the struts and rudders aft of it. How and why does this happen? If we ask the propeller to absorb too much power— to develop more lift than that for which it is designed, we get cavitation. As we increase RPM's— move the "air foil section" through the water faster —the pressure over the "fat" side gets less and less until a point is reached where the water passing over the blade literally boils—yes, it turns into *steam!* This sounds pretty far out, but a dish of water in a vacuum chamber in a laboratory can be made to boil not by increasing the temperature but by reducing the pressure acting on it. A highly loaded propeller does the same thing, not in a lab, but on your boat! The "cavity" limits the amount of thrust we can get from our propeller, but a *cavitating wheel still produces a lot of thrust.* The trouble comes because there is a peak of low pressure about ⅓ of the way aft of the blade's leading edge. After that, the pressure is greater and the steam bubbles condense violently. This "implosion" hammers on the blade and can erode it away over a period of time. Some of the "implosions" may even take place on the struts and rudder aft of the propeller and erode these as well.

In a supercavitating propeller, the pitch, diameter and blade shape are designed so that high horsepower can be used efficiently under high cavitation. But the trailing edge of the blades are "chopped" away so that the "implosions" have nothing on which to hammer. The detail design of a supercavitating propeller and a regular non-cavitating propeller is very different. Loading an ordinary propeller to the cavitating point makes it operate in conditions for which it is not suited and reduces its efficiency sometimes quite suddenly and may lead to engine overspeed and other problems.

Almost all single-screw boats have right-handed propellers. There is no advantage in efficiency from a right-handed propeller but most boatmen are used to it and its low speed maneuvering characteristics. A left-handed propeller can cause practical operator problems for one who is used to a right-handed propeller and often requires re-training of the boatman. Twin-screw boats usually have "outboard turning" propellers. This is important in low speed handling characteristics because of the complex interaction of propeller and hull. The explanation of the reasons would be lengthy and technically "deep" but it is a proven fact that *inboard* turning propellers make a boat extremely difficult to handle at low speeds. Twin-screw boats are far more maneuverable at slow speeds than single screw craft. Beside being able to apply varying amounts of power to each propeller separately, the propellers of twin screw boats are placed on either side of the centerline, giving them greater turning leverage.

The Rudder

An inboard powered vessel is steered by means of a vertical blade called the rudder which can be pivoted to either side of the centerline. The size and shape of the rudder have a considerable effect on its operating characteristics. Boats which are designed for relatively slow speeds usually have large rudders, while higher speed boats have smaller ones. The rudder is generally placed directly behind the propeller, or nearly so. Modern twin screw pleasure craft almost always have twin rudders, each of which is placed behind its respective propeller.

The pivotal shaft to which the rudder is attached is called the stock. On most rudders, the stock is attached to the forward edge of the blade. Certain rud-

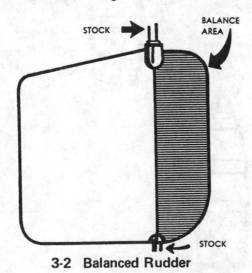

3-2 Balanced Rudder

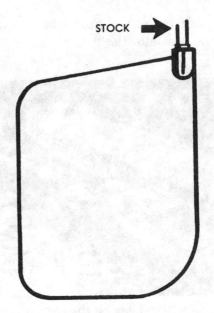

3-3 Rudder

ders are designed with a portion of the blade projecting ahead of the stock. These are called balanced rudders. When a balanced rudder is pivoted off the center line, the portion of the blade which is ahead of the stock is placed on the opposite side of the centerline. Although this may be only 15 to 20% of the surface area of the blade, it has the effect of taking a considerable amount of strain off the steering gear and thus makes the boat easier to handle.

The rudder is another lifting surface. It can be either a symetrical airfoil or a flat plate. As we turn the rudder from its amidships position while the vessel is making headway, it creates a lift, just like an airplane wing, and the resultant force tends to move the stern of the boat sideways.

Even good symetrical airfoil rudders lose their efficiency when turned too far off the centerline, and much of the turning force is lost. It is for this reason that most rudders are limited mechanically to a "hard over" angle of about 35° from amidships.

Practical Effects of Propellers and Rudders

The first thing to remember when operating a powerboat, or any boat for that matter, is the fact that when the rudder is moved off centerline, it is the *stern* and not the bow that changes direction first. This becomes especially important when getting underway (under headway) from a float or pier. Under this circumstance, putting the rudder away from the side nearer the float will only drive the stern of the boat into the float.

3-4 Leaving the Dock

Manuevering at Speed

Maneuvering at speed is usually a "rudder only" operation. When we put the rudder over, the lift force tends to force the stern sideways. The boat pivots at a point which is usually forward of amidships and the bow is initially slightly inside the turn track line with the stern outboard.

Boats at speed usually settle into a turn nicely because of the forces of the water on the moving hull.

As long as the lifting force of the rudder is applied the boat will continue to turn. Returning the helm to amidships will slow the turn and the boat will tend to straighten out. But in a very heavy boat, a bit of opposite rudder (meeting her) may be helpful in settling on the new course.

Low Speed Maneuvering

Single Screw

If our boat is dead in the water, there is no flow over the rudder. The rudder can be moved from hard over to hard over without effect. As we put the engine ahead, the propeller's lift tries to move the boat ahead—but the boat has inertia—it resists a change in motion, and the propeller acts practically in a different manner than it does at speed.

Without going too deeply into the analysis of propeller action, we should be aware of the fact that a rotating propeller develops a component of torque in addition to the component of thrust. The thrust component propels the boat while the torque component generates a transverse force through the shafting which may tend to force the stern to port or starboard. When a boat is dead in the water, and the engine is placed ahead, both thrust and torque

3-5 TURNING PIVOT

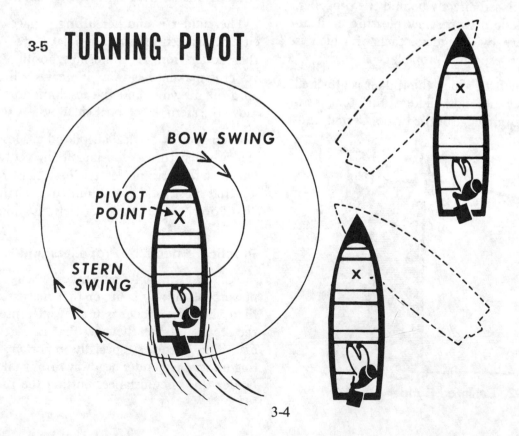

BOW SWING

PIVOT POINT

STERN SWING

are initially large. Most of the initial thrust is overcome by the vessel's fore-and-aft inertia, but the torque is relatively free to react and the stern may be forced to the side.

The initial practical effect of the right-hand turning propeller of a single-screw boat is to force the stern to starboard. There are exceptions but this is the general rule. The propeller wash also forces water over the rudder. More than one boatman who didn't realize that his rudder was hard over when he hit the throttle has had a big surprise. The sideways propeller forces grow less important as speed builds up and a boat with any significant forward motion handles quite normally.

Backing the engine of a "right-handed" boat tends to swing the stern to port. This is caused by an interaction of the propeller and the hull which decreases the effectiveness of the portion of the propeller which is "on top," nearest the hull. It is a complex phenomena which depends to some extent on hull design as well as propeller tip clearance from the hull and other factors. There are boats which will back dead straight, some which back to starboard (although this is most unusual for a "right-handed" boat) and a few which will do the unexpected. There are many factors involved, so each boatman should learn his own boat's behavior patterns. It is the wise boatman who realizes that most "right-handed" boats back to port, but *who doesn't always count on it!*

When backing down it is good practice to have the rudder amidship initially. This is especially true if there is a direct "tiller line" steering system as is

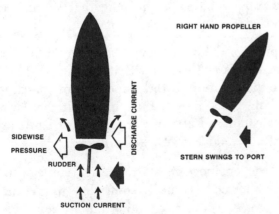

3-6 Single Screw Vessel with Headway, Propeller Backing

sometimes found on older boats. The resultant "kick" on the wheel from a hard backdown of one of these boats with the rudder part way over can damage the steering system and has been known to break a boatman's wrist. In any case the strain on the steering system can be considerable.

Rudder Action While Going Astern

As sternway builds up the rudder begins to have a marked effect on maneuvering and the boat backs just like a car. There are many rules on the "reverse" effect of the rudder but this is the simplest: When backing down, right rudder will swing the *stern* to the right. The bow, of course, will go to the left. If the stern motion is stopped and the boat is put ahead, the rudder must be shifted to keep the bow swinging in the same direction.

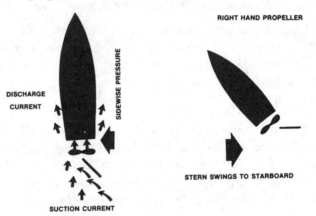

3-7 Single Screw Vessel with Sternway, Propeller Backing

Twin Screw Boats

Since a twin-screw boat has two "thrust producers" (propellers), one on each side of the centerline, it is usually a joy to maneuver at low speeds. By going ahead on one screw and backing down on the other, the boat can be turned very easily and practically within her own length.

Outboards and In/Out Drives

These boats are steered by turning the line of thrust of the propellers. They have no rudders, although the lower units and shaft housings have some slight rudder effect. They pose no special problems in handling except that power is required to turn the boat. One cannot coast alongside and control the heading of the boat by rudder action alone as is easily done with a conventional propeller and rudder system. They are responsive and handy. For example, the stern can be moved toward or away from a pier or float by positioning the thrust angle properly and applying just a touch of power. Thus, maneuvering is much simpler with an outboard or I-O drive than with an inboard driven boat. Even backing down is easier though most outboard driven craft steer poorly while reversing because the bow tends to swing away from the line of travel. When making a partial or complete turn with an outboard, reduce speed and turn in an arc of sufficient width so the boat will stay on an even keel. Never attempt short turns at high speed. Countless capsizings have resulted from this foolhardy practice.

The Technique of Docking and Maneuvering

One of the best ways to judge the competence of a boatman is to observe the manner in which he gets his craft underway from a float or pier, and how he places his boat alongside the float when returning to his dock.

One boat is seen to get underway as the result of much running back and forth and much pushing and pulling, all to the accompaniment of much shouting of orders, generally by everyone aboard to nobody in particular. Another boat is seen to get underway with all persons comfortably seated, the lines quietly let go, and the craft skillfully maneuvered clear of the float or pier. Both of these vessels have gotten underway successfully. Both have accomplished the same result—but what a difference in technique!

At this point, the reader might argue that the first boatman could be comparatively new to the sport, while the second boatman obviously was an "old pro." It is conceded that this might well be the case but one does not advance from the first situation to the second without a thorough understanding of the forces at work, which may be encountered under varying conditions.

Before Getting Underway

Before getting underway, the prudent boatman will be found to be quite busy. Sailboat skippers generally check their rigging—stays, shrouds, hal-

yards and sheets. Sails are made up and ready to hoist. Both sail and powerboat skippers should check all of the vessel's systems and gear, usually with the aid of a check list. The fuel in the tanks should be measured (or the gauges read) and the engine oil level should be determined. All lights, including running lights, should be seen to be operating properly. The whistle or horn should be sounded briefly. (One possible exception to this would be if the departure were from a crowded anchorage and scheduled for 0500 hours!) The condition of the bilges should be checked. Hand lines should be broken out, ready for use. Anchors should be bent on and ready to let go. Lifesaving devices should be taken out of their lockers and placed in readily accessible places. All electronic gear which will be used should be turned on. Hatch covers should be open to allow engine and fuel tank spaces to ventilate and bilge blowers, if any, should be operating. A heaving line and boat hook should be available for instant use. In short, all equipment aboard should be determined to be in satisfactory operating condition. Only when this is done, is the vessel in condition to start the engine or engines.

Starting Engines

When ready to start engines, special precautions are taken. Even though the engine and fuel tank compartments have been thoroughly ventilated, it is still necessary to test for gas vapors which may be present in these spaces. This can be done by activating an electronic vapor detector, or by activating our built-in vapor detector—the nose! The nose is generally far more sensitive than a device in detecting gasoline vapors, and it is the nose that should be satisfied that no vapors are present.

The proof of the pudding will be when the starter is engaged. It is at this point that ignition is introduced to the situation. If the proper mixture of gasoline and air exists, it is at this point that the day's activities could end abruptly in a flash of flame as the mixture explodes with great force.

Once the engines are started, the temperature should be allowed to come up somewhat, to prevent stalling. However, excessive idling should be avoided. It is usually best to allow the engines to warm up under a load.

Getting Underway

With the engines started, and all gauges reflecting desired readings, it is time to get underway. Before casting off the mooring lines, a careful inspection should be made of the immediate surroundings. All hazards and obstructions should be noted, and the direction and strength of the wind and current should be known.

This chapter will develop situations which will be encountered while docking and getting underway. Before getting into this, however, the boatman should be reminded that a slow speed should be maintained through crowded anchorage or marina areas. The boatman is legally responsible for any damage caused to others by his vessel's wash. Most marinas have a 5-knot speed limit but this may be too fast if the wash doesn't flatten appreciably within a few feet from the stern. All fenders (which may be dangling) should be taken in. Mooring and hand lines, and all loose gear about the decks, should be secured.

Leaving the Dock

Leaving a dock and returning to it require a certain level of skill on the part of the boat operator. In all of the maneuvers involved in docking and leaving a dock, it is imperative that certain facts be kept clearly in mind. The first and most important point to remember is that the stern is the only part of the boat that can be steered. As stated earlier in this chapter, the stern moves sideways and must always be watched. This is not to say that the bow must not also be watched but all too many boatmen concentrate on the bow and in this concentration, slam the stern into the wharfs and floats with damaging results.

Wind and Current

There are also other factors at work however, if the boatman is alert, he can make these forces work for him. These forces, which are almost always present, are wind and current. Most boatmen (other than our sailboat friends) think of wind and current as hindrances. Both wind and current can be considerable help in maneuvering if the boatman knows how to employ them.

One of the first surprises experienced by the newcomer to powerboat operation is the relatively great effect the wind has on his vessel. Deep draft boats, with comparatively low freeboard, are far less affected by the wind than by the current. This is because there is more underwater body for the current to work against on deep draft boats, while there is less topsides area (and cabin structure) against which the wind can work. Most powerboats are not deep draft vessels, and present high topsides and relatively large cabin areas to the wind. Many powerboats may be affected more by the wind than by the current. This is important to remember while underway; but it is most important to remember when maneuvering in close quarters.

Generally, the bow of a powerboat has higher freeboard than the stern and is considerably less heavy. Consequently, the bow will almost always be blown downwind at a faster rate than the stern. This accounts for the characteristic of most powerboats to turn their stern into the wind if left to themselves. In some marina areas, where maneuvering is necessarily restricted to close quarters, it is not physically possible to get up enough way to bring the bow up into the wind. Under these conditions, the boatman has no choice but to go into reverse and cooperate with the wind instead of attempting to resist its effects.

The Use of Lines

We generally think of lines as simply a means of keeping a boat tied to a pier. These lines are known

DOCKING LINES

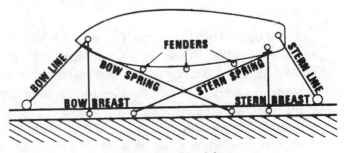

3-8 Mooring Lines

as mooring lines, and it might be well to think about lines briefly before continuing on.

The most often used mooring lines are the bow line and the stern line. These are simple to employ and are usually sufficient, provided that fenders are suspended from the hull at strategic points to keep the hull from chafing against the float.

If the vessel is to be left alongside a pier or float for a long time, as with a permanent mooring, the use of breast lines and spring lines should be considered. Breast lines prevent sideways movement and spring lines limit the fore-and-aft movement of the vessel. If moored to a pier or wharf in tidal areas, it is important to leave sufficient slack in all lines to accomodate the rise and fall of the tide.

Spring lines may also be used in close quarters to help the vessel into or out of a slip or to facilitate maneuvers alongside a wharf. If the spring line is to be handled by those aboard the boat, both ends of the line should be aboard, with the bight around a bollard or cleat on the wharf. A spring line is let go by hauling in on one end of the line. If used under these conditions, a spring line must be tended carefully to be certain that it does not become fouled on the rudder or propeller. Under no conditions should a spring line, which is being used to assist a maneuver, be tied off to a cleat or bitt aboard the boat. A half turn around the bitt or cleat is usually all that is required. The spring line should be able to be adjusted as necessary and cast off quickly when no longer needed.

Leaving a Slip

In this case, and in all cases to follow, it is assumed that the vessel is a right-hand single-screw craft of inboard propulsion.

Some boats depart from their slips by backing out and little trouble should be encountered with this maneuver. Once the engine has been started and all is ready, all lines are cast off. The rudder is placed amidships, with the engine in slow astern. The boat will back down slightly to port. At this point, the starboard bow should be tended carefully, as it might swing into the right hand finger pier or float. When the bow is clear, apply hard left rudder. The turn will become more pronounced. When suf-

ficiently clear, apply hard right rudder and go ahead with a short burst of power. This should check the sternway and stop the boat. The rudder is now placed amidships (or as necessary to pick up the desired heading) and the boat proceeds under slow speed ahead.

Getting Underway from a Float, Pier or Wharf

In many cases, a simple maneuver such as getting underway can be complicated by the presence of other craft immediately ahead or astern of your boat, thus severely restricting your choice of alternatives. Wind or current could also become a factor in the sense that the boat is being blown onto or away from the float.

Leaving a Dock, Wind Blowing off the Float

In this case, the wind will be of considerable help in getting clear. Cast off the stern line, then the bow line. The boat will drift clear, with the bow falling off more rapidly than the stern. When sufficiently clear of all obstructions, place the engine in slow ahead and proceed in the desired direction.

Leaving a Dock, Wind Blowing onto the Float

Getting away from a float, when the boat is being set onto it by the wind, will generally require the use of a spring line. Cast off the stern line and hold an after bow spring line. Have fenders over the starboard bow and tend the line carefully. Go ahead slowly with full right rudder. The spring line should check the forward movement and the stern will swing away from the float and into the wind. Adjust the engine speed as necessary to overcome the

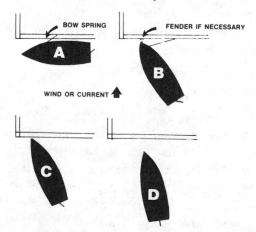

3-9   Leaving a Dock, Wind Blowing onto the Float

force of the wind. When the stern is clear of all obstructions, put the rudder over to hard right, place the engine in slow astern, and cast off the spring line. The boat will back directly into the wind. Adjust the helm as necessary to avoid over-steering and, when sufficiently clear of the float, go ahead with a short burst of power to check the sternway. From this position, come right or left to the desired heading under slow ahead.

Leaving a Dock, Wind on the Bow

In this case, the wind can be of considerable help. Cast off the bow line and hold a forward quarter

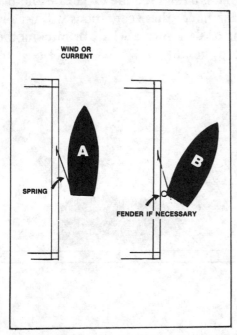

3-10 Leaving a Dock-Wind on the Bow

spring line. This will allow the bow to fall off, away from the float. It might be necessary to start this by a gentle push with a boat hook against the float. When the bow has fallen off sufficiently to be clear of all obstructions, cast off the spring line and go ahead slowly with left rudder.

If the desired direction of travel is downwind, execute the above maneuver with the spring line on the outboard quarter cleat. Hold the spring line until the wind has blown the bow sufficiently clear. Cast off the spring and go ahead slowly with right rudder.

Leaving a Dock, Wind on the Stern

Cast off the stern line and hold an after bow spring line. Have fenders over the port bow and tend the line carefully. Go ahead slowly with full left rudder. The stern will swing away from the float. When the stern is sufficiently clear of all obstructions, place the rudder amidships, cast off the spring line and place the engine in slow astern. The boat will back into the wind with the bow tending to fall off to starboard. When clear, go ahead with a short burst of power to check the sternway. Go ahead slowly with right rudder.

In close quarters, where there is little room to maneuver, it is usually not practical to attempt to bring the bow into the wind. If the desired direction of travel is upwind, it is generally best to travel under sternway to a point where there is more space to maneuver.

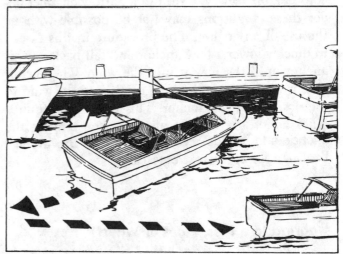

3-11 Using the Bow Spring Line

Turning in a Narrow Channel

In some cases it may be necessary to make a complete 180° turn in a channel that is too narrow when compared to the boat's minimum turning circle. If the boat is a right-hand-screw vessel, start the turn as close to the left hand side of the channel as possible, Put the rudder over to hard right and LEAVE IT THERE. Alternately go ahead and reverse until the turn is complete. When the boat is properly aligned with the channel in the opposite direction, put the rudder amidships and proceed under slow speed ahead.

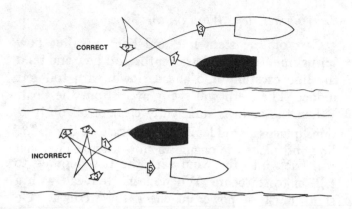

3-12 Turning a Right Hand Screw Boat in a Narrow Channel

If the desired new direction of travel is into the wind and if the wind is sufficiently strong to cause considerable leeway, a turn in a narrow channel under these conditions may not be possible without the use of an anchor. The procedure in this case is to quickly lower a bow anchor and fall back on this anchor until the bow is into the wind. The anchor rode is picked up as the boat heads into the wind to the position of the anchor. This maneuver requires quick action on the part of the person tending the anchor and is not recommended for the average boatman except in extreme cases.

Mooring to a Pier, Float or Wharf

Docking a boat can be a source of pride or embarassment. Frequently, a would-be salt approaches a pier at breakneck speed, throws everything into reverse and if he doesn't plow through the pier, he gets alongside just in time for his own wake to pound his boat against the pilings.

Don't be a "hot rodder." Make the landing approach cautiously and slowly. All that is needed is enough speed for the boat to respond to the rudder. It may not look as spectacular but it is certainly better seamanship, safer and in many cases, much cheaper. It is also good seamanship to have fenders, mooring lines, a heaving line and at least one long line ready well in advance of actual docking.

Because of the varied construction of piers and floats, you will not always have a choice of which side of the pier or float to make your landing. With a right-handed screw vessel, is is usually easier to get alongside port-side-to than to get in starboard-side-to. Whenever wind or current is a factor in the situation, the approach should, if possible, be made from downwind or downstream. In this way, the bow will be headed into the wind or current. Downwind landings are difficult and require a higher degree of skill than landings into the wind but there may be certain situations where this cannot be avoided. All landings should be carefully planned in advance but downwind landings require extra care and planning. A mistake under these conditions will usually cause the boat to slam into a wharf or into another boat with costly results.

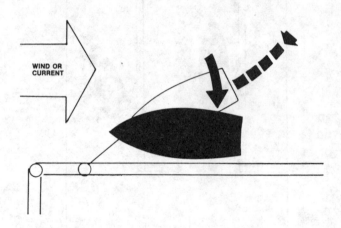

3-13 Docking Against Wind or Currents

Docking with no Wind or Current

A landing is usually made by bringing the bow alongside the wharf or float under slow headway and reversing to stop the boat. If there is no wind or current, a boat with a right-hand screw should land portside to the wharf. When the port bow is put alongside and the boat is backed to check the headway, the sidewise pressure of the backing screw sends the stern alongside. In a starboard-side-to landing, the same propeller effect sends the stern away from the float. It is obvious then, that a

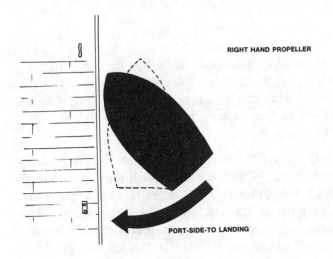

RIGHT HAND PROPELLER

PORT-SIDE-TO LANDING

3-14 Effect of Backing Propeller

starboard-side-to landing must be made at a very flat angle to the float and with as little headway as possible so that little or no backing is necessary.

Docking, Wind Blowing off the Float

The approach must be made at a relatively sharp angle since the wind will tend to blow the bow down. It will be necessary to hold a certain amount of right rudder to maintain the correct heading. A fender should be rigged on the starboard bow.

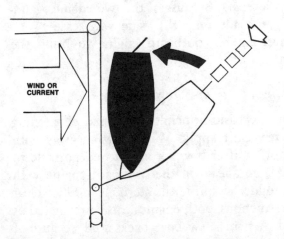

WIND OR CURRENT

3-15 Docking from Leeward

When close aboard, send the bow line ashore and put the rudder over to hard left. Go ahead on the bow line, which will act as an after bow spring. The stern will come alongside the float. Send the

stern line ashore and secure the engine. Adjust mooring lines as ncessary.

Docking, Wind Blowing onto the Float

The approach should be made at a flat angle, keeping in mind the tendency of the wind to blow the boat toward the float. Since the bow will fall off more than the stern, a certain amount of left rudder must be held to maintain the desired heading. Plenty of fenders should be rigged along the starboard side. When in the proper position, reverse the engine to check the headway. The boat will come alongside parallel to the float. This could be a hard landing, depending on the strength of the wind. DO NOT use arms or legs to fend off as the boat approaches the float. Many an arm and leg has been broken or crushed in this manner. The fenders should cushion the shock, with an assist from a judiciously employed boathook or two. When alongside, send mooring lines ashore and adjust as necessary.

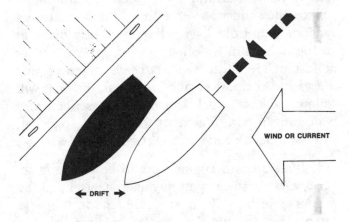

WIND OR CURRENT

← DRIFT →

3-16 Docking from Windward

Twin-Screw Maneuvering

Up to this point, we have been concerned only with the handling characteristics of right-hand-single-screw boats. The great majority of pleasure power craft fall within this category. However, twin-screw boats are rapidly increasing in popularity and a few words on the handling characteristics of twin-screw boats are in order.

On twin-screw boats with inboard-outdrive units, both propellers are right-handed; but on most twin-screw inboards the starboard propeller is right-handed and the port propeller is left-handed. The first thing to remember about an inboard twin-screw boat is that it is infinitely more maneuverable than a single-screw boat in close quarters. There are two propellers, turning outboard, positioned on either side of the center line. Twin rudders, which are found on almost all modern twin-screw pleasure boats, are positioned directly behind each propeller. The basic principles which apply to single-screw craft with regard to propeller action also apply to each propeller of a twin-screw boat. The important difference is that, with counter-rotating screws, each propeller can be made to cancel out the undesirable effects of the other. This concept can be used to advantage in maneuvering in close quarters since the effects of the two propeller thrusts can be individually controlled.

In order to understand the principles of twin-screw boat handling, it is necessary to observe the effects of each screw individually. Let's assume that the starboard engine is going ahead, the port engine is in neutral and the rudders are amidships. (Since the rudders operate in unison and are not separately controlled, we will refer to the movement of the rudders in the singular — simply as "rudder amidships.") With the starboard engine going ahead and the port engine in neutral, the boat will follow a course which can best be described as a wide turn to port. The craft will tend to follow an extension of the curve of the starboard gunwale.

If the starboard engine were to be placed in reverse, again with the port engine in neutral and the rudder amidships, the boat would tend to follow an extension of the curve of the starboard gunwale but under sternway.

If the port engine were engaged, with the starboard engine in neutral, the boat would tend to follow an extension of the port gunwale, both in ahead and in reverse.

A twin-screw boat can be made to turn completely in little more than her own length by going ahead on one engine and astern on the other. In the case of the starboard engine going ahead and the port engine backing, the combination of the reactions set up will turn the vessel without recourse to the rudder, and without the necessity of having either headway or sternway.

Since a boat is more efficient when going ahead

than when going astern, the effect of the propeller going ahead is greater than that of the one going astern. If both engines are set at the same rpm's, a certain amount of headway will be made while pivoting. This can be cancelled out by increasing the rpm's of the backing engine just enough to offset the headway.

If the craft has single lever controls, the pivoting maneuver is simple enough, with only two controls for the operator to manipulate. If the throttles and the transmissions are separately controlled, the first-time twin-screw operator may find that he has too many controls to operate at the same time. Most twin-screw boat operators set both engines at a fast idle and forget about them. Since the rudder is not used in the maneuver, it too can be forgotten. This leaves only the two gear levers for the operator to manipulate.

Docking the Twin-Screw Boat

The approach to a float, pier or wharf is similar to the previously discussed techniques for a single-screw boat since the ever-present wind is non-selective and will cause the bow of a twin-screw craft to fall off just as it does with a single-screw boat. When the bow is alongside, the outboard engine is reversed to bring the stern in toward the wharf. On a portside- to landing, the starboard engine is reversed; and on a starboard-side-to landing, the port engine is reversed. Because of the two engines, landing can be made on either side with ease by always reversing the outboard engine to bring the stern in.

Undocking the Twin-Screw Boat

Again, the basic principles discussed concerning single-screw craft apply. When getting away with the use of an after bow spring (if tied portside to the float), go ahead on the starboard engine with full left rudder to spring the stern clear. Once clear of all obstructions, both engines can be regulated as to speed. A twin-screw boat backs well because of the counter rotation of the propeller blades which cancel out the effects of individual propeller torque.

Underway with a Twin-Screw Boat

While underway, the advantages of the twin propellers may appear to have been lost. This is not so.

By adjusting (increasing) the rpm's of the leeward engine, the effects of leeway caused by wind or current can be overcome without constantly holding a right or left rudder to maintain the desired heading. Increase the rpm's of the leeward engine a little at a time until the bow ceases to fall off. The boat will now maintain heading with little or no rudder correction necessary.

If the rudder is damaged in any manner while underway, the twin-screw boat can be steered quite efficiently by judicious use of the throttles. Either the port or the starboard engine is set at a desired speed and the other is speeded up or slowed down to accomplish steering. Assuming that we set the port engine at 2800 rpm's (or any convenient speed), the boat can be turned to the left by speeding up the starboard engine, or turned to the right by decreasing the starboard engine's rpm's.

The average boatman who "graduates" from a single-screw to a twin-screw boat historically tends to become "lazy" in his maneuvering. This is due to the fact that less precision is required. With a single screw boat, he had to carefully pre-plan his landings, or other maneuvers, since he could generally depend on getting only one opportunity to make his move. On a landing for instance, if he made a mistake, he could try to back down and recover but in most instances, he was committed on his first approach. A mistake in landing with a single-screw boat usually results in a collision, with subsequent damage to his boat or to some other object.

On the other hand, the twin-screw boat operator can make a mistake on his approach, stop, back down, and make another approach. Since the twin-screw boat will back to port, to dead astern or to starboard, the operator tends to be more relaxed. He

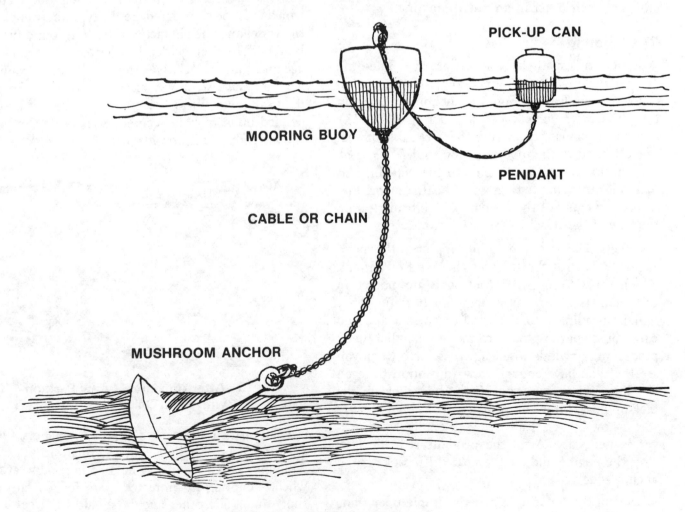

3-17 Typical Mooring Rig

can, with equanimity, become "lazy" and, because of the forgiving qualities and the versatility of his vessel, can usually get away with it.

Mooring to a Buoy

Mooring buoys, like all buoys, are secured to permanent anchors sunk deeply into the bottom. Mooring buoys are usually found near a yacht club, in a harbor, or other places where vessels congregate. It should be noted that mooring buoys are established and maintained specifically for mooring purposes and that they are the only buoys to which pleasure boatmen may legally moor their vessels. Mooring to an aid to navigation is illegal and if the aid is that of a public agency, it is a violation of public law. Mooring buoys offer safe, convenient anchorages, eliminating the need for the boatman to use his own anchor. These buoys also have the effect of keeping many craft anchored in close proximity of each other in an orderly manner.

The Mooring

A mooring usually has four major parts. These are (1) an anchor (usually very heavy); (2) an anchor cable or chain leading from the anchor to a buoy on the surface which is called a mooring buoy; (3) a mooring pendant consisting of a wire cable or fiber line attached to the mooring buoy; and (4) a small pick-up float which is attached to the pendant and makes it quite simple to grasp. A boat is moored by securing the end of the pendant to a bitt or cleat on the bow of the vessel.

When picking up a mooring, approach the mooring buoy against the force of the wind or current, whichever is stronger. If other boats are moored in the vicinity, observe how they are heading. They will be heading into the wind or current and you can adjust your approach to roughly parallel them, proceeding upwind. Disengage the clutch when you see that you have enough forward motion to reach the buoy. Have a person on the bow pick up the pick-up float, bring the pendant aboard, and secure it to a bow bitt or cleat. Use your engine to maneuver as necessary. After the pendant is made fast, stop the engine and let the boat drift back on the anchor rode.

Leaving the mooring is a fairly simple operation. About the only difficulty you may have is the possibility of getting the pendant fouled in your rudder or propeller. When the pendant is let go, go astern slowly until you have enough room to maneuver without hitting the buoy or fouling the pendant.

Anchoring

The art of anchoring should be mastered by every boatman, if only for his own protection. Many pleasure boatmen become very proficient in navigation and boat handling but neglect the important problem of anchoring once their destination has been reached. The general term applied to all equipment used for anchoring a vessel is *ground tackle*. A large percentage of pleasure boats are poorly equipped in this respect. The selection of ground tackle must be made with due regard to a number of factors.

There are so many variables in the requirements for adequate ground tackle that it is not possible to establish a firm set of rules. Among the factors which must be considered are the type and weight of the vessel and the character of bottom found in the locality. The average depth of water in the anchorage area and the relative strength of the prevailing wind and current should also be considered. Suffice it to say that, unless the ground tackle can be depended upon to hold securely even while the boat is unattended, it is not adequate for the task.

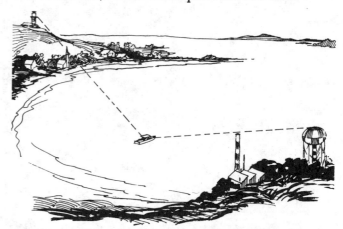

3-18 After Anchoring Check Position with Land Objects

Each boat should carry at least two anchors. One anchor may be of light weight and small size for easy handling. This anchor may be used in good weather when anchoring in protected areas for a relatively short time. The other anchor should be larger and heavier for use during bad weather conditions or when you intend to anchor overnight when there might be danger of dragging the anchor. The size of the anchors will depend on the size of the boat on which they will be used. Do not trust your own judgement in selecting these anchors. Get expert advice or use the manufacturers' recommendations.

Types of Anchors

There are many types of anchors available on the market. For the average pleasure boat, the so-called "patent" anchor is recommended. These anchors may be known by the names of their manufacturers and have great holding power for their weight. The following types of anchors are available for the pleaure boatman of today.

Yachtsman's Anchor

The yachtman's anchor is an adaption of the age-old kedge, redesigned to overcome some of the kedge's objectionable features. The plane of the stock is perpendicular to that of the arm and the stock is at the head. It has a sharp bill for good penetration of the bottom and the fluke is diamond-shaped to permit the cable to slip past it without fouling as the boat swings with changing current or shifting tide.

Mushroom Anchor

The mushroom is stockless, with a cast iron bowl at the end of the shank. The mushroom anchor is used principally for permanent moorings. This anchor will gradually sink deeply into the bottom and when so embedded, has tremendous holding power.

Fisherman's Anchor

This is a small mushroom type anchor which depends mainly on weight for holding power. It is used principally by small boat and skiff fishermen for deep or protected anchoring.

Grapnel

The grapnel has a straight shank with four or five curved claw-like arms. It is used mostly for recovering lost articles or objects. When used as an anchor, it is used on bottoms of rock or coral, with the deliberate intention of hooking it under a rock or coral head. A trip line, attached to the crown, is a *must* for retrieving it from the bottom.

Northill

The Northill anchor has a stock at the crown instead of at the head. The arm is at right angles to the shank and the broad flukes are set at an angle carefully designed to assure a quick bite and and penetration. The sharp point on the bill causes the anchor to dig into the bottom as soon as a pull is placed on the cable.

CQR Plow

This anchor is of British design and takes its name from the design of its flukes, which resemble a plow. This anchor is designed to lie on its side on the bottom. When a pull is placed on the cable, the flukes dig in quickly and deeply. The CQR Plow is an efficient anchor but is clumsy to handle and stow. It is now manufactured in this country and is gradually gaining favor among boatmen.

Danforth

The Danforth anchor is a by-product of World War II. Many thousands of these anchors (up to 3,000 lbs.) were used to pull landing craft off the beachheads of the Pacific. The Danforth anchor is lightweight and is characterized by long narrow twin flukes pivoted at one end of a relatively long shank. The stock is attached to the rear of the flukes. The flukes engage the bottom quickly and the anchor tends to bury completely under heavy strain.

Navy

The Navy anchor is found principally on large vessels. Because it is stockless, it stows conveniently in hawse pipes. Large

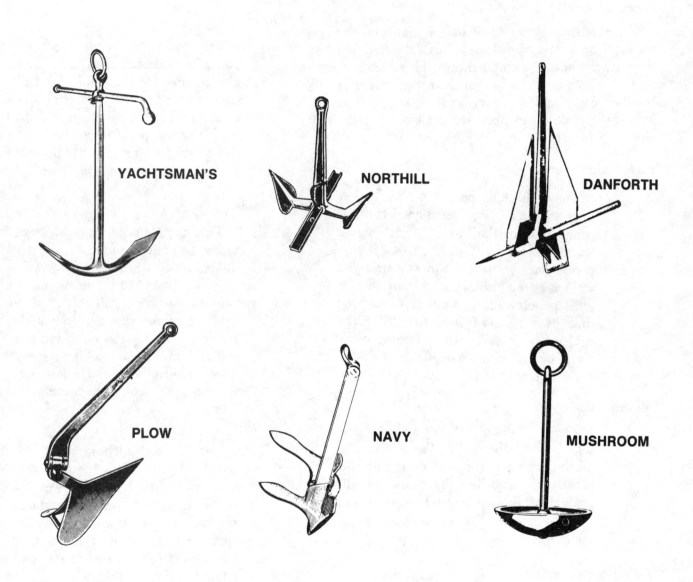

3-19   Various Types of Anchors

vessels have an ample supply of power to handle heavy anchors. The Navy anchor has a very high ratio of weight to holding power. On small craft, a Navy anchor heavy enough to provide adequate holding power is a backbreaker to handle. If the weight is kept down to make it easier to handle, its holding power is highly questionable. Several adaptations of the Navy type are on the market today, designed specifically for small craft. Some of these are quite adequate.

Rode and Scope

The size and length of the anchor rode will depend on the size of the anchor and the depth of the water. The *rode* is the anchor line and chain on which a boat is riding. *Scope* is the length of the anchor rode. Anchors hold best when the pull of the rode on the shank of the anchor is as near to horizontal as possible. For this reason, the holding power of an anchor increases as the scope is increased. A ratio of 7 to 1, that is a scope equal to seven times the depth of the water, is considered best for most anchoring purposes. A ratio of 5 to 1 is adequate but 3 to 1 is poor unless the weather is excellent, the consistency of the bottom is also excellent and the rise and fall of the tide is not excessive.

How to Anchor Your Boat

There are just a few simple rules to remember when anchoring. Head your boat into the wind or current. Reduce speed and make sure your anchor cable is ready for free running. Reverse the engine and when the boat starts to make a slight sternway through the water *lower* the anchor.

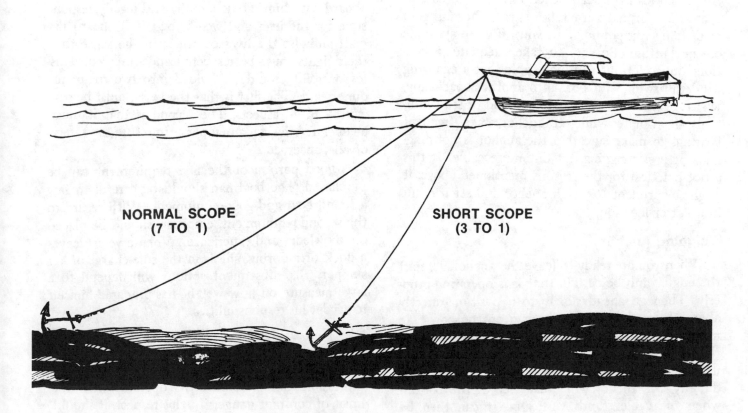

NORMAL SCOPE
(7 TO 1)

SHORT SCOPE
(3 TO 1)

3-20 Proper Anchoring

Make sure that you are not standing on any part of the line as it goes over the side and always be sure that the end of the anchor cable is secured to the boat. This end of the cable is known as the bitter end. Perhaps one reason for this term is that you would feel quite bitter as you watched the end of the line slither over the side. Actually, it is so named because it is the end of the line that is tied to the bitt. The loss of anchor and line in this manner has embarrassed more than one boatman.

When sufficient cable is out, usually five to seven times the depth of the water, stop the engine and make the cable fast to a forward cleat or bitt to make the anchor dig into the bottom. A definite halt in the drifting of the boat should be felt as the anchor digs in. It is wise at this time to take a sight on some stationary object on shore to make certain that your anchor is not dragging on the bottom. If the anchor is not holding, it can usually be made to bite in by letting out more line. Bear in mind that an anchor will usually hold better in mud than in sand, so it is good practice to check the character of the bottom. This can be done by either looking on your chart or lowering an armed lead. An armed lead is a lead which has a hollowed bottom and is armed with tallow, wax, chewing gum or bedding compound. This will bring up a sample of the bottom. Be sure to take adequate precautions not to let out so much cable that a changing wind will swing your boat into another boat, buoy, wharf, or onto the shore. If the wind or sea conditions deteriorate while at anchor, take frequent bearings to make sure that the anchor is not dragging. If it is dragging, let out more cable. If this is not practical for the reasons mentioned above, it might be prudent to weigh anchor and set it again in a better location.

Weighing Anchor

When you are ready to leave the anchorage, start the engine and be certain that it is operating properly. Then go ahead slowly to a position directly above the anchor. Have a person on the bow take up the slack in the cable as you proceed. Whipping the line up and down as it comes up will help free it of weeds and grass before it comes on deck. Ordinarily, the anchor will break free of the bottom when the cable stands vertically. It can then be raised to the deck and stowed.

If the anchor does not break free as the result of a good vertical heave, secure the line to a bitt and go ahead slowly for a few yards. If the anchor still does not break free, it is probably fouled. One way to attempt to clear it is to make the line fast to a bitt, and then run the boat slowly in wide circles on a taut line. In those cases where the anchor will not break out under any circumstances, the boat should be run up as close as possible, the anchor cable cut and a marker float attached to mark the remaining end. This will make it possible to attempt to retrieve the anchor later.

Heavy Weather Boat Handling

Although recreational boating is intended primarily to provide recreation, it also entails responsibilities. To some, responsibility is a part of the pleasure of boating. To others, it is accepted as a necessary part of the sport. However, a few boatmen fail to assume the necessary responsibility, and these persons become contributors to the accidents, and resultant tragedies, which occur on our waters. The small boat owner/operator cannot escape the responsibility he assumes when he takes persons aboard with him. He is morally and legally responsible for the lives and well-being of all aboard his craft and also the lives of others in the sense that their rights must be respected and observed. This responsibility could be divided into two major requirements. The first is that the vessel must be seaworthy in all aspects. The second is that it must be operated in such a manner as to insure the safety of all concerned.

A good portion of the first requirement can be purchased. The boatman should be careful to buy a sound boat and good equipment. With regard to the second requirement, emphasis should be placed on knowledge and experience. When a vessel leaves a dock or mooring, she is in the sole charge of her skipper. His subsequent actions will depend to a large measure on how well he has prepared himself to accept his responsibilities.

In United States Coast Guard Auxiliary public education courses, great emphasis is placed on safety. This might very well give the student the impression that pleasure boats operate under the threat of constant danger. In this respect, it should be pointed out that little skill is required to operate a well-found boat on a calm day in uncongested waters. Adverse conditions, caused by weather or some failure of equipment or personnel, require skillful judgement based on knowledge and understanding of the potential hazards of the sea and the means of combatting them.

Waves

Waves are undulations on the surface of the water This phenomenon is most widely observed but least understood by the average boatman. Consequently, a few words about waves, their causes and effects, should be in order.

Waves are caused principally by the wind. Other causes are submarine earthquakes, volcanic eruptions and the tides. Ripples form if a breeze of less than two knots blows across the surface of the water. If this breeze were to stop suddenly, the ripples would soon disappear. If the wind exceeds two knots, more stable gravity waves are formed. These progress in the direction of the generating wind. Unlike wind or current, gravity waves are not affected by the rotation of the earth. When the wind ceases to blow, energy is no longer transferred to the wave (now called a "swell") and its height begins to diminish. This reduction takes place quite slowly. If a wave is of sufficient strength, it will continue to travel until it reaches shore. In the deep waters of the open seas, "old" waves tend to take on a characteristic shape known as a cycloid. These have gentle slopes, rounded troughs and crests that are somewhat sharper than the slopes. The term employed to describe this type of wave is "swell" or "ground swell."

The distance between consecutive crests is called the wave length and the vertical distance between the crest and the trough is called the wave height.

Small craft are generally quite comfortable in this type of sea as they move smoothly up and down without any violent motions.

As the waves approach the shore and the water begins to shoal, the waves start to feel bottom. When the depth of the water shoals to about one-half of the wave length, the wave begins to decrease in velocity and increase in height. As the depth of the water becomes more shallow, the velocity continues to decrease, while the crests become sharper and the wave length becomes shorter. Eventually, the waves begin to "pile up" on the shore. At this point, the velocity will begin to increase again, and when the wave's height is about one-seventh of its length, the top of the wave will begin to curl and break. Shallow water breakers have a strong horizontal flow in addition to their vertical motion. Also, a strong return flow opposes the base of the advancing waves.

Except in very shallow waters, the horizontal flow of water caused by a wave is negligible. Wave motion at sea is energy moving through the water, not the water itself rushing along. This can best be visualized if you have ever seen the waves caused by wind in a field of wheat. Each stalk sways back and forth but the wheat does not pile up at the downwind end of the field. The motion of a given particle of water in a wave is quite similar to the action of the wheat. If this particle of water were on the surface, it would rise as the wave crest approached, with a slight forward motion. As the crest passed, it would descend, with a slight backward motion. The speed of this slight horizontal motion would increase at the crest and slow down in the trough. When added to the vertical motion of rising and falling, a given particle of water would roughly describe a circle (in a vertical plane) as each wave passes.

Because of the many independent wave systems in the sea at the same time, the surface acquires a complex and irregular pattern. Longer wave systems outrun shorter ones as the systems interfere with one another. This is the principal reason that successive wave crests are not the same height. This may be further accentuated by wave systems crossing each other at an angle. On occasion, this condition will produce peak-like rises.

In very heavy weather, waves with breaking crests may form well out to sea. This is an extremely dangerous condition for the small boat operator and should be avoided if at all possible. The boatman should get weather information before setting out.

Heavy Weather

At the first warning of heavy weather, whether it be by observation of the skies or by radio warnings, the boatman should rig for heavy weather by taking certain precautions before the weather hits. All hatches and portholes should be secured and all loose gear lashed down. Life lines should be rigged and extra lines should be readily available. If you are in shallow water, be certain that the ground tackle is in condition to let go quickly. If in deeper water, the sea anchor should be broken out and made ready for use if necessary. If you are towing a dinghy, either bring it aboard or set it far back on a heavy tow line. Set the tow line so that the dinghy will ride in step with your boat. The sea characteristics of your vessel and your dinghy are simply not the same. In many cases during a blow, a dinghy has become troublesome and difficult to control. In extreme cases, cut the dinghy painter and abandon it. Be sure the first aid kit is available and if is to be a strong blow, put on your personal flotation devices. Secure the galley and put out all fires. It might be a good idea to prepare sandwiches or other food rations against the time when they will be most welcome. Finally, just before the weather hits, get the best navigational fix that you can. In the decreased visibility, you might not be able to see landmarks as well as you could in clear weather.

Heavy weather, in itself, does not place the small craft in danger. It will, however, test the mettle of both the vessel and her crew. It is comforting to note that a well-found boat, manned by a knowledgeable skipper and an able crew, is usually equal to the task.

Running Into a Sea

As the seas build up, the bow of your boat will be driven into the waves with increasing force instead of being lifted, as is the case in calmer water. This causes the boat to take a tremendous pounding. Heavy objects could break loose and become veritable battering rams. The violent action of the hull could cause serious falls within the boat. Injuries caused at this time are most difficult to treat because of the boat's unpredictable and violent motion. The propeller is alternately submerged and out of the water, causing the engine to be loaded one moment and racing wildly the next. In this condition, the boat, her crew, and all the boat's gear are under extreme stress and steps must be taken immediately to reduce this stress.

The first thing to do is slow down. Many inexperienced boatmen, caught in their first storm, are unable to resist the temptation to run helter skelter for

the nearest port. This would have been an excellent idea before the storm arrived, provided a safe harbor were near enough to reach in time. But now, it is too late! By slowing down, the bow will tend to lift with the waves, as the natural force of buoyancy is again allowed to function. Take the seas slightly off the bow, preferrably at an angle approaching 45°. This will cause the boat to roll and pitch, but it is far easier on both boat and crew than the violent motions of pitching alone. If unable to make headway under these conditions, it is advisable to lay to. Most power craft, if left to their own resources, turn their stern into the wind. This is patently unacceptable in these circumstances, so it will be necessary to use enough power to keep the bow up into the wind, adjusting the speed so that you will be making neither headway nor sternway. If the storm is of long duration, fuel may become a real problem. If this causes concern, it might be best to fall back on a sea anchor. The sea anchor should be securely attached to the rode and the bitter end of the rode should be secured to a bow bitt or cleat *before the sea anchor is set out.* A trip line should be tied to the cone end of the sea anchor, to facilitate its retrieval when necessary. The sea anchor is hauled in backwards by pulling in the trip line. When the sea anchor is set out, the boat will fall back on the line, and the bow will be held into the wind. This may not be very comfortable, but it is the best you can do under the circumstances. Depending on the size of the sea anchor, the drift will be drastically reduced. Try to keep the center of gravity as low as possible by keeping all persons down or near the bottom of the boat. This will make the boat more stable and reduce the chance of capsizing.

3-21 Use of a Sea Anchor

Running in a Beam Sea

Running in a beam sea or "in the trough," as it is commonly called, is an acceptable procedure only under conditions of comparative calm. In a beam sea, the waves are acting directly on the vessel's sides (coming from abeam) and, in rough water, could roll some boats over on their side. If the required course is laid so that you are in the trough and the action of the boat becomes excessive, it might be best to change course slightly to take the seas off the bow or quarter. In order to make the desired landfall it may be necessary to sail a "zig-zag" course, taking the seas off the bow for awhile, then off the quarter. The distance travelled over the water will be longer and your time of arrival will be later, but this change of plan is highly preferable to a change of plan occasioned by capsizing at sea with all hands ending up in the water.

3-22 Zig-Zagging Through Heavy Seas

Running Before the Sea

When a vessel sails in the same direction that the seas are running, it is running before the sea or running in a following sea. On the high seas, a following sea is usually no more than a nuisance. Precise attention to the rudder is required, as the turning action of the hull appears to be more lively and difficult to control. Inexperienced boatmen in their first following sea, tend to overcontrol, with the result that they find themselves wandering all over the ocean.

In shallow bays and large shallow lakes, following seas often build up to the point where it becomes extremely dangerous for small craft. This danger is confined principally to power craft, which usually have large transom areas. Sailing vessels and craft with "double ender" hulls generally experience little difficulty in following seas because of their streamlined underwater shape. The force of the water, acting on the relatively large non-streamlined transom of a power cruiser can cause the boat to yaw wildly from side to side. On some boats, the rudder and propeller can be lifted clear of the water as the stern is picked up by an approaching wave. If the boat is yawing at the time the stern is lifted clear of the water, the boat is completely out of control and could be thrown broadside into the trough and rolled over by the next wave. This is known as going into a broach and should be avoided at all costs.

3-23 Broaching

The secret of avoiding a broach is to keep yawing under control at all times. It is important to keep sideways motion to a minimum. This can be accomplished only when the rudder is in the water. The rudder can be kept "wet" by slowing down as the wave approaches the stern and allowing the wave to pass under. The rpm's are then increased slightly until the next wave approaches the stern. rpm's are again reduced long enough to let the next following wave pass under. By judicious use of the throttle and the rudder, yawing can be kept to a minimum. It is important to remember that a yaw can quickly become a broach. Once the broach has started, it is almost impossible to stop.

At this point, one might arrive at the conclusion that running before the sea is a lot of hard work. The fact is that it *is* a lot of hard work. Both the throttle and the rudder must be tended constantly. In a very heavy following sea, rudder action has been known on occasion to become reversed. Hard right rudder, in these circumstances could send the stern to the right instead of to the left. Under conditions as extreme as this, a heavy line or small sea anchor

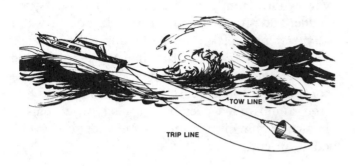

3-24 Drogue Used with Following Seas

trailed far astern will help to "nail the stern down" and make the yawing tendency easier to control.

Control of the engine rpm's in a heavy following sea cannot be over-emphasized. Unless the boat is slowed down appreciably as the wave approaches the stern, the vessel will be picked up by the wave and may find itself racing down the forward face of the wave at a greatly increased speed. While this might seem exciting, it could become *too* exciting as the boat races forward and plows into the trough, burying the bow well under in the process. The following wave might well pick up the stern and, with the bow deeply set in the water, flip the boat end over end. This is known as pitchpoling and is extremely dangerous. It is a sad fact that either a broach or a pitchpole has an air of finality about it. The usual result of either is loss of life and property. Needless to say, either can happen instantly in a strong following sea and makes running before the sea potentially the most dangerous point of cruising.

Impaired Visibility

When the subject of impaired or restricted visibility is brought up, most boatmen immediately think of fog. While it is true that fog is the most common impairment to visibility, other conditions such as heavy rain, sleet, hail and snow also fall within this category. The techniques for cruising in im-

3-25 Pitchpoling

paired visibility are common to all of these conditions. For convenience of the author (if for no better reason), we will include all of the foregoing conditions under the general term "fog." Consequently, when we consider fog, we will be inferentially including heavy rain, sleet, hail and snow. On second thought, and in deference to our modern civilization with its effects on our atmosphere, we will also include "heavy smog" in our general classification of "fog."

The first and most obvious rule for safe boat operation in conditions of impaired visibility is not to go out on the water in the first place. If it's too foggy to see, it follows that it is too foggy to cruise. Fog has a habit of burning off eventually and the boatman is well advised to be patient until the visibility improves a bit. The inexperienced boatman, caught out on the water when these conditions close in, will find himself in a whole new world. If it's his first time in a real "pea soup" fog, he will find himself struggling mightily with the temptation to panic.

Even if the fog closes in rapidly, the impending condition can generally be observed for a short time beforehand. This time should be employed in making an accurate determination of the vessel's position. In the section on Plotting we will learn how to do this, but at this time we emphasize the need for determining a position as accurately as possible. Also, if a cruise log has not been maintained up to this point, it is an excellent idea to start one now. If you don't have a log book, the back of an envelope or the back page of your engine manual will do. Record the compass heading, the speed (as accurately as possible) and the *time*. Unless you know where you were at the time the fog closed in, you will have absolutely no idea where you are at any subsequent time. Further, unless you know in what direction you are heading and how fast (or slow) you are cruising, you will have absolutely no idea where you are going or when you might get there.

Today, many vessels are equipped with radar. Almost all commercial vessels and many pleasure craft now have this equipment. The owner of a boat not equipped with radar can increase his own margin of safety in fog by rigging a radar reflector as high as possible above the hull. A radar reflector is made of thin light-weight metal sheets or fine-mesh metal screen arranged in three mutually perpendicular planes. These reflectors can be purchased commercially or they can be homemade. They are usually constructed so they can be folded flat for easy storage. If the area of each plane is only two feet square the device will reflect a radar image which is comparable to that of a medium sized steel vessel. By placing the radar reflector as high as possible on a mast or in the rigging, vessels equipped with radar will be able to detect the presence of your boat in the fog. This greatly increases your margin of safety.

With your position determined and the log entered you are as ready for the fog as you will ever be. As soon as things close in, slow down. Your speed will be determined by the visible distance. The law requires that you be able to stop in not more than one half of your visible distance. In theory, if all fogbound vessels could stop in half of their distance of visibility, there would be no collisions in fog. For instance, if the visibility were 500 feet, and two vessels on a collision course were to sight each other at 500 feet, each would be able to stop in less than 250 feet. Granted, the vessels would come precariously close—but they would not collide!

Regardless of weather conditions, the law requires that you maintain an efficient watch at all times when you are underway. This becomes more important than ever in a fog. A lookout should be posted on the bow, or as far forward as possible. The bow lookout should be as far removed from the engine noise as possible so that he will be able to hear other sounds around him. Since the fog has deprived all hands from the use of their eyes in the navigation of the vessel, great dependence must be placed on the use of their ears. In extreme cases, it will become necessary to stop the engine frequently to afford all hands a series of silent listening periods.

It might be well to mention that the behavior of sound travelling through fog is most deceptive and unpredictable. In heavy fog, sound has been known to travel long distances and "skip" large areas in the process. A bell or horn, for instance, has been heard clearly a mile away and not heard at all at a distance of 100 yards. Further, when the sound is heard, it can often be interpreted as coming from more than one direction. If the sound is faint, it could appear to come successively from all points of the compass. To compound this even further, our ears are not directionally oriented. Whether we realize it or not, the average human being has grown accustomed to depending on his eyes as an aid to determine the direction from which a sound is coming. Those of you who do not believe this, are invited to try a simple experiment. Stand upright and close your eyes tightly. (Better still, put on a blindfold, since this will keep you from peeking.) Ask someone to snap a pair of coins directly in front of you or directly behind you. Have him do this a few times, both front and back. You will discover, to your surprise, that you will not be able to tell with certainty whether the sound was coming from in front or from behind. And so it is in fog—you must depend on your ears and your ears are not very dependable. However, there are several ways of aiding the directional ability of your ears. One way is to cup your hands behind both ears and then turn your head until the sound is loudest. You are then looking in the direction of the sound. Another way is to place the small end of a megaphone up to one ear, plug the other ear and turn your head until the sound is loudest. The sound is then coming from the direction the megaphone is pointing.

According to law, you must sound proper fog signals on the whistle. This becomes quite an accomplishment if you don't have a whistle. Vessels under 16 feet must sound fog signals even though the law does not specify that a whistle must be carried aboard. Accordingly, if your boating area is plagued by foggy seasons you should have a whistle (and a bell, as we shall see later) even if your craft is less than 16 feet long. Your whistle signals warn others of your presence. Since all craft are similarly bound to sound fog signals, their signals should warn you of their presence. Upon hearing the fog signal of another vessel, stop immediately and do not start again until you have determined to your full satisfaction that it is safe to proceed. Other sounds that may be heard are fog horns of sailboats, fog horns of lighthouses, bells, sirens, diaphragm horns, the sounds of breakers and other land sounds. Identification of the sound is important as it could possibly be related to an object found on your chart. For instance, a boatman caught in a real "pea souper" off the coast of Southern California, exchanged whistle signals with the Los Angeles Lighthouse for over thirty minutes before he came to the realization that this was, in fact, a lighthouse and not another vessel!

Depending on the depth of the water and the configuration of the shore, an anchor could be lowered from the bow and allowed to hang straight down with sufficient cable out to engage the bottom before the boat runs up on the shore. If you have a radio direction finder aboard and if you have become proficient in its use (it's too late to learn now), it can be of great help in determining your position and in "homing in" on the radio signal. A word of caution to those using this "homing in" technique. Be sure to *stop* before you arrive at the transmitter. Many radio beacons are situated on the ends of breakwaters or piers and many hapless boatmen have "homed in" on these aids with such precision that they smashed right into the pier or ended up holed on a rocky breakwater.

If possible, the best thing to do in a heavy fog is to get well clear of channels and shipping lanes and lower the anchor. When you anchor, you are not underway. However, you are required to sound proper anchor signals when anchored in a fog. Anchor signals are sounded on a bell. Here again, if your boat is less than 26 feet long, you are not legally required to have a bell aboard. In the chapter on *Rules of the Road*, you will study the whole subject of right-of-way, sound signals and fog signals. These rules differ according to where you do your boating. Your instructor will advise you con-

cerning which set of rules apply to your waters. However, the forgoing comments apply to all waters since they are related strictly to the use of common sense.

Running Narrow Inlets

No text on the art of seamanship and safety would be complete without a few words concerning the running of narrow inlets. Many rivers and coves are connected to the sea by narrow inlets. While no two inlets are alike, they have a lot in common. Shoaling is not gradual as it is along most coasts. At the mouth of most narrow inlets shoaling is quite rapid and it is usually confused by bottom irregularities known as sand bars with deeper pools in between.

As the waves approach narrow inlets, their height increases rapidly and breakers form over the shallowest areas, indicating the location and (to some extent) the size of the sand bars. Further, these sand bars are constantly shifting, thus thwarting all attempts to define the limits of the navigable channel by the use of buoys. Every narrow inlet in existence has its own peculiarities and it is here more than anywhere else that local knowledge and intimate familiarity with existing conditions come into play.

It is not possible to learn the techniques of running narrow or breaking inlets from the printed page. Anyone who has ever had the experience of shooting a "hair raiser" will agree with this statement. Narrow inlets come in all shapes and sizes. Some are reserved only for experts even under the best of conditions. Others present only minimum difficulty at best and require a high degree of skill only under the worst of sea conditions. In all narrow inlets, the water is confused and irregular and no prudent boatman would attempt his first run in an unfamiliar inlet without having a "native" aboard to point out known hazards and indicate the areas where the safe channel could most probably be found.

One point to remember when contemplating running a narrow inlet is that you may be required to use bursts of high power to maintain the proper attitude in relation to the seas. This would automatically rule out sailboats (even sailing auxiliaries) and low powered displacement-hull power craft. These types of vessels do not have the necessary quick response to run anything but the mildest form of narrow inlet.

While standing off the inlet, prepare a sea anchor or drogue. Use a heavy line for the drogue and be certain that a smaller trip line is attached to the narrow opening. Having determined (by observation) the cadence of the waves, select a small one and run up onto its back surface. The drogue is streamed astern *by the trip line*, ready for use. As the wave moves forward you must maintain your position exactly on the back of the wave. Set the drogue by *letting out* the trip line if you feel the boat is moving toward the crest of the wave. Use bursts of high power if you feel the boat sliding backward into the trough. Maintain your position on the wave until it eventually breaks ahead of your boat. Trip the drogue (if it is still set) and apply full power as you enter the turbulent water. As calmer water is reached, slow down and haul in the drogue by the trip line.

Do not attempt to tow a dinghy astern of your boat while entering a breaking inlet. It can only cause trouble. If possible, the dinghy should be brought aboard and secured bottom up. If this is not possible it might be better to abandon the dinghy and attempt to retrieve it later.

Conclusion

In conclusion, use good common sense when it comes to deciding whether or not you should use your boat when the wind and sea are increasing in velocity and size. If there is the least doubt in your mind, decide against it. Strangely enough, the more a man goes to sea, the greater respect he has for it. Don't tempt fate. Don't take chances on becoming another statistic. The sea has always seemed mysterious. Let the professional seaman seek out its mysteries—he is far better equipped for it.

CHAPTER 4

Legal Requirements

Introduction

The Congress of The United States has recognized the need for safety in boating and has enacted into law certain basic requirements for motorboats. In addition, there are numerous state and local regulations which amplify the federal requirements. As in all other areas of our society, ignorance of the navigation laws does not exempt you from prosecution if you violate them. You must become aware of your responsibilities on the water and equip your craft according to federal and state requirements.

This chapter deals with federal laws and regulations applicable to boats and boatmen. State and local requirements vary so much across the country that it is impossible to cover them in this chapter. You can obtain information concerning these from the nearest state or local boating law enforcement agency.

Numbering of Vessels

Boats propelled by machinery and operated on the navigable waters of the United States must be numbered, regardless of length and whether fitted with inboard or outboard engines.

This numbering requirement excludes boats used exclusively for racing and vessels documented as yachts. Other exceptions include public vessels, state and municipal vessels and ships' lifeboats. Vessels that have a valid temporary certificate may operate without displaying the registration number on the bow while awaiting issuance of a permanent certificate.

In general, the term "navigable waters of the United States" refers to waters which provide a "road" for transportation between two or more states or to the sea.

Under the Federal Boating Act of 1958, most states have assumed this numbering function. Their systems are compatible with the federal system. If you intend to operate principally on waters in a state which has received federal approval of its numbering system you must determine that particular state's requirements. The state has jurisdiction and may, for example, require all pleasure craft, regardless of type of waters, to be numbered. For information regarding individual states with approved systems, consult your marine dealer, the Coast Guard, the Coast Guard Auxiliary, or the State Boating Law Administration.

If your boat must be numbered, the place of application depends upon the waters of principal use. Where these waters are within a state that has a federally approved numbering system, application is made in accordance with that state's instructions.

When a boat is used principally on ocean or gulf waters, the place where it is normally moored becomes the determining factor in where the application is made. If the state where the boat is moored has a federally approved system, application is made to that state. When the state system has not been federally approved, application is made to the Commandant (G-BLC-4), U.S. Coast Guard, Washington, D.C. 20590. However, most states have enacted numbering laws approved by the federal government.

The number assigned by the certificate is to be painted on or attached to each side of the forward half of the vessel (the bow), and no other numbers may be displayed thereon. Numbers are to read from left to right, to be of block character, of contrasting

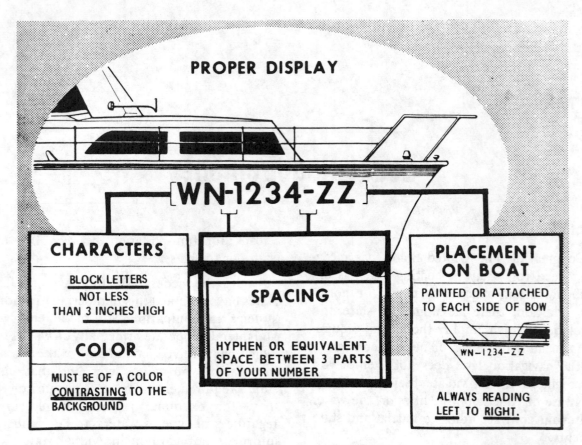

4-1 Proper Number Placement

color to the background and not less than three inches in height. Between the prefix, the numerals, and the suffix, there must be a hyphen or space equal to the width of any letter or number except "I" or "l".

The number shall not be placed on the obscured underside of a flared bow where the angle is such that the number cannot be easily read. When the vessel configuration is such that the number cannot be so placed on the bow, it will be placed on the forward half of the hull or on the permanent super-structure located on the forward half of the hull, as nearly vertical as possible, and where easily ob-served. If the above will not provide ready identifi-cation, the number may be mounted on a bracket or fixture firmly attached to the forward half of the vessel.

Sales and Transfers

Boat numbers and Certificates of Number are not transferable from person to person, nor from boat to boat. This number stays with the boat unless the state of principal use is changed. When numbered by the Coast Guard, a new application with a $6.00 fee must be filed by each owner for every boat (except dealers) with the Commandant G-BLC-3, U.S. Coast Guard, Washington, D.C. 20590.

Documenting of Vessels

Under navigation laws administered by the U. S. Coast Guard, a vessel of 5 net tons or over owned by a citizen of the United States and used exclu-sively for pleasure may be documented as a yacht.

The principal privileges are:

(a) Authority to fly the yacht ensign.
(b) Provision for recording and retaining copies of mortgages, bills of sale, and other instru-ments of title with the U. S. Coast Guard. Mortgages which are so recorded may, upon compliance with the applicable require-ments, become preferred mortgages, thus giving additional security to the mortgagee.

A documented yacht must display her name and hailing port on some conspicuous portion of the hull, usually the stern, and her official number and net tonnage must be carved or otherwise permanently marked on her main beam.

Sales to Aliens

Under Federal law, the sale, transfer, mortgage, or lease by a U. S. citizen to an alien of a vessel of more than 65 feet in length and/or designed for propulsion by an engine or engines totalling more than 600 horsepower, must be specifically approved by the Maritime Administration.

The same stipulation applies to the sale, transfer, mortgage, or lease (to an alien) of any vessel presently documented or last documented in the United States, regardless of its length or specified horsepower.

Specific advance approval by the Maritime Administration is also necessary for the sale of any vessel to a citizen or resident of certain Communist-controlled countries.

For approvals or further information, communicate with the Foreign Transfer Branch, Office of Ship Operations, Maritime Administration, Washington, D. C. 20235.

Length of Motorboats

The federal government has, through the Motorboat Act of 1940, as amended, set forth minimum equipment for different lengths of boat. Before you can determine your boat's needs to conform with the requirements of federal law, you first have to accurately determine the length of the boat. "Motorboat" means any vessel 65 feet in length or less which is propelled by steam. The word "motorboat," also means a boat temporarily or permanently equipped with a motor and, although few and far between, a boat propelled by steam.

For determining "official length", the length is measured from end to end over the deck excluding sheer. This means a straight line measurement of the overall length from the foremost part of the vessel to the aftermost part of the vessel, measured parallel to the centerline. Bow sprits, bumpkins, rudders, outboard motor brackets, and similar fittings or attachments are not to be included in the measurement. Length is stated in feet and inches.

After determining your boat's length, the next step is to equip it with at least the minimum requirements by the law. It is important to remember that this equipment is the minimum required to be on board your boat to conform with federal law.

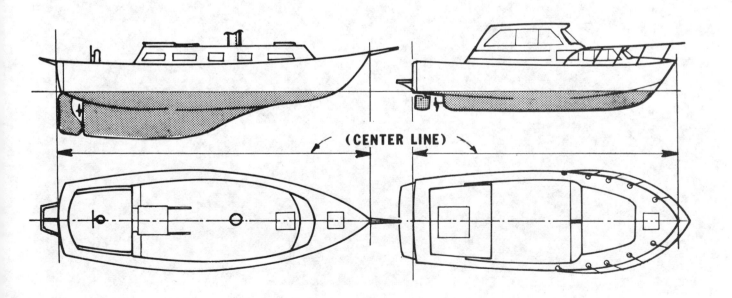

4-2 Measuring the Boat

All motorboats may be required to carry up to six different items of equipment: fire extinguishers, personal flotation devices, flame arresters, ventilation devices, bells, and whistles.

Lights

By day, a vessel's course, change of course or progress on her course is fairly obvious. By night, practically nothing can be determined about another vessel unless the vessel is lighted according to the rules. As with the rules for maneuvering, the provisions for lights vary according to the place, the size of the vessel and her use. Lights for vessels will be discussed in Chapter V, *Rules of the Road*.

Fire Extinguishers

Fire extinguishers are classified by letter and roman numeral according to their size and the type of fire they are designed to put out. The letter indicates the type of fire: "A" for combustible solids; "B" for flammable and combustible liquids; "C" for electrical fires and "D" for combustible metals. Motorboats are required to have either hand portable or semi-portable units capable of extinguishing fires involving flammable liquids and grease (class "B" fires). The table below makes it easy to understand the classifications you will use:

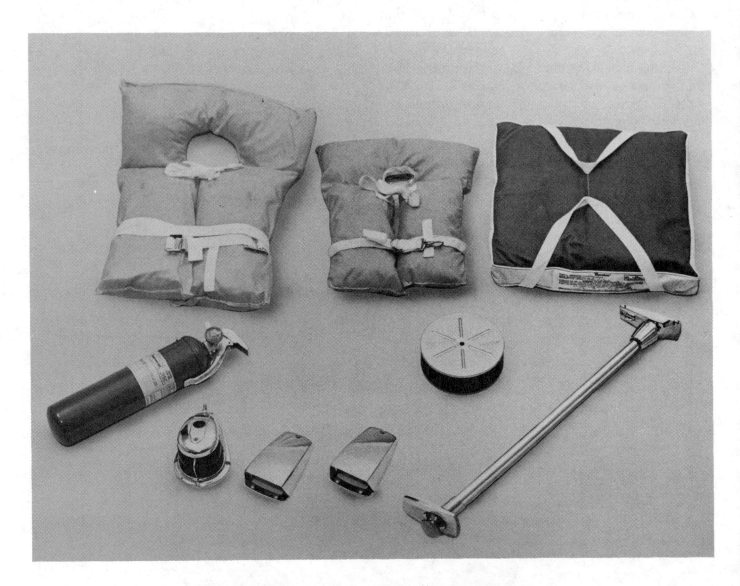

4-3 Equipment for boats less than 16 feet in length.

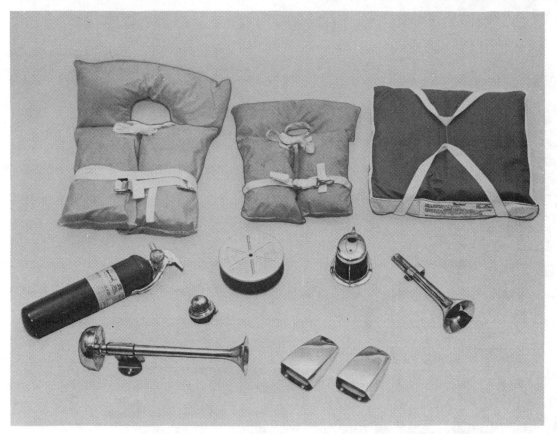

4-4   Equipment for boats 16 feet to less than 26 feet in length.

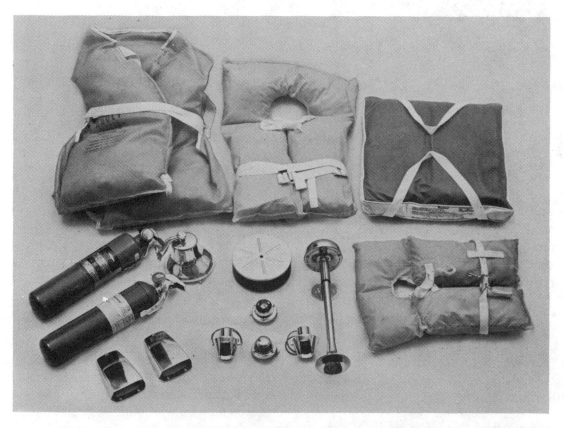

4-5   Equipment for boats 26 feet to less than 40 feet in length.

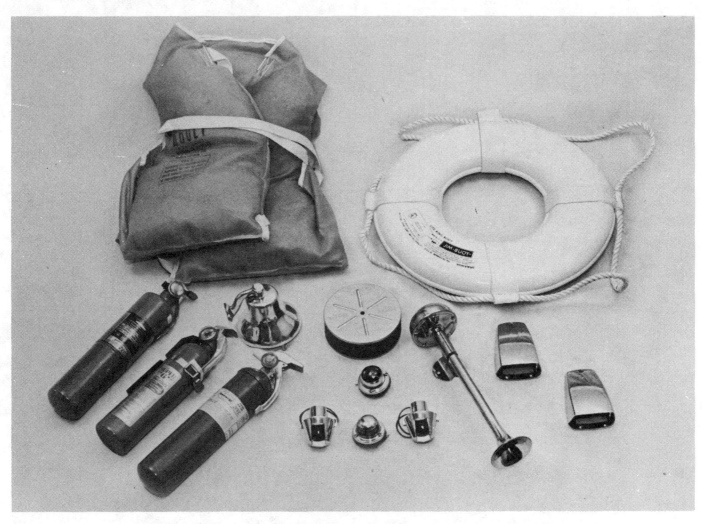

4-6 Equipment for boats 40 feet to not more than 65 feet in length.

Classification (type – size)	Foam	Carbon Dioxide	Dry Chemical	Freon
B-I	1¼ gals.	4 lbs.	2 lbs.	2½ lbs.
B-II	2½ gals.	15 lbs.	10 lbs.	—
B-III	12 gals.	35 lbs.	20 lbs.	—

To meet equipment requirements, portable fire extinguishers must be Coast Guard approved. Portable fire extinguishers bearing the "Marine Type" label of Underwriters' Laboratories Inc., are approved for use on motorboats. Example: "Marine Type, USCG Type B, Size 1, Approval No. 162. 028/EX. . . ."

For current listings of marine type portable fire extinguishers, consult the Fire Protection Equipment List published by the Underwriters' Laboratories, Inc., 207 East Ohio Street, Chicago, Illinois.

Most fire extinguishers manufactured prior to 1 January 1965, do not have the Coast Guard approval number on the nameplate. When a fire extinguisher does not show the Coast Guard approval number, the nameplate should be checked against the listing in CG-190, Equipment Lists at Coast Guard Marine Inspection Offices, or Underwriters' Laboratories, Inc., Fire Protection Equipment List. To be acceptable by the Coast Guard for use, they must be in good and serviceable condition.

If there is doubt about the approval status of any fire extinguisher, you should contact the nearest Coast Guard Marine Inspection Office.

You should make frequent checks to be sure your extinguishers are in their proper stowage brackets and undamaged. Cracked or broken hose should be replaced and nozzles should be kept free of obstructions. Extinguishers having pressure gauges should show pressure within the designated limits. Locking pins and sealing wires should be checked to assure that the extinguisher has not been used since last recharge. Extinguishers should never be tried merely to see if they are in proper operating condition because in many cases the valves will not properly reseat, thereby resulting in a gradual discharge. A discharged extinguisher should be recharged at the first opportunity.

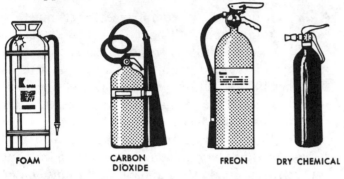

4-7 Typical Fire Extinguishers

The following tests and inspections should be made by qualified persons:

Foam

Once a year discharge the extinguisher. Clean the hose and inside of the extinguisher thoroughly. Recharge and attach a tag indicating the date of servicing.

Carbon Dioxide or Freon

Twice a year weigh the cylinder and recharge if the weight loss exceeds 10% of the weight of the charge. Inspect hose and nozzle to be sure they are clear. Inspect the lead seals on the operating levers to insure they are not broken. Attach a tag to indicate when the extinguisher was serviced or inspected.

Dry Chemical

With visual pressure indicator

Regularly check the pressure indicator to insure the extinguisher has the proper amount of pressure. Occasionally invert the extinguisher and shake it to insure that the powder has not packed and caked due to vibration. Check the nozzle to insure that there is no powder in it; if there is, weigh the extinguisher to insure that it has a full charge. Check the seals to insure that they are intact.

Without indicator

Once every six months the extinguisher must be taken ashore to be checked and weighed. If the weight is ¼ ounce less than that stamped on the container it must be serviced. The seals indicating that it has not been tampered with must be intact. If there is any indication of tampering or leakage such as powder in the nozzle, the extinguisher must be serviced. All servicing must be indicated by the servicing station on an attached tag.

Fire Extinguisher Requirements

If, owing to the nature of its construction, a boat will tend to trap explosive vapors, it is required to carry a fire extinguisher. There is increased possibly of explosion if any of the below listed conditions exist. Motorboats less than 26 feet in length having one or more of these areas are required to carry a fire extinguisher.

1. Closed compartments under thwarts and seats wherein portable tanks may be stored.

2. Double bottoms not sealed to the hull or which are not completely filled with flotation material.

3. Closed living spaces.

4. Closed stowage compartments in which combustible or flammable materials are stowed.

5. Permanently installed fuel tanks.

The conditions numbered below do not, by themselves, require fire extinguishers on outboard motorboats less than 26 feet in length·

1. Bait wells.
2. Glove compartments.
3. Buoyant flotation material.
4. Open slatted flooring.
5. Ice chests.

All motorboats 26 feet or greater, and those motorboats less than 26 feet which are required to be equipped with fire extinguishers, must be equipped according to the following table:

MINIMUM NUMBER OF
HAND PORTABLE FIRE EXTINGUISHERS REQUIRED

Length of vessel	No fixed system in machinery space	Fixed fire extinguishing system in machinery space
Less than 16′	1 B-1	None
16′ to less than 26′	1 B-1	None
26′ to less than 40′	2 B-1 or 1 B-11	1 B-1
40′ through 65′	3 B-1 or 1 B-11 and 1 B-1	2 B-1 or 1 B-11

Hull Identification Number

A hull identification number must be displayed on all recreation boats the construction of which began after October 31, 1972. The number consists of 12 characters no less than one-fourth of an inch in height and must be affixed to the outboard side of the transom or, if there is no transom, to the outermost starboard side at the end of the hull that bears the rudder or other steering mechanism. The hull identification number must be affixed above the waterline of the boat in such a way that alteration, removal, or replacement would be obvious and evident. Additional characters may be displayed after the hull identification number if they are separated from the hull identification number by a hyphen.

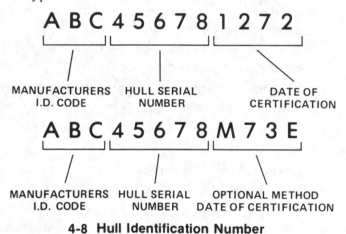

4-8 Hull Identification Number

Display of Capacity Information

All monohull recreational boats less than 20 feet in length the construction of which began after October 31, 1972, except sailboats, canoes, kayaks, and inflatable boats, must have a legible capacity marking permanently displayed where it is clearly visible to the operator when he is getting the boat underway. The information required to be marked must be displayed in the following manner:

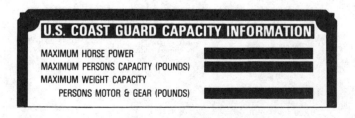

4-9 Capacity Plate for Outboards

U.S. COAST GUARD CAPACITY INFORMATION

MAXIMUM PERSONS CAPACITY (POUNDS)

MAXIMUM WEIGHT CAPACITY

PERSONS & GEAR (POUNDS)

4-10 Capacity Plate for Inboards, etc.

Manufacturer Certification of Compliance

A certification of compliance label must be affixed to all monohull boats less than 20 feet in length except sailboats, canoes, kayaks, and inflatable boats construction of which began after 31 October 1972. Each label must contain (1) the name and address of the manufacturer who certifies the boat or associated equipment and (2) the words "This ('Boat' or 'Equipment') complies with U.S. Coast Guard Safety Standards in effect on the Date of Certification. Letters and numbers must be no less than one-eighth of an inch in height. The certification of compliance label may be affixed at any easily accessible location on the boat or associated equipment. This label may, at the manufacturer's option, be combined with the capacity plate.

THIS BOAT COMPLIES WITH U.S. COAST GUARD SAFETY STANDARDS IN EFFECT ON THE DATE OF CERTIFICATION

MODEL NO.   SERIAL NO.

MFD. BY

4-11 Certificate of Compliance

U.S. COAST GUARD CAPACITY INFORMATION

MAXIMUM HORSE POWER

MAXIMUM PERSONS CAPACITY (POUNDS)

MAXIMUM WEIGHT CAPACITY

PERSONS MOTOR & GEAR (POUNDS)

THIS BOAT COMPLIES WITH U.S. COAST GUARD SAFETY STANDARDS IN EFFECT ON THE DATE OF CERTIFICATION

MODEL NO.   SERIAL NO.

MFD. BY

4-12 Combination Capacity Plate and Certificate of Compliance

Personal Flotation Devices

As of 1 October 1973, a new Federal personal flotation device (PFD) regulation became effective. The new law requires that (1) all recreational boats less than sixteen (16) feet in length, including sailboats and rowboats, and all kayaks and canoes, carry at least one Type I, II, III, or IV PFD for each person on board, and (2) all recreational boats sixteen (16) feet or over in length, including sailboats and rowboats, carry at least one Type I, II, or III (wearable) PFD for each person on board *and* one Type IV (throwable) PFD in each boat.

The new regulation below defines the various types of PFD's for recreational boats:

Type I – A Type I PFD is a Coast Guard approved device designed to turn an *unconscious* person in the water from a face downward position to a vertical or slightly backward position, and to have more than 20 pounds of buoyancy. This is the familiar collar-type lifejacket, bulky and less wearable than other PFD types, but designed to keep the wearer afloat for extended periods of time in rough water. Type I PFD's are recommended for off-shore cruising. They are acceptable for all size boats.

Type II – A Type II PFD is a Coast Guard approved device designed to turn an *unconscious* person in the water from a face downward position to a vertical or slightly backward position, and to have at least 15.5 pounds of buoyancy. This is a more wearable device than the Type I and is recommended for closer, in-shore cruising. Type II PFD's are also acceptable for all size boats.

Type III – A Type III PFD is a Coast Guard approved device designed to keep a *conscious* person in a vertical or slightly backward position. Like the Type II PFD, Type III must have at least 15.5 pounds of buoyancy. However, it has a lesser turning ability than either Type I or Type II. Type III PFD's are recommended for in-water sports, or on lakes, impoundments, and close in-shore operation. They are acceptable for all size boats.

Type IV – A Type IV PFD is a Coast Guard approved device designed to be *thrown to a person in the water and not worn.* It must have at least 16.5 pounds of buoyancy. Type IV PFD's are acceptable for boats less than 16 feet in length and canoes and kayaks, and at least one Type IV PFD is required for boats 16 feet and over in length.

All Coast Guard approved personal flotation devices bear markings indicating the manufacturer, the type, and an approval number. However, since the above type designations were adopted in 1973, there are many kinds of Coast Guard approved PFD's in existence which are not marked as "Type I, II, III, or IV." The following "conversion" table gives equivalent "type" information for previously existing devices.

Number on Label	Devices Marked	are Equivalent to
160,002	Life preserver	Performance Type I personal flotation device
160,003	Life preserver	Performance Type I personal flotation device
160,004	Life preserver	Performance Type I personal flotation device
160,005	Life preserver	Performance Type I personal flotation device
160,009	Ring life buoy	Performance Type IV personal flotation device
160,047	Buoyant vest	Performance Type II personal flotation device
160,048	Buoyant cushion	Performance Type IV personal flotation device
160,049	Buoyant cushion	Performance Type IV personal flotation device
160,050	Ring life buoy	Performance Type IV personal flotation device
160,052	Buoyant vest	Performance Type II personal flotation device
160,055	Life preserver	Performance Type I personal flotation device
160,060	Buoyant vest	Performance Type II personal flotation device
160,064	Special purpose water safety buoyant devices	A device intended to be worn may be equivalent to Type II or Type III. A device that is equivalent to Type III is marked "Type III Device – may not turn unconscious wearer." A device intended to be grasped is equivalent to Type IV.

All personal flotation devices can have excellent flotation materials, be expertly manufactured and be in serviceable condition without being a good personal flotation device. Why? The proper use of any personal flotation device requires the wearer to know how it will perform. The only way to gain this knowledge is through personal experience. Every person going out on the water in a boat should first understand how to properly fit and wear the personal flotation device intended for his use. He should then understand how the device will react when the wearer and device are in the water. Only then can he be sure he and the device are ready for an emergency which would cause him to leave the boat. Children, especially, require this practice. Any wearable PFD shall be of an appropriate size for the person who intends to wear it. Child size devices are acceptable only for persons weighing less than 90 pounds.

Life Preservers (Type I PFDs)

Life preservers will last for many years if they are given reasonable care. They should be dried thoroughly before being put away and should be stowed in a dry, well-ventilated place. Do not stow in the bottom of lockers or deck storage boxes where moisture might accumulate. Frequent airing and drying in the sun is also recommended. Life preservers should not be tossed about haphazardly, used as fenders or cushions, or otherwise roughly treated.

Life preservers are most often of the kapok type, although buoyant fibrous glass, cork, balsa wood, and unicellular plastic foam are used. They are either jacket or bib design.

The jacket type is constructed with pads of buoyant materials inserted in a cloth covering. This covering is fitted with the necessary straps and ties.

Bib type life preservers are constructed of unicellular plastic foam with a vinyl-dip surface or cloth cover. They are fitted with an adjustable strap. Adult and child sizes are available. All Coast Guard approved life preservers (Type I) are required to be Indian Orange colored.

The jacket type life preserver should be put on the same as a coat with all ties and fasteners secured to obtain a snug fit. When the bib type is worn the body strap should be drawn snugly.

All life preservers are required to be ready for use and readily accessible. This means they should be ready to be worn without adjustments as well as being within reach. The straps should be adjusted for the person for whom it is intended and the fasteners unhooked to eliminate that step when time is most critical.

When underway in a small open boat, life preservers should be worn by children and non-swimmers. When rough weather is encountered on any type of boat, or when in hazardous waters, life preservers should be worn by everyone. As a matter of good seamanship and common sense, all *unsatisfactory* lifesaving equipment should be left ashore. Its replacement should be Coast Guard approved equipment. An emergency is no time to conduct an inspection to determine whether or not the equipment is serviceable.

Buoyant Vests (Type II PFDs)

Coast Guard approved buoyant vests are manufactured in several designs. They can be constructed of pads of kapok, fibrous glass or unicellular plastic with cloth covering, with straps and ties attached. The kapok and fibrous glass pads are enclosed in plastic bags. Other models of buoyant vests are made of unicellular plastic foam which has a vinyl-dip coating. They are made in three sizes: adult, child (medium) and child (small), and may be any color.

Buoyant vests are identified by a Coast Guard approval number and the model number which are contained on a label attached to the vest. Vests must be in good and serviceable condition.

As with life preservers, buoyant vests have a variety of adjustable straps which should be adjusted to fit before leaving the mooring. Be sure to make children's adjustments for proper fit, too. Vests should be worn snugly with all ties and fasteners

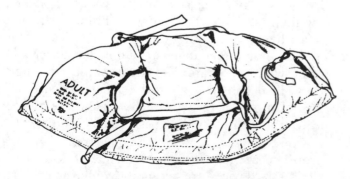

4-13 Type I Personal Flotation Device

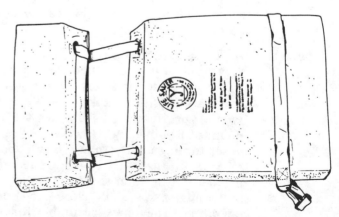

4-14 Type II Personal Flotation Device

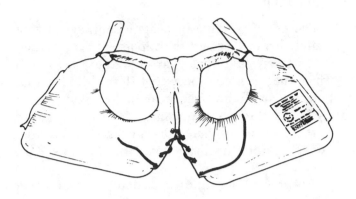

4-15 Type III Personal Flotation Device

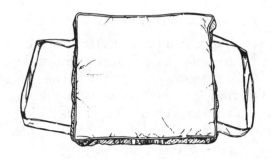

4-16 Type IV PFD (Buoyant Cushion)

pulled tight and worn by children and non-swimmers when underway in small boats or open construction type craft. They should be dried thoroughly before being put away, and when stowed on board should be in a readily accessible location which is dry, cool, and well ventilated. Buoyant vests should not be tossed about haphazardly, used as fenders or cushions, or otherwise roughly treated.

Buoyant Cushions (Type IV PFDs)

Buoyant cushions approved by the Coast Guard contain kapok, fibrous glass or unicellular plastic foam, come in a variety of sizes and shapes, may be any color, and are fitted with grab straps. Some unicellular plastic foam buoyant cushions are vinyl-dip coated.

Buoyant cushions are generally more readily accessible since they are sometimes used as seat cushions. However, the kapok or fibrous glass cushions used as seats become unserviceable rather rapidly because the inner plastic envelope may be punctured.

Cushions are usually available in time of emergency. However, they are difficult to hang on to in the water and do not afford as great a degree of protection as a life preserver or buoyant vest. For this reason, buoyant cushions are not recommended for use by children or non-swimmers. The straps on buoyant cushions are put there primarily for holding-on purposes. However, they may also be used in throwing the cushion. Cushions should never be worn on a person's back since this tends to force

the wearer's face down in the water.

Approved buoyant cushions are marked on the side (gusset), showing the Coast Guard approval number and other information concerning the cushion and its use.

Ring Life Buoys (Type IV PFDs)

These personal flotation devices can be made of cork, balsa wood or unicellular plastic foam, and are available in 30, 24, and 20-inch sizes. Their covering is either canvas or specially-surfaced plastic foam. All buoys are fitted with a grab line and may be colored either white or orange.

It is desirable to attach approximately 60 feet of line to the grab rope on the ring buoy. When throwing a ring buoy, care should be taken not to hit the person in the water. Ring buoys should be stowed in brackets topside, readily accessible for emergencies.

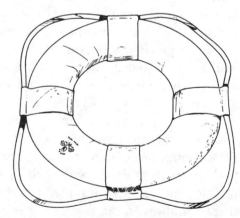

4-17 Type IV PFD (Ring Buoy)

Cork and balsa wood ring buoys must bear two markings, the manufacturer's stamp and the Coast Guard inspector's stamp. Plastic foam ring buoys bear only one marking, a nameplate attached to the buoy.

Special Purpose Water Safety Buoyant Devices (May be Type III PFD's)

Approved special purpose water safety buoyant devices are manufactured in many designs depending on the intended special purpose. These include water ski jump vests, hunters' vests, motorboat racing vests, flotation jackets, and others. Additional strength is added where needed for the intended purpose of the device.

The devices are made for either wearing or grasping. Wearing devices are available in adult and child sizes. Their markings include the Coast Guard approval Number 160.064/ . . . as well as the special purpose for which the device is intended, instructions for use and maintenance, and other necessary information. Some devices intended for grasping also are marked with the wording: *Warning—Do not wear on Back."*

Ventilation Systems

No foolproof ventilation system has been developed. The efficiency of various shaped cowls and ducts, the location of system components, the capacity of blowers, and the choice of materials are all related to safety. There is no such thing as a ventilation system "approved" by the Coast Guard. There has been, however, a great deal of study and thought, some testing, and years of experience upon which to form recommendations. These lead to the conclusion that, as a minimum, fresh air should be ducted into each engine and fuel tank compartment and dangerous fumes ducted out of the vessel. To create a flow through the ducting system, at least when underway or when there is a wind, cowls (scoops) or other fittings of equivalent effectiveness are needed on all ducts. A wind-actuated rotary exhauster or mechanical blower is considered equivalent and preferred to a cowl on the exhaust duct. To scavenge gases from ventilated spaces and avoid undesirable turbulance within the spaces, at least one inlet duct must be installed to extend to a point at least midway to the bilge, or at least below the level of the carburetor air intake. At least one exhaust duct must extend from the open atmosphere to the lower portion of the bilge. Ducts should not be installed so low in the bilge that they may become obstructed by normal accumulation of bilge water.

Open Boats

The use of gasoline in boats will always present a safety hazard because the vapors are heavier than air and may find their way into the bilges from which there is no escape except through the ventilation systems. In an open boat these vapors may be dissipated through the scouring effect of exposure to the open atmosphere. Open boats are, therefore, exempted from the above ventilation requirements.

All three of the following conditions should be met in order to consider a boat "open":

1. Engine and fuel tank compartments shall have as a minimum 15 square inches of open area directly exposed to the atmosphere for each cubic foot of net compartment volume.
2. There must be no long or narrow unventilated spaces accessible from such compartments in which a flame could propagate.
3. Long, narrow compartments (such as side panels), if joining engine or fuel compartments and not serving as ducts thereto, shall have at least 15 square inches of open area per cubic foot provided by frequent openings along the full length of the compartment formed.

Technical Details

Most boat owners, on learning that fires and explosions of fuels cause more property damage in pleasure boating than any other type of accident, and run a close second to collisions in personal injuries, are anxious to improve the ventilation system on their boats. They want to protect their families, friends and investments by installing a ventilation system that at least meets the safety standards recommended by the boat building industry. To accomplish this the following should be considered and installed if not present.

Intake (Air Supply)

There must be one or more intake ducts into each fuel and engine compartment, fitted with a cowl (scoop), extending from the open atmosphere to a level midway to the bilge (fuel compartment) or at least below the level of the carburetor (engine compartment).

Exhaust

There must be one or more exhaust ducts from the lower portion of the bilge of each fuel and engine compartment to the free atmosphere, fitted with a cowl or an equivalent such as a wind actuated rotary exhauster or a power exhaust blower.

Ducting Materials

For long life and safety, ducts should be constructed of nonferrous, galvanized ferrous, or sturdy high temperature resistant nonmetallic materials, routed clear of and protected from contact with hot engine surfaces.

Positioning of Cowls

Normally, the intake cowl will face forward in an area of free underway airflow, and the exhaust cowl will face aft where a suction effect can be expected. They should be located with respect to each other so as to avoid the pick up of vapors while fueling.

Carburetion Air

Openings in engine compartment for entry of air to the carburetor are additional to the ventilation system requirements.

Ducting Size

There should be no constriction in the ducting system which is smaller than the minimum cross sectional area required for reasonable efficiency.

Small Motorboats

To determine the minimum cross sectional area of the air conduits (cowls and ducting) for motorboats having small engine and/or fuel tank compartments see table 1, which is based on net compartment volume.

Cabin Cruisers and Larger Boats

For most cabin cruisers and other large motorboats, Table 2, which is based on the vessel's beam, is a practical guide for determining the minimum cross sectional area of the air conduits (ducts and cowls).

General Precautions

Ventilation systems are not designed to remove vapors caused by breaks in fuel lines or leaking tanks. If gas odors are detected repairs are generally indicated. Prior to each starting of the engine, espec-

ially on calm days and where a power exhaust system is not installed, the engine compartment should be opened to dissipate vapors which may be present. The smaller the compartment the quicker an explosive mixture of gasoline vapors can be expected to develop.

TABLE I

ONE INTAKE AND ONE EXHAUST SYSTEM			TWO INTAKE AND TWO EXHAUST SYSTEMS
Net Volume (cu. ft.)	Minimum Inside Diameter for Each (inches)	Area (sq. in.)	Minimum Inside Diameter for Each (inches)
Up to 8	2	3	
10	2¼	4	
12	2½	5	
14	2¾	6	
17	3	7	
20	3¼	8	
23	3½	10	2½
27	3¾	11	3
30	4	13	3
35	4¼	14	3
39	4½	16	3
43	4¾	19	3
48	5	20	3

NOTE: Determine gross compartment volume, then determine the volume of tanks, engine and other items in that compartment. The difference is the net compartment volume.

TABLE 2
TWO INTAKE AND TWO EXHAUST SYSTEMS

Vessel Beam (feet)	Minimum Inside Diameter for Each Duct (inches)	Area (square inches)
7	3	7
8	3¼	8
9	3½	9
10	3½	10
11	3¾	11
12	4	12
13	4¼	13
14	4¼	14
15	4½	15
16	4½	16
17	4½	17
18	5	18
19	5	19

Play it Safe—Keep Your Boat Free of Explosive Vapors!

Note: Vessels which are intended for carrying more than six passengers for hire are subject to special regulations. Owners should contact the nearest Coast Guard Marine Inspection Office for inspection requirements.

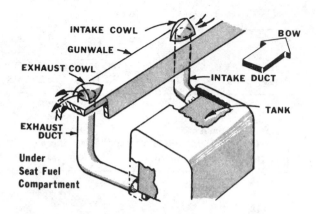

4-18 Ventilation

Example of Ventilation Arrangements On Small Motorboats

Natural System

The above features provide for ventilation without mechanical assistance. Efficiency is greatest when there is a breeze from forward of the beam, which will normally occur when underway or at anchor, and some of the time when moored. Although less efficient when the wind is abaft the beam, some scouring effect may even then be expected.

Mechanical Blowers

To provide a positive means of exhausting vapors when there is little or no movement of air (calm days) and especially before starting engines when the explosion risk is greatest, mechanical blowers are recommended for engine spaces. It is suggested that ducting separate from the natural ventilation system be installed. Exhaust blowers should be of the sealed or arcless type and, if located within the compartment being ventilated, be as high as possible. Blower fan blades or impellers should be non-sparking and, if installed in the exhaust duct of the natural system, should not interfere with the functioning of the ducts as natural ventilators. Exterior terminations of power exhaust ducts may be fitted with louvered fittings instead of cowls.

Backfire Flame Arresters

4-19 Backfire Flame Arrester

Gasoline engines (other than outboard engines) that have been installed since April 25, 1940, must have an acceptable means of backfire flame control. The usual method is by installation of a Coast Guard approved flame arrester. Alternate methods are a special Coast Guard approved reed valve system or a closed metallic duct system which would carry all backfire flames outside the vessel in a manner to permit dispersion without endangering the vessel, persons on board, or nearby vessels or structures.

4-20 Whistle and Horns

Whistle or Horn

Whistle signals are required to be given by all boats under certain circumstances. Equipment requirements vary according to the length of the boat.

Less than 16 feet	No whistle required.
16 feet to less than 26 feet	Mouth, hand or power operated, capable of producing a blast of 2 seconds or more duration and audible for a distance of at least ½ mile.
26 feet to less than 40 feet	Hand or power operated, capable of producing a blast of 2 seconds or more duration and audible for a distance of at least 1 mile.

| 40 feet through 65 feet | Power operated, capable of producing a blast of 2 seconds or more duration and audible for a distance of at least 1 mile. |

Note that even though a boat less than 16 feet in length is not required to have a whistle on board, it still must give the proper whistle signals when needed.

4-21 Bell

Bell

Bell signals are required when a vessel is at anchor under conditions of restricted visibility. All vessels 26 feet or greater but not more than 65 feet in length are required to carry a bell on board. No specific size is stipulated but it must be capable of giving a clear, bell-like tone. Even though boats less than 26 feet in length need not have a bell aboard, this does not exempt them from the requirement to give the proper signals if the occasion arises.

Your Responsibility as a Boatman

You are responsible for any damage your boat may cause other craft or for any injuries suffered by your passengers or others. For instance, if you pass close to a cruiser at high speed and your wake rocks this vessel so that the dishes in the galley are broken, you may be held responsible. If this should happen when hot foods are being prepared or served on board the cruiser and someone suffers serious burns as a result of the violent rocking caused by your wake, you may be held liable. You could be summoned into court and equitable civil damages assessed against you. In addition, you might also be cited for negligent or grossly negligent operation.

Water Pollution and the Recreational Boatman

The recreational boatman has an important stake in the effort to keep the nation's waters free from pollution. You must help to provide and protect clean water not only for your own recreation but also for the enjoyment of sport fishermen, divers, swimmers, and all who appreciate a beautiful and bountiful natural resource. An important part of the responsibility to protect the marine environment is observing the Federal water pollution laws.

The Refuse Act of 1899 prohibits the throwing, discharging, or depositing of any refuse matter of any kind (including trash, garbage, oil, and other liquid pollutants) into the waters of the United States to a distance of three miles from the coastline. The Federal Water Pollution Control Act prohibits the discharge of oil or hazardous substances into the waters of the United States to twelve miles offshore. You must immediately notify the U.S. Coast Guard if your vessel or facility discharges oil or hazardous substances into the water.

Federal regulations issued under the Federal Water Pollution Control Act require:

(1) All vessels under 100 gross tons must have a fixed or portable means to discharge oily bilge slops to a reception facility. A bucket or bailer is considered a portable means.

(2) Vessels 26 feet in length and over must have posted a placard at least 5 by 8 inches, made of durable material, fixed in a conspicuous place in the machinery spaces, or at the bilge and ballast pump control station, stating the following:

DISCHARGE OF OIL PROHIBITED

The Federal Water Pollution Control Act prohibits the discharge of oil or oily waste into or upon the navigable waters and contiguous zone of the United States if such discharge causes a film or sheen upon, or discoloration of, the surface of the water, or causes a sludge or emulsion beneath the surface of the water. Violators are subject to a penalty of $5,000.

---

(3) No person may drain the sumps of oil lubricated machinery or the contents of oil filters, strainers, or purifiers into the bilge of any U.S. vessel.

You must also help to ensure that others obey the law. You are encouraged to report polluting discharges which you observe to the nearest U.S. Coast Guard office. Report the following information:

a. location,
b. source,

c. size,
d. color,
e. substance,
f. time observed.

Do not attempt to take samples of any chemical discharge. If uncertain as to the identity of any discharge, avoid flame, physical contact, or inhalation of fumes.

Boating Accident Reports

The operator of any boat involved in an accident must stop, render assistance and offer identification. Reports must be made for any accident which results in death, personal injury (a person loses consciousness or receives medical treatment or is disabled for more than 24 hours), property damage in amount greater than $100, or the disappearance of a person (that indicates death or injury). In accidents involving death or disappearance, the nearest reporting authority must be notified immediately (and in writing within 48 hours); all other accidents must be reported within 5 days.

Boating accident report forms (CG-3865) may be obtained from any Coast Guard office or unit. They must be submitted by the operator to the nearest Coast Guard Officer in Charge, Marine Inspection, unless the operator is required to file an accident report with a state having an approved numbering system. Accident reports furnish information for use in compiling accident prevention data. Information from individual reports will not be publicly disclosed.

Law Enforcement

Coast Guard boarding vessels will be identified by the Coast Guard ensign and personnel will be in uniform. A vessel underway, upon being hailed by a Coast Guard vessel or patrolboat, is required to stop immediately and lay to or maneuver in such a way as to permit the boarding officer to come aboard. Failure to stop to permit boarding may subject the operator to a penalty which may be as much as $100.

The owner or operator of a vessel which is not numbered as required or who fails to file notice of transfer, destruction or abandonment of a vessel or fails to report a change of address, is liable to a penalty which could be as much as $500.

A civil penalty may be imposed by the Coast Guard for negligent or grossly negligent operation, for failure to obey the Rules of the Road or failure to comply with regulations.

The law also provides for a fine of up to $1,000 and imprisonment of not more than 1 year for the criminal offense of reckless or negligent operation of a vessel which endangers the life or property of any person.

Courtesy Motorboat Examination

As a courtesy to pleasure boat owners and operators, members of the Coast Guard Auxiliary check thousands of boats each year for legal and safety requirements. These members are qualified as Courtesy Examiners under strict requirements set by the Coast Guard and are very knowledgeable in their field. The examinations are performed as a courtesy and only with the consent of the pleasure boat owner. To pass the examination, a vessel must satisfy not only federal equipment requirements but also certain additional safety requirements recommended by the Auxiliary. If the boat passes the examination it is awarded a safety decal which is placed conspicuously on the vessel.

Federal Boat Safety Act of 1971

In August 1971 major Federal legislation, PL 92-75 or the Federal Boat Safety Act of 1971 was enacted into law. This law manifested the mandate given the U.S. Coast Guard by the Congress of the United States to improve recreational boat safety. Federal regulations which are being or have been developed will bring about a number of changes designed to improve boating safety. A few of these changes affecting sections in this chapter are:

a. Establish a new system for numbering boats. The Act requires any vessel, if undocumented, equipped with propulsion machinery of any type, regardless of horsepower, to be numbered.

b. Establish a uniform system for reporting boating accidents. Existing regulations defining reportable accidents and reporting procedures will be changed.

c. Establish specific safety standards which boat manufacturers must follow in the manufacture of boats. These will encompass such areas as capacity, flotation, safe powering and fire and explosion, among others.

d. Establish specific standards of performance for certain associated equipment normally carried by recreational boats.

e. Require a boat manufacturer to report non-compliance with a standard or any defect which creates a substantial risk of personal injury to the public to purchasers of boats by means of a defects notification system.

f. Require that each boat manufactured be assigned a hull identification number.

Regulations have already been issued under the new law and became effective April 17, 1972, requiring the carriage of Coast Guard approved personal flotation devices on all recreational boats.

The law also authorizes a Coast Guard Boarding Officer, when in his judgment continued unsafe use of a boat creates an especially hazardous condition, to direct the operator to correct the hazardous condition immediately or return to a mooring and to remain there until the situation creating the hazard is corrected or ended. Reasons for using the authority are insufficient personal flotation devices or firefighting equipment aboard and overloading. Other unsafe conditions that may create especially hazardous conditions will be defined in future regulations. Failure to comply with the orders of the Boarding Officer subject the offender to penalties provided for under the law.

Additionally the law authorizes any Coast Guard District Commander (not his staff) to issue regulations for a specific boat designating that boat unsafe for a specific voyage on a specific body of water when he has determined that such a voyage would be a manifestly unsafe voyage.

CHAPTER 5

Rules of the Road

Introduction

Men have been sailing the seas since the beginning of history. For thousands of years, the open ocean was a lonely place to be. Vessels rarely met on the high seas and the sight of an occasional sail on the horizon was an event guaranteed to break the monotony of the long voyage. As the world's trade increased and traffic became more regular on established shipping lanes, the chances of vessels meeting became greater. In 1863, Great Britain and France adopted a code of uniform regulations for preventing collisions at sea. In 1864, the Congress of the United States adopted a similiar set of rules. In 1865, other countries adopted these rules but it was not until 1889 that representatives from the world's seafaring nations met in Washington D. C. to create an international code of rules for vessels on the high seas. The language barrier must have been formidable since these men were attempting to define exact shades of meaning. Since maritime customs of that day differed widely, it is to their everlasting credit that they managed to agree on a code of rules for vessels at sea. This code was known as the International Rules of the Road and was in use until the International Rules of 1948 were adopted and put into effect. There have been revisions since then but, by and large, the changes have been comparatively minor. The latest revision, The 1972 International Regulations for Preventing Collisions at Sea (effective in International waters in mid-1977), makes a number of further minor changes, including the designation of measurements in meters rather than feet. Existing vessels, now in compliance, will not be required to reposition their lights because of the conversion to metric measurements. Neither will they be required to conform to new requirements for light ranges for a period of four years.

It is important to point out that the above mentioned rules apply to the international waters of the high seas only. Territorial waters were left to the jurisdiction of each country involved. The United States has legislated in this area, although no single code could be expected to cover all regions and special situations in U. S. waters. Consequently, we have several codes. These codes are commonly known as the Inland Rules, the Great Lakes Rules and the Western Rivers Rules. Each code applies to certain waters and each contains rules for special situations peculiar to these waters. In addition to these, we also have Pilot Rules, the Department of the Army Rules and Regulations, the Act of April 25, 1940, better known as the Motorboat Act, and others. While these Rules are not being changed at once, they will undoubtedly be reviewed and modifications made at a later date to bring them into closer conformity with the new International Rules.

Enough rules to sink a ship? Not really. The primary purpose of each and every one of them is to prevent collisions at sea and on our navigable waters. There are almost as many rules as there are possible situations but, strangely enough, they work! When the early draftsmen of these rules gave sailing craft the right-of-way over power driven vessels, they did so for a very good reason. Sailing vessels do not enjoy the relative ease of maneuverability of powered craft since they depend on the wind for their propulsion. When our Inland Rules were written (in 1897), they were patterned closely on the International (high seas) Rules and that feature giving sailing vessels the right-of-way (most of the time) over powered vessels was retained. The writers of our early Inland Rules can be forgiven for not having the foresight to envision a confrontation between an 8 foot long sail boat and a 1,000 foot long ocean liner. Until a few years ago, your teen-aged daughter, out for a day's sail in a sailing dinghy, could force the RMS Queen Mary to give way in the congested waters of New York harbor. This is not so today but one cannot blame the "Mary" for finally giving up in sheer desperation and consenting to spend her declining years in the sedate comfort of the Port of Long Beach, California.

For the student who is about to tackle the subject of Rules of the Road for the very first time - a word of encouragement. You will not be expected to know them all. However, regardless of where you do your boating, other skippers have the right to assume that you know what you're doing. So the Rules that you will have to learn are those which apply to *your boat* and the waters on which you will sail or cruise. Remember, when you take the wheel or tiller, there is a *presumption of knowledge!* If you fail to observe the rules, the fact that you did not know them will not be accepted as a valid defense in any citation which may result as a consequence of your actions.

Jurisdiction

All vessels are required to observe the rules of the road which apply to the waters on which they navigate. These codes, mentioned briefly heretofore, are to be found in the following U. S. Coast Guard publications and apply to the waters described below:

Rules of the Road, International—Inland (CG-169)

The Coast Guard has included the Rules for both these waters in the one publication, CG-169.

International Rules apply on the high seas seaward of the established boundary lines between International and Inland waters, and on certain foreign waters. Inland Rules apply to all waters inshore of these boundary lines except the Great Lakes and the Western Rivers. The boundary lines for Inland Rules of the Road are established by the Commandant of the Coast Guard. A boundary line is designated for most bays, sounds, harbors, rivers or estuaries in U. S. waters which connect to the high seas. These lines are described in the back of CG-169 and CG-184 and, where appropriate, on various charts of coastal waters.

Rules of the Road, Great Lakes (CG-172)

Great Lakes rules apply to the waters of the Great Lakes and their connecting tributaries as far east as Montreal.

Rules of the Road, Western Rivers (CG-184)

Western Rivers rules apply to the waters of the Mississippi River between its source and the Huey P. Long Bridge and all of its tributaries emptying thereinto and their tributaries, that part of the Atchafalaya River above its junction with the Plaquemine-Morgan City alternate waterway, and the Red River of the North.

Some Definitions

As we develop the subject, we will be using terms which may be unfamiliar or new. Because these rules are in fact *laws*, exact definitions become very important. The following terms will appear throughout this Chapter, so let's "define our terms" before we proceed further:

Vessel—Every description of watercraft used or capable of being used as a means of transportation on the water.
Power Vessel—Any vessel propelled by machinery, including any sailing vessel under sail AND power.
Steam Vessel—Any vessel propelled by machinery.
Sailing Vessel—Any vessel which is under sail alone, including any power vessel under sail and not under power.
Underway—Not at anchor, aground, or made fast to the shore.
Danger Zone—The area from dead ahead of a vessel or two points abaft her starboard beam.
Right-of-Way—The right and duty to maintain Course and Speed.
Privileged Vessel—The vessel which has the right-of-way.
Stand-on Vessel—Same as privileged vessel.
Burdened Vessel—The vessel which must keep clear of the privileged vessel.
Give-way Vessel—Same as burdened vessel.
Visible (when applied to lights)—Visible on a dark, clear night.
Short Blast (on whistle)—A blast of about one second's duration.
Prolonged Blast (on whistle)—A blast of from four to six seconds' duration.
Distinct Blast (on whistle)—A clearly audible blast of any length.
Engaged In Fishing—Fishing with nets, lines or trawls, but does not include fishing with trolling lines.
Point—An arc of 11¼° of the horizon (32 points equal the full circle 360°).

General Categories

As we study the Rules of the Road, we will divide them into three general categories; (1) Lights and Shapes; (2) Steering and Sailing Rules, and Sound

Signals; and (3) Fog Signals. The latter two will be separated into four sections, one for each set of Rules. The first category, Lights and Shapes, will be separated into two sections, one for the "Motorboat Act" waters and the other for international waters of the high seas.

Lights and Shapes

Your lights convey information to others under conditions of restricted visibility or at night when your vessel is not otherwise visible. The lights that you must carry and display depend on whether your vessel is under power or under sail, its length and the waters on which you do your boating. The regulations for lights for boats navigating on all Inland waters, the Great Lakes and the Western Rivers, fall under the jurisdiction of the Motorboat Act for vessels not over 65 feet in length. If you do your boating on international waters, the Inter-

national Rules apply. Lights prescribed under the International Rules may be carried and displayed on all inland waters, including the Great Lakes and the Western Rivers but not the reverse. So, if your boating is done sometimes on inland and sometimes on international waters, you should equip your craft with international lights.

It might be well to mention at this point that a motorboat (under the Motorboat Act) is any vessel not over 65 feet in length that is propelled by machinery. A sailing auxiliary (a sailboat which has an engine installed or which has an outboard engine aboard which can be mounted and used for propulsion) is considered to be a motorboat within the meaning of the Motorboat Act and must display the lights of a motorboat of its class while underway under power, reglardless of whether the vessel is under sail and power or under power only.

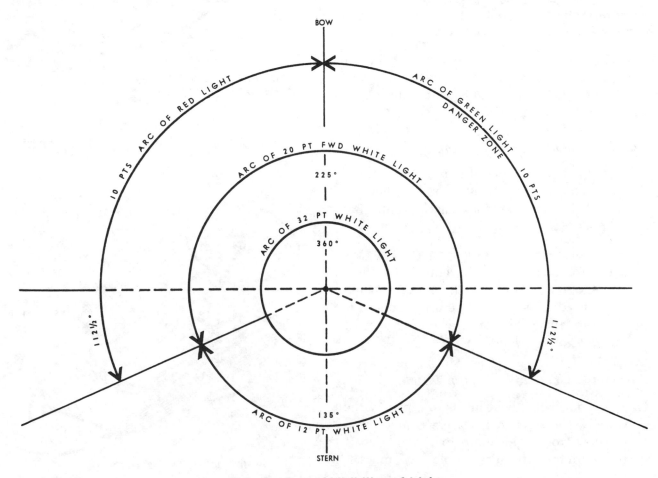

5-1 Degrees of Visibility of Lights

5-3

Arc of Visibility of Lights on Vessels

Lights carried on vessels are defensive in the sense that they are not intended for illumination but for identification or warning. The law requires that these lights be clearly visible throughout their prescribed arc of visibility and that they be effectively screened so that they will not be visible through the balance of the circle. The arc of visibility for lights on vessels is called out in points, each point being equal to 11¼° of the circle. Thirty-two points equal a complete circle. The arc of visibility for prescribed lights on vessels are as follows:

10 points (112½°) Visible from right (dead) ahead to 2 points abaft the respective beams.

12 points (135°) Visible from right (dead) astern to 2 points abaft the beam on both sides.

20 points (225°) Visible from right (dead) ahead to 2 points abaft the beam on both sides.

32 points (360°) Visible throughout the complete circle of the horizon.

Lights under the Motorboat Act (Inland, Western Rivers and Great Lakes)

These lights must be carried and exhibited by all motorboats in all weathers from sunset to sunrise when underway. No other lights which can be mistaken for these lights may be displayed.

Motorboats under 26 Feet in Length

1. A 32-point white light aft, visible for 2 miles, high enough to be seen all around the horizon. This light may be carried off the center line if necessary.

2. A combined lantern in the forepart of the vessel, lower than the white light aft, showing green to starboard and red to port, of 10 points each, fixed so as to show from right ahead to 2 points abaft the beam on their respective sides, visible for 1 mile.

Motorboats 26 Feet to 65 Feet in Length

1. A 20-point white light in the fore part of the vessel as near the stem as practicable, fixed to show from right ahead to 2 points abaft the beam on both sides, visible for 2 miles.

2. A 32-point white light aft to show all around

the horizon, visible for 2 miles. This light must be higher than the white light forward.

3. Separate red and green side lights, red to port and green to starboard, of 10 points each, fixed to show from right ahead to 2 points abaft the beam on their respective sides, visible for 1 mile.

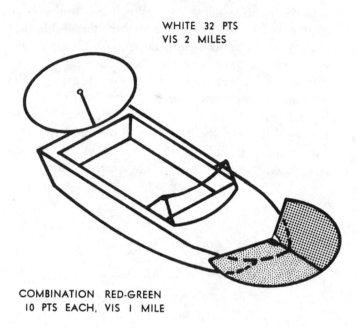

WHITE 32 PTS
VIS 2 MILES

COMBINATION RED-GREEN
10 PTS EACH, VIS 1 MILE

5-2 Motorboat Under 26 Feet in Length

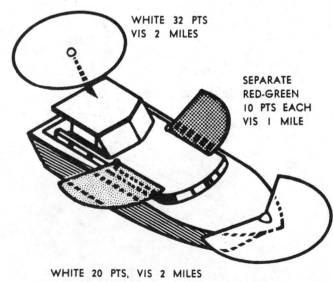

WHITE 32 PTS
VIS 2 MILES

SEPARATE
RED-GREEN
10 PTS EACH
VIS 1 MILE

WHITE 20 PTS, VIS 2 MILES

5-3 Motorboat 26 Feet through 65 Feet in Length

Sailing Auxiliaries

Under Sail and Power, or Power Alone

A sailing auxiliary not over 65 feet in length must carry and exhibit the same lights as a motorboat of its class while underway under sail and power or power alone.

Under Sail Alone, Under 26 Feet in Length

When under sail alone, a sailing auxiliary under 26 feet in length must carry and exhibit the following lights:

1. A combined lantern in the forepart of the vessel, showing green to starboard and red to port, of 10 points each, fixed so as to show from right ahead to 2 points abaft the beam on their respective sides, visible for 1 mile.
   NOTE: Separate 10-point red and green side lights may be carried in lieu of the combined lantern.

2. A 12-point white light aft, visible for 2 miles, fixed so as to show from right astern to 2 points abaft the beam on both sides of the vessel.

NOTE: Under Great Lakes Rules, the 12-point white stern light is not required for a vessel underway under sail alone; but a white light must be available to display on the quarter from which a vessel is approaching. This light must be shown in time to prevent a collision.

Under Sail Alone, 26 Feet Through 65 Feet in Length

When under sail alone, a sailing auxiliary 26 feet in length through 65 feet in length must carry and exhibit the following lights:

1. Separate red and green side lights showing red to port and green to starboard, of 10 points each, fixed to show from right ahead to 2 points abaft the beam on their respective sides, visible for 1 mile.

2. A 12-point white light aft, visible for 2 miles, fixed so as to show from right astern to 2 points abaft the beam on both sides of the vessel.

WHITE 12 PTS
VIS 2 MILES

COMBINATION
RED-GREEN
10 PTS EACH, VIS 1 MILE

5-4 Sailing Auxiliary, Under Sail Alone, Under 26 Feet in Length

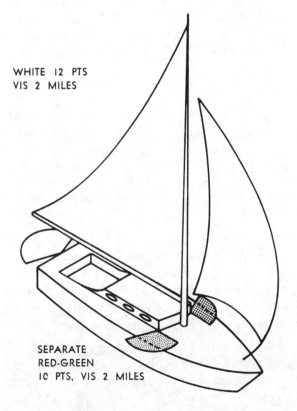

WHITE 12 PTS
VIS 2 MILES

SEPARATE
RED-GREEN
10 PTS, VIS 2 MILES

5-5 Sailing Auxiliary, Under Sail Only, 26 Ft. to 65 Ft. in Length

NOTE: Under Great Lakes Rules, the 12-point white stern light is not required for a vessel underway under sail alone; but a white light must be available to display on the quarter from which a vessel is appproaching. This light must be shown in time to prevent a collision.

Sailboats

Sailboats (sailing vessels with no engines aboard) must carry and exhibit the following lights:

1. Separate red and green side lights, showing red to port and green to starboard, of 10 points each, fixed to show from right ahead to 2 points abaft the beam on their respective sides, visible for 2 miles.

2. A 12-point white light aft, visible for 2 miles, fixed so as to show from right astern to 2 points abaft the beam on both sides of the vessel.

   NOTE: Under Great Lakes Rules, the 12-point white stern light is not required for a vessel underway under sail alone; but a white light must be available to display on the quarter from which a vessel is approaching. This light must be shown in time to prevent a collision.

Rowing Boats

Rowing boats, whether under sail or under oars, shall have ready at hand a lantern showing a white light which shall be temporarily exhibited in sufficient time to avert a collision.

Lights under the International Rules of the Road

Except for minor details, the 1972 Rules call for the same lights on all vessels less than 20 meters (65.6 feet) in length. These lights must be carried and exhibited by all vessels in all weathers from sunset to sunrise when underway. No other lights which can be mistaken for these lights may be displayed.

However, it should be noted that existing vessels, now in compliance, will not be required to reposition their lights because of the conversion to metric measurements. Neither will they be required to meet new requirements for light ranges for a period of four years.

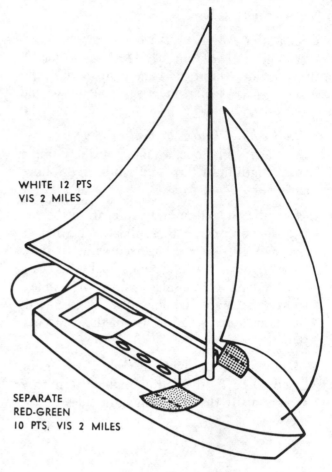

WHITE 12 PTS
VIS 2 MILES

SEPARATE
RED-GREEN
10 PTS, VIS 2 MILES

5-6 Sailboat

Motorboats

Lights required include:

1. Masthead light. A 20 point white light over the centerline in the forepart of the vessel. This must be visible from right ahead to 2 points abaft the beam on both sides of the vessel. For a vessel under 12 meters (39.4 feet) in length this must have a visibility of 2 miles and be located at least 1 meter (3.3 feet) higher than the colored lights. For a vessel from 12 meters to 20 meters in length the visibility must be 3 miles and the light must be located at least 2.5 meters (8.2 feet) above the gunwale.

2. Side lights. These are separate side lights, red to port and green to starboard, fixed so as to show from right ahead to 2 points abaft the beam on their respective sides. Visibility must be 1 mile for vessels under 12 meters (39.4 feet) in length and 2 miles for vessels 12 meters to 20 meters (65.6 feet) in length. If desired, a combined

lantern may be substituted for the separate side lights.

3. Stern light. This is a 12 point white light placed as nearly as practicable at the stern of the vessel. It must be fixed to show from right astern to 2 points abaft the beam on both sides of the vessel. Visibility must be 2 miles.

Small Motorboats

Small motorboats under 7 meters (23.0 feet) in length whose maximum speed does not exceed 7 knots may, in lieu of the lights specified above, exhibit an all-round (32 point) white light. Such vessel should, if practicable, also exhibit side lights.

Sailing Auxiliaries

A sailing auxiliary under sail and power or power alone must carry and exhibit the same lights as a motorboat. In practice, the 20 point white mast-head light is generally fixed on the foremast, high enough so that it will not be obscured by the jib.

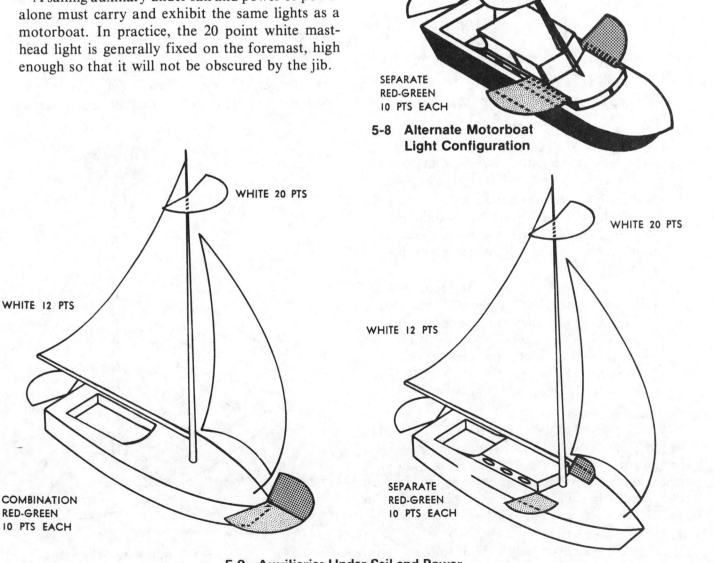

WHITE 12 PTS

WHITE 20 PTS

COMBINATION
RED-GREEN
10 PTS EACH.

5-7 Motorboat

WHITE 12 PTS

WHITE 20 PTS

SEPARATE
RED-GREEN
10 PTS EACH

5-8 Alternate Motorboat Light Configuration

WHITE 20 PTS

WHITE 12 PTS

COMBINATION
RED-GREEN
10 PTS EACH

WHITE 20 PTS

WHITE 12 PTS

SEPARATE
RED-GREEN
10 PTS EACH

5-9 Auxiliaries Under Sail and Power

Vessels Under Sail Alone

A vessel under sail alone must carry and exhibit the same lights as a motorboat except the 20 point white masthead light which is extinguished. Two modifications to this are authorized:

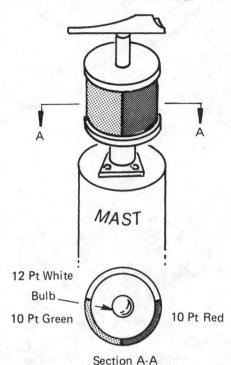

Section A-A

5-10 New Combination Masthead Light For Sailboats Under 12 Meters (39.4 Feet)

1. If the sailing vessel is less than 12 meters (39.4 feet) in length, the colored lights and the white sternlight may be combined in one lantern at or near the top of the mast where it can best be seen.

2. A sailing vessel not using this combination lantern may, if desired, display at or near the top of the mast, where they can best be seen, two all-round (32 point) lights in a vertical line, the upper being red and the lower green. They shall be separated by at least 1 meter (3.3 feet) and visibility shall be at least 2 miles.

Small Sailing Vessels

A sailing vessel of less than 7 meters (23.0 feet) in length shall, if practicable, exhibit the lights prescribed above. If she does not, she shall have ready at hand an electric torch or lighted lantern showing a white light which shall be exhibited in sufficient time to prevent collision.

Vessels Under Oars

A vessel under oars may exhibit the lights prescribed for sailing vessels. If she does not, she shall have ready at hand an electric torch or lighted lantern showing a white light which shall be exhibited in sufficient time to prevent collision.

Large Vessels

Large vessels carry lights which should be of some interest to the small boat skipper. Large vessels develop strong wave patterns which the small boat skipper will do well to keep clear of, particularly at night. Large vessels underway at night may be identified by their range lights. Power driven vessels over 150 feet in length underway in international waters carry a 20-point white light, visible 5 miles, in the forepart of the vessel and, abaft this white light and in line with and over the keel, another 20 point white light, also visible 5 miles, and at least 15 feet higher than the forward white light. When a large vessel is approaching at night, these range lights will be seen one above the other. The vessel's heading with relation to your boat can be determined by the position of these range lights. For instance, if these range lights appear exactly above one another, the vessel is heading straight for your boat and it's important to get out of its way as soon as possible!

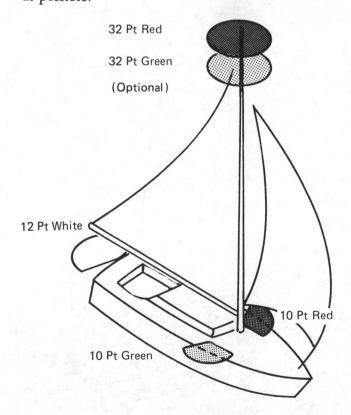

5-11 Alternate Sailboat Light Configuration

In inland waters, the after range light is optional for seagoing steam vessels. On steam vessels, an after range light must be shown. This range light is a white, 32-point light.

Ferryboats plying Inland waters are usually double-ended and have a specific set of lighting requirements. Two sets of colored side lights are carried and one set is used according to which direction the ferry is moving. The white lights are seen all around the horizon (32 points) and, in addition, they may carry a special light assigned to it by the officer in charge of Marine Inspection. This special light may be of any color and will usually be carried amidships, at least 15 feet above the range lights, visible all around the horizon.

Tow boats and the barges they push or tow are lighted according to each set of rules in a different manner. Our rivers and our harbors are constantly being dredged. Dredges have equipment protruding from them and pipelines or barges which carry away the waste. These units are lighted to warn you to keep clear at night. Buoy tenders and vessels working over wrecks also have their own set of lighting requirements. Certain prescribed areas have special lighting combinations which are peculiar to the area. For instance, on the Gulf Intracoastal Waterway the rules governing towed vessels in Western Rivers are followed. Another set of rules governs the waters around New York harbor and the Hudson River. Specific lighting requirements are prescribed for vessels which are on pilot duty, either on station or on their way to station. The lights which will be seen on vessels which denote their occupation will usually be vertically arranged and will be white or red or a combination of these colors. It is important to realize that whenever you see a lighting arrangement other than the regular running lights on vessels in your area, the vessels thus lighted are unable to maneuver except with difficulty. In some cases, they cannot maneuver at all. It is always a good idea to approach these vessels cautiously and keep well clear of any equipment which might be projecting from them. The student is advised that lighting patterns on various working vessels vary greatly and would require a considerable mental effort to memorize. Rather than attempt to do this, play it safe and give them a wide berth.

Anchor Lights

Certain anchorage areas have been designated by the Secretary of the Army as "special anchorage areas" and vessels not over 65 feet in length may anchor in these areas without being required to show an anchor light at night. Under all other conditions, all vessels must display one or more lights while at anchor at night. All four sets of rules require a vessel under 150 feet in length to display a white 32-point light, carried forward, where it can best be seen. In International, Inland, and Western Rivers, this light must be visible for 2 miles. On the Great Lakes, the visibility requirement for this anchor light is 1 mile. Large vessels over 150 feet in length are required by International, Inland and Western Rivers Rules to carry two anchor lights, the forward light being carried higher than the after light. On the Great Lakes, the anchor lights are carried in pairs, two forward at the same height, arranged so that one or the other, or both, are visible all around the horizon, and two aft, similarly arranged but lower than the forward lights. In addition, Great Lakes Rules require vessels over 150 feet in length to display white deck lights at 100 ft. intervals along the deck, visible from any angle of approach.

Shapes (Day Signals)

In the daytime, vessels engaged in certain specific occupations are required to display signals or shapes. The list of these signals is long and there would be no point in attempting to memorize them. Shapes are usually fabric-covered frames in the shape of balls, cones, diamonds or cylinders. Day signals and shapes are used to indicate vessels which are given special privileges by the Rules of the Road (such as vessels engaged in fishing—Rule 26). If a vessel is entitled to a privilege, it must display the proper shape to obtain it. A good rule-of-thumb would be to consider all vessels which display such shapes as being incapable of maneuvering except with difficulty, and thus unable to react quickly to situations imposed upon them by other vessels. There is one situation, however, where this rule-of-thumb does not apply. Rule 14 of the International Rules requires a sailboat underway under sail and power to display by day a black conical shape, point downwards, carried forward where it can best be seen. This exception to the rule-of-thumb is not serious since the signal just described will seldom, if ever, be encountered. Thus for all practical purposes the rule-of-thumb remains inviolate. Whenever you see a vessel at anchor or underway displaying a day signal, approach it with caution or stay away from it if possible.

Steering and Sailing Rules and Sound Signals

These rules determine which vessel has the right-of-way in situations where vessels are meeting, crossing or overtaking. In each case (except for vessels meeting bow-on or nearly so) one vessel is "privileged" and has the right-of-way and the other is "burdened" and must keep clear of the privileged vessel.

Privileged Vessel Duty

The vessel which has the right-of-way (the privileged vessel or the stand-on vessel) has a duty to maintain course and speed. This is logical in the sense that it gives the burdened vessel an opportunity to base its actions on a known set of conditions. The privileged vessel's duty to maintain course and speed ends abruptly the instant a collision is imminent. The general prudential rule, mentioned later in this chapter, will explain this but for the moment it is important to realize that the privileged vessel also becomes burdened when a collision is imminent and the situation is considered to be "in extremis."

Burdened Vessel Duty

The vessel which does not have the right-of-way (the burdened vessel or the make-way vessel) has a duty to take positive and timely action to keep out of the way of the privileged vessel. *This does not mean to increase speed and cross ahead of the privileged vessel!* In fact, the rules state that the burdened vessel shall, if possible, avoid crossing ahead of the privileged vessel. The burdened vessel, when changing heading to comply with the Rules of the Road, should make such changes in heading smartly and definitely in order that its action can be easily observed by those aboard the privileged vessel. The burdened vessel usually conforms to the rules in crossing situations by changing course briefly or slowing down (or both) and passing astern of the privileged vessel. However, before we get into this, let's take a good look at a very important rule.

The General Prudential Rule

The General Prudential Rule is found in all four sets of Rules of the Road. It is called Article 27 in the Inland Rules. It is called Rule 27 in the International Rules and also in the Great Lakes Rules. It is called "Rule Numbered 25" in the Western Rivers Rules. In each case, however, its wording (and meaning) is almost the same.

'In obeying and construing these rules due regard shall be had to all dangers of navigation and collision, and to any special circumstances, which may render a departure from the above rules necessary in order to avoid immediate danger. . . ."

Thus we see that the General Prudential Rule does not apply only on such occasions as it may appear convenient. The steering and sailing rules must be observed under all normal circumstances. It is only when a collision is imminent, and would certainly occur if both vessels continued on their present course and speed, that the General Prudential Rule applies. The Courts have held . . .

". . . When such departure becomes necessary, neither vessel shall have the right-of-way and both vessels shall navigate with caution until the danger of collision is over."

As we have seen, the privileged vessel is obliged to maintain course and speed under normal conditions until such time that a collision becomes imminent. At that instant, the privileged vessel also becomes burdened and is obliged to take all actions necessary to avoid the collision. To put it simply, the privileged vessel does not, at any time, have the right-of-way *through the hull* of another vessel!

When Rules of the Road Apply

It has been said (in jest) that risk of collision exists whenever two vessels are on the same ocean at the same time. While we know this to be a gross exaggeration, the exact time when steering and sailing rules must be applied is difficult to define. Mr. Justice Clifford, in N.Y. & LIVERPOOL vs RUMBALL, said, "Rules of navigation are obligatory on vessels approaching each other, from the time the necessity of precaution begins, and continue to be applicable as the vessels advance, so long as the means and opportunity to avoid danger remain. They are equally inapplicable to vessels of any description while they are yet so distant from each other that measures of precaution have not become necessary to avoid a collision."

From this, it is comparatively simple to define the time when steering and sailing rules of the road *do not* apply. They do not apply when the vessels are so far apart that a danger of collision will not arise *regardless of the actions of either vessel.* Thus, by elimination, we can safely deduce that if the vessels are sufficiently close to each other that a departure from the rules by either vessel will create a danger of collision, steering and sailing rules must be applied from that point in time until both vessels are again clear of each other.

We should keep in mind that compliance with the rules is *mandatory* upon each vessel, and not optional. There is no choice of action by either vessel until the danger of collision is so imminent that *both* vessels must take evasive action.

The Situations

Steering rules between power vessels are based on all possible situations. In each case, both vessels must observe the rules until they are well clear of one another. Basically, there are three main situations which can lead to a collision afloat. These situations are:

> The meeting situation
> The crossing situation
> The overtaking situation

All of the situations between power vessels are shown in the diagram on this page. Remember, rules apply when two or more vessels are in sight of one another and only when the vessels are sufficiently close that for both vessels to continue on their present course and speed would create a danger of collision.

You are the skipper of the vessel in the center of the diagram. You must keep out of the way of any vessel approaching you in the arc from dead ahead (or right ahead) of you to 2 points abaft your starboard beam. All the other vessels in the diagram — except the meeting vessel — must keep clear of you. Both you and the meeting vessel must alter course as necessary to pass clear of each other.

Normally, all the situations can be observed in the making by simply taking a series of bearings on the other vessel or its lights at night. Unless the vessels are sailing on courses which parallel one another, if the bearings do not change substantially between sights, a collision is almost inevitable. The

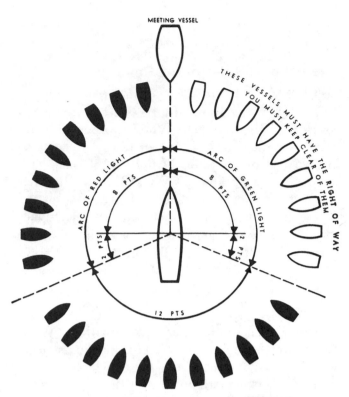

5-12   Right of Way in a Crossing Situation

"burdened" vessel is required to change course or speed, or both, while the "privileged" vessel is required to hold her course and speed. Where small craft are concerned, good sense is one of the best rules. In other words, when you can, seek to avoid a situation instead of frantically searching your mind for the exactly proper rule to get you safely out of it.

Generally speaking, the right-of-way situations between vessels are quite similar in all four sets of Rules. In order that you might more easily learn the rules which apply to your boat and to your waters, the balance of this chapter will be divided into separate subdivisions — International, Inland, Great Lakes and Western Rivers. In addition, we have included a section on sailboat rules for those of you who operate sailboats. Power boat skippers may be interested in this section since it should help to clear up some of the mystery which surrounds the actions of sailboats seen nearby. Your instructor will tell you which set of Rules apply to your waters. These should be learned thoroughly since there usually isn't enough time to "look it up" when two boats are converging at a speed of 15 knots each. The combined speed of approach in this situation is 30 knots, which means that you will have a minute at most to decide what you are going to do.

International Rules of the Road

Power Vessels Meeting End on (or Head on)

Rule 18 of the International Rules of the Road covers this situation well. When two power driven vessels are meeting head on, or nearly so, so as to involve risk of collision, *neither vessel shall have the right-of-way*, and each vessel shall alter her course to starboard so that each may pass on the port side of the other. Remember, this rule applies only if the vessels are meeting head on in such a way as to involve risk of collision. It does not apply if both vessels, keeping to their respective courses, will pass safely clear of one another.

Power Vessels Crossing

Rule 19 takes care of crossing situations. When two power driven vessels are crossing, so as to involve risk of collision, the vessel which has the other on her own starboard side shall keep out of

the way of the other. In the daytime, a vessel approaching on your starboard side can be easily seen. At night, if you see the red side light of another vessel which is crossing your course on your starboard side, that vessel has the right-of-way and you must keep clear.

Power Vessels Overtaking

If a vessel is overtaking another, it is burdened until the overtaken vessel has been passed and is clear. Rule 24 states that every vessel coming up with another vessel from any direction more than 2 points abaft her beam shall be deemed to be an overtaking vessel. No subsequent alteration of the bearing between these two vessels shall relieve the overtaking vessel of her duty of keeping clear of the overtaken vessel until she is finally past and clear. If the overtaking vessel is in doubt whether she is forward or abaft the direction of 2 points abaft the beam of the overtaken vessel, she shall assume that she is an overtaking vessel and shall keep clear. At night, if you are unable to see the

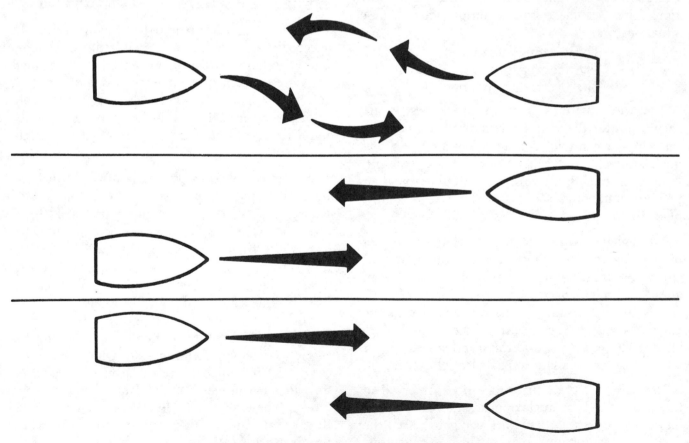

**5-13 Meeting Situations Under International Rules
Neither Vessel Has The Right-Of-Way.**

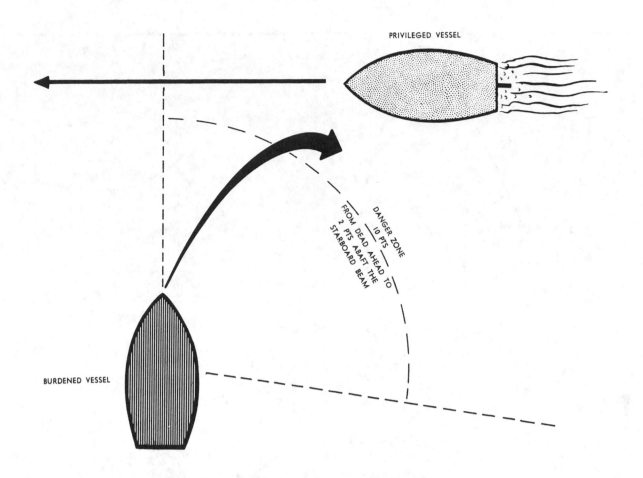

PRIVILEGED VESSEL

DANGER ZONE
10 PTS
FROM DEAD AHEAD TO
2 PTS ABAFT THE
STARBOARD BEAM

BURDENED VESSEL

5-14 Crossing Situation Under International Rules

overtaken vessel's side lights (red or green), you should assume that you are overtaking and keep clear.

Power Vessels in Narrow Channels and Bends

In a narrow channel, every power vessel shall keep to the right side of the channel when it is safe and practicable to do so. When a power vessel is nearing a bend in a narrow channel where a vessel approaching from the other direction might not be seen, at about the time she arrives within one-half mile of the bend she shall sound one prolonged blast (4 to 6 seconds) on the whistle as a signal. If another vessel is within hearing around the bend, this other vessel shall answer the signal with a similar blast. However, even if no reply is heard to the original signal, the vessel shall navigate the bend with alertness and caution.

In a narrow channel, a power vessel of less than 65 feet in length shall not hamper the safe passage of a vessel which can navigate only inside such

channel. In other words, don't play "right-of-way games" with large vessels in a narrow channel. It is not only against the law but it could be costly. Large deep-draft vessels are difficult to maneuver in narrow channels and must, of necessity, remain within the limits of the channel. Your boat is extremely more maneuverable in the channel and so the rules state that you do not have the right-of-way. This is only common sense.

Right-of-Way of Fishing Vessels

All fishing vessels which are fishing with nets, lines or trawls are considered to be fishing vessels under the International Rules. Vessels fishing with trolling lines are *not* considered to be fishing vessels. Fishing vessels have the right-of-way and all other vessels shall keep out of their way. However, a fishing vessel shall not impede the passage of another vessel navigating within a narrow channel or fairway. The student is reminded that the fact that he might be trolling a lure aft of his boat or from out-

5-13

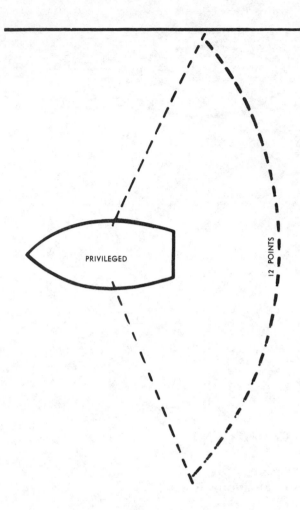

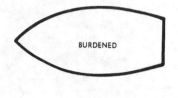

**5-15 Overtaking Situation Under
International Rules**

riggers does not make his vessel a fishing vessel under the rules. A fishing vessel must display a basket or two black cones in the rigging. When you see these, it's a good idea to keep well clear.

Sailing Vessel Right-of-Way

When a power-driven vessel and a sailing vessel (under sail only) are proceeding in such directions as to involve risk of collision, the power-driven vessel shall keep clear of the sailing vessel except in the following situations:

1. When a sailing vessel is overtaking a power-driven vessel the overtaken vessel (in this case the power vessel) has the right-of-way, and the sailing vessel shall keep out of the way.

2. A sailing vessel shall keep clear of any vessel engaged in fishing with nets, lines or trawls.

3. In a narrow channel, a sailing vessel shall not hamper the safe passage of a power-driven

vessel which can navigate only inside such channel.

Sailboat skippers should realize, however, that even though power boats are far more maneuverable than sailboats, power boats do not have power brakes. It is foolhardy to defy fate by tacking immediately under the bow of a power boat in the comforting assurance that you have the right-of-way. The power boat's transmission could fail to engage in full reverse and an accident could very likely result. Having the right-of-way is small comfort when viewed in the light of a damaged hull and possible injury to those aboard.

*Sound Signals Under the International Rules
  of the Road*

On the international waters or the high seas, one, two and three blast sound signals are considered "course indicating signals" and are accompanied by a change of course or some other action on the part of the vessel sounding such signals. These signals are given only when vessels are in sight of one another. There are three such signals, and they are as follows.

One short blast (1 second) means "I am altering my course to starboard. . . . Two short blasts (1 second each) means "I am altering my course to port. . . . Three short blasts (1 second each) means "My engines are going astern. . . .

Whenever a power vessel which, under the rules, is to keep her course and speed (a privileged vessel), and she is in doubt whether sufficient action is being taken by the other (burdened) vessel to avert a collision, she may indicate such doubt by giving the danger signal. This signal is as follows:

Five or more short blasts (1 second each) on the whistle.

The fact that a vessel sounds the danger signal does not relieve her of her obligations to keep a proper lookout and to observe the general prudential rule.

As stated earlier, sound signals under International Rules are signals indicating an action or doubt and as such are normally not answered by the other vessel. Any whistle signal under the rules may be further indicated by a visual signal consisting of a white light visible all around the horizon (32 points) at a distance of at least five miles, which will operate simultaneously with the whistle and remain lighted and visible during the same period as the sound signal.

Conduct in Restricted Visibility Under the International Rules

Radar

The development of RADAR has made it possible to "see" through fog to a limited degree. The student is cautioned, however, that even though his vessel may be equipped with RADAR, under the International Rules of the Road the information obtained from RADAR does not relieve the vessel so equipped from the obligation of conforming strictly with the rules in conditions of restricted visibility.

Signals in Restricted Visibility

Fog signals are required to be sounded by all vessels (power and sail) in fog, mist, falling snow, heavy rainstorms or any other condition of restricted visibility, whether by day or night. Power-driven vessels shall sound fog signals on the whistle and sailing vessels shall sound fog signals on the fog horn.

A prolonged blast is specified as one of from four to six seconds' duration. A short blast is specified as of about one second's duration.

A power vessel making headway through the water shall sound one prolonged blast (4 to 6 seconds) on the whistle at least every 2 minutes.

A power vessel underway but stopped and making no way through the water shall sound two prolonged blasts on the whistle, with an interval of about two seconds between blasts, at least every two minutes.

A sailing vessel, a vessel not under command, a vessel restricted in her ability to maneuver, and a vessel engaged in towing or pushing another vessel shall, instead of the signals indicated above, sound one prolonged blast followed by two short blasts at intervals of not more than 2 minutes. A vessel being towed shall sound one prolonged blast followed by three short blasts at intervals of not more than 2 minutes. When practicable, this signal shall be made immediately after the signal made by the towing vessel.

Vessels at Anchor

When at anchor, every vessel shall ring the bell rapidly for at least five seconds at intervals of not more than one minute. Large vessels (over 350 feet in length) also sound a gong at the stern when anchored in a fog. All vessels may, in addition, sound three blasts on the whistle or fog horn as follows: One short, one prolonged and one short blast, to give warning of her position and of the possibility of collision to any vessel which appears to be standing into danger of a collision.

Speed in Fog

In conditions of impaired visibility, all vessels shall proceed at a moderate speed, having careful regard to the existing circumstances and conditions. A vessel which hears the fog signal of another vessel apparently ahead of her beam shall stop, reverse her engines if necessary, and proceed with caution until danger of collision has passed. In conditions of impaired visibility, speed should be governed to a great extent by the visible distance. It would appear logical to give one-half of the visible distance to the other vessel. Under this assumption, any vessel underway in fog should be able to stop in half of her visible distance. The speed, thus determined would be the *maximum* speed allowed under the rules of good seamanship in the circumstances.

Inland Rules of the Road

Power Vessels Meeting Head-on

When two power vessels are approaching each other head-on, and a danger of collision arises, neither vessel is privileged and each should alter course to the right to pass clear. One vessel will sound one short (1 second) blast on her whistle, indicating her intention to pass port to port. This signal will be immmediately answered by the other vessel with one short blast. On waters under the Inland Rules of the Road, these whistle signals are signals of intent and assent. As such, each whistle signal shall be answered. The first vessel indicates her intention by a whistle signal and the other vessel answers with a similar signal to indicate that she understands and agrees. Thereupon, both vessels alter their course to starboard smartly and keep the other vessel to port during the passing. If the vessels are meeting, but not on a collision course, and would clear each other with plenty of room to spare without a change of heading, there would be no necessity for either vessel to alter course and they would pass port to port or starboard to starboard simply by exchanging signals. On a starboard-to-

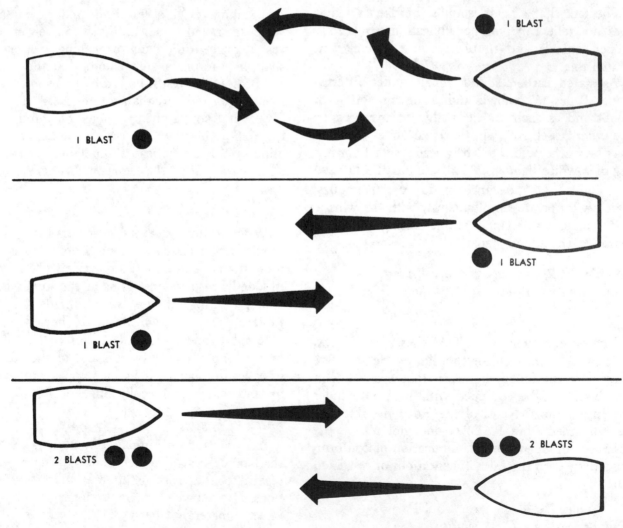

5-16 Meeting Situations Under Inland Rules

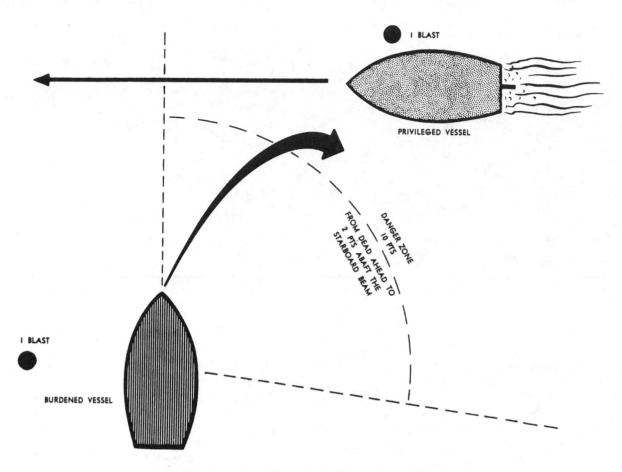

5-17 Crossing Situations Under Inland Rules

starboard passing the signals are two short blasts (1 second each) given by each vessel. In any meeting situation, if either vessel does not understand the other's signals or feels that the type of passage signaled for will be dangerous, she should sound the "Danger Signal," which consists of four or more short blasts (1 second each) on her whistle. When a danger signal is given or heard, both vessels shall stop and continue to exchange signals until they are understood by both vessels before either vessel may proceed again. The cause of most head-on-collisions between vessels is usually carelessness, stubborness or ignorance of the rules.

Power Vessels Crossing

When two power vessels are crossing so as to involve a risk of collision, the vessel which has the other on her starboard side shall keep out of the way of the other. At night, if you see the red light of another vessel which is crossing your course, that vessel has the right-of-way and you must keep clear. In the situation in Illustration 5-17, the privi–

leged vessel will sound one short blast (1 second) on her whistle to indicate that she has the right-of-way and will maintain course and speed. The burdened vessel will answer with one short blast on her whistle to indicate that she has heard and understood the signal and will keep clear. If there is any doubt in the mind of the skipper of either vessel concerning the safety of the crossing or the intentions of the other, either vessel will sound the danger signal. When this signal is given or heard, both vessels must stop and exchange signals until the situation is clear to both skippers.

Power Vessels Overtaking

If a vessel is overtaking another, it is burdened until the overtaken vessel has been passed and is clear. Every vessel coming up with another vessel from any direction more than 2 points abaft her beam shall be deemed to be an overtaking vessel. No subsequent alteration of the bearing between these two vessels shall relieve the overtaking vessel of her duty of keeping clear of the overtaken vessel until she is finally past and clear. If the over-

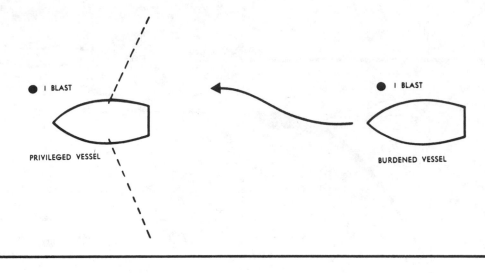

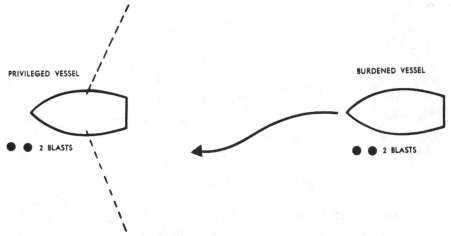

5-18 Overtaking Situations - Inland Rules

taking vessel is in doubt whether she is abaft the direction of 2 points abaft the beam of the overtaken vessel, she shall assume that she is an overtaking vessel and shall keep clear. At night, if you are unable to see the overtaken vessel's side lights (red or green) you should assume that you are overtaking and keep clear. During an overtaking situation, the privileged vessel (the one being overtaken) must maintain course and speed. If the burdened vessel (the one which is overtaking) wishes to pass on the privileged vessel's starboard side, she will sound one short blast (1 second). If the privileged vessel agrees to the starboard passage, she will answer with one short blast. If the burdened vessel desires to pass on the privileged vessel's port side, she will sound two short blasts. Again, if the privileged vessel agrees to the port passage, she will answer with two short blasts. If

for some reason it is not safe for the overtaking vessel to pass on the side signalled for, the privileged vessel will sound the danger signal. In this case it is usually not necessary for both vessels to stop. They simply continue to exchange signals until they have agreement on which side the passage will be made. In no case may a vessel answer a signal with a different signal. A signal of one short blast must be answered with one short blast or the danger signal. It is illegal to answer one blast with two, or two blasts with one. This is known as a "cross signal." It keeps everyone in doubt concerning the exact intentions of the other vessel and is quite dangerous.

Power Vessels in Narrow Channels and Bends

In a narrow channel, every power vessel shall keep to the right side of the channel if it is safe and practicable to do so. When a power vessel is nearing a bend in a channel where a vessel approaching from around the bend would not be seen due to cliffs or some other obstruction, Inland Rules require the vessel to sound one long blast at about the time she arrives one-half mile from the bend. The duration of time for a long blast is not spelled out in the Inland Rules but it is traditionally a blast of eight to ten seconds duration. If this signal is answered by a vessel around the bend, both vessels shall immediately give and answer proper signals for meeting and passing. If the signal is not answered, the channel is to be considered clear and the vessel giving the signal may act accordingly.

A vessel leaving her berth shall give the same signal as a vessel nearing a bend.

In narrow channels, a power vessel of 65 feet or less in length shall not hamper the safe passage of a vessel which can navigate only inside such channel. Large deep-draft ships are difficult to maneuver and almost impossible to stop in response to situations imposed upon them by other vessels while they are navigating in a narrow channel. The Inland Rules give these larger vessels the right-of-way in narrow channels. This is only common sense.

Right-of-Way of Fishing Vessels

All fishing vessels which are fishing with nets, lines or trawls are privileged under the Inland Rules. Vessels fishing in this manner may be underway or at anchor. In any case, it's dangerous to approach too close, so you should keep well clear. If you happen to be streaming a jig from astern in the hope that you might catch a fish, this fact does not make your boat a fishing vessel under the rules. You will be able to tell a fishing vessel by the fact that she must display a basket aloft where it can best be seen.

Sailing Vessel Right-of-Way

When a power-driven vessel and a sailing vessel (under sail only) are proceeding in such directions as to involve risk of collision, the power-driven vessel shall keep clear of the sailing vessel except in the following situations:

1. When a sailing vessel is overtaking a power-driven vessel, the overtaken vessel (in this case the power vessel) has the right-of-way, and the sailing vessel shall keep out of the way.

2. A sailing vessel shall keep clear of any vessel engaged in fishing with nets, lines or trawls.

3. In a narrow channel, a sailing vessel shall not hamper the safe passage of a power-driven vessel which can navigate only inside such channel.

Sailing vessels do not exchange whistle signals with each other, nor do they exchange such signals with a power vessel. Sailboat skippers should realize that, even though power boats are far more maneuverable than sail boats, power boats do not have power brakes. It is foolhardy to defy fate by tacking immediately under the bow of a power boat in the comforting assurance that you have the right-of-way. The power boat's transmission could fail to engage in full reverse and an accident could very likely result. Having the right-of-way is small comfort when viewed in the light of a damaged hull and possible injury to those aboard.

Sound Signals Under Inland Rules of the Road

On Inland waters, sound signals required when meeting, crossing or overtaking are signals of intent and assent. The vessel which signals first does so to indicate her proposed action. When the signal is answered by the other vessel, she is indicating that she understands the signal and that she agrees with the proposed maneuver by the other vessel and will govern her own actions accordingly. Only after this agreement is reached does either vessel change course.

Sound signals of intent and assent are only exchanged between power vessels in sight of one another, and then only when they are close enough that a risk of collision might arise.

All sound signals under Inland Rules are sounded on the whistle. Whistle signals have many meanings, such as in a head to head situation.

One short blast means "I intend to alter my course to starboard."

Two short blasts mean "I intend to alter my course to port."

Three short blasts mean "My engines are going at full speed astern."

Inland Rules do not define the exact length of time for a short blast. These signals are intended to be given as "short, rapid blasts." A period of about one second each would appear to suffice.

When power vessels are approaching each other, if either vessel fails to understand the course or intention of the other, from any cause, the vessel which is in doubt shall immediately signify the same by sounding four or more short rapid blasts on the whistle. This is the danger signal (or doubt signal) under the Inland Rules. When this signal is heard from any vessel which is approaching, both vessels should stop and not proceed until the proper signals have been given and understood.

Conduct in Restricted Visibility Under the Inland Rules

Fog Signals

All vessels, power or sail, are required by the Inland Rules to sound proper fog signals in fog, mist, falling snow or heavy rain storms, whether by day or night. Power vessels sound fog signals on the whistle; sail vessels sound fog signals on the fog horn.

A power vessel underway shall sound one prolonged blast on the whistle at least every minute.

Towing vessels sound a series of three blasts in succession every minute, namely, one prolonged blast followed by two short blasts. A vessel being towed may give the same signal.

A sailing vessel underway shall sound, at intervals of not more than one minute, the following signals on the fog horn.

If on the starboard tack — one blast.

If on the port tack — two blasts in succession.

If the wind is abaft the beam — three blasts in succession. The rules do not specify the length of time for each blast.

Vessels at Anchor

When at anchor, a vessel shall ring the bell rapidly for at least five seconds at intervals of not more than one minute. This is not required of vessels not over 65 feet in length when anchored in a special anchorage area as specified by the Secretary of the Army.

Speed in Fog

In conditions of impaired visibility, all vessels shall proceed at a moderate speed, having careful regard to the existing circumstances and conditions. A vessel which hears the fog signal of another vessel apparently ahead of her beam shall, as far as the circumstances of the case permit, stop her engines and then navigate with caution until danger of collision is over. In conditions of reduced visibility, the speed shall be governed to a great extent by the visible distance. It would appear logical to give one-half of the visible distance to the other vessel. Under this assumption, any vessel underway in fog should be able to stop in half of her visible distance. This speed, that is a speed at which you would be able to stop in half of the visible distance, would be the *maximum* speed allowed under the rules of good seamanship in the circumstances.

Great Lakes Rules of the Road

Power Vessels Meeting in Narrow Channels and Rivers

When two power vessels meet (going in opposite directions) in narrow channels where there is a current, the "less maneuverable" or descending vessel has the right-of-way. The privileged vessel is required to signal as to which side she plans to take, which signal shall be given at about the time the two vessels approach to within one-half mile of each other. If the privileged vessel elects to pass the burdened vessel port-to-port, she shall signal this intention by sounding one "distinct blast" on the whistle. This shall be promptly answered by the burdened vessel by a similar blast on her whistle. If the privileged vessel elects to pass starboard-to-starboard, she shall sound two distinct blasts on her whistle, which shall also be promptly answered by the burdened vessel by two distinct blasts. These signals could be considered signals of intent and understanding in the sense that the privileged vessel signals her intention and the burdened vessel signals her understanding of the privileged vessel's intentions.

In all channels of less than 500 feet in width, when power vessels proceeding in opposite directions are about to meet, both vessels shall slow down to a moderate speed, according to the circumstances.

A power or sail vessel of 65 feet or less in length shall not hamper the safe passage of a vessel which can navigate only inside that channel.

Vessels Overtaking in Narrow Channels

In channels less than 500 feet in width, the rules do not permit one vessel to overtake and pass another unless the overtaken vessel is disabled or signals her permission for the overtaking vessel to pass. If the overtaking vessel desires to pass the overtaken vessel's starboard side she shall signal by sounding one distinct blast on the whistle. If the overtaken vessel agrees to the starboard passing, she shall answer with one distinct blast. If the overtaking vessel desires to pass the overtaken vessel's port side, she shall signal by sounding two distinct blasts on the whistle. If the overtaken vessel agrees to the port passing, she shall answer with two distinct blasts. If the overtaken vessel decides that either passing is unsafe, she shall answer by sound-

ing several short and rapid blasts on the whistle, not less than five. In this case, the overtaking vessel may not pass until permission has been received from the overtaken vessel by a properly answered whistle signal.

Special Rules for the St. Mary's River

Special anchorage and navigation requirements for the St. Mary's River in Michigan supplement the general rules and regulations applicable to vessels on the Great Lakes. These are set forth in a separate section of the Great Lakes Pilot Rules (contained in Coast Guard publication CG-172.) and will not be enumerated here.

Power Vessels Meeting End-on

When two power vessels are meeting end-on or head-on so as to involve risk of collision, neither vessel shall have the right of way and each shall sound one distinct blast on the whistle and shall

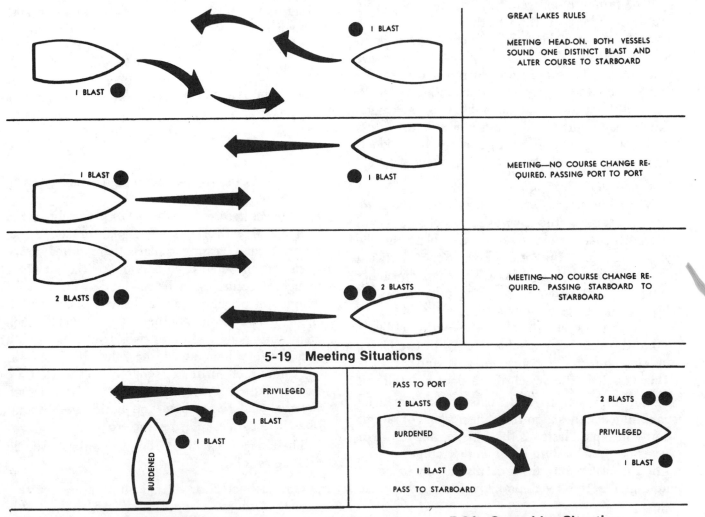

5-19 Meeting Situations

5-20 Crossing Situation

5-21 Overtaking Situation

alter her course to starboard so that each shall pass on the port side of the other.

If the vessels are passing in opposite directions and an alteration of course will not be required in order to pass safely, whistle signals indicating course must be given and answered. If the vessels will pass port-to-port, each shall sound one distinct blast on the whistle. If they will pass starboard-to-starboard, each shall sound two distinct blasts on the whistle. These signals shall be sounded as the vessels approach within one-half mile of each other.

Power Vessels Crossing

When two power vessels are crossing so as to involve risk of collision, the vessel which has the other on her starboard side shall keep out of the way of the other. The vessel having the right of way shall blow one distinct blast on the whistle as a signal of her intention to cross the bow of the other, holding her course and speed, which signal shall be promptly answered by the other vessel by one distinct blast on the whistle as a signal of her intention to direct her course to starboard so as to cross the stern of the other vessel or otherwise keep clear. If for some reason it is not possible for both vessels to comply with each other's signals, this shall be made apparent by blowing the danger signal (five short rapid blasts) and both vessels shall stop, engines backed if necessary, until signals for passing with safety are made and understood.

Power Vessels Overtaking

When one power vessel desires to overtake another by passing the overtaken vessel's starboard side, she shall sound one distinct blast on the whistle to signal this desire and, if the overtaken vessel answers with one blast, she shall direct her course to starboard and pass the other vessel. If the overtaking vessel desires to pass the overtaken vessel's port side, she shall sound two distinct blasts and, if the overtaken vessel answers with two blasts, she shall direct her course to port and pass the other vessel. If the vessel ahead does not think it safe for the vessel astern to pass at that time, she shall immediately sound the danger signal of several short and rapid blasts on the whistle, not less than five. The vessel astern shall not attempt to pass until the overtaken vessel deems it safe to do so and signifies this by a properly answered whistle signal.

Sailing Vessel Right-of-Way

When a steam vessel and a sailing vessel (under sail alone) are proceeding in such directions as to involve risk of collision, the power vessel shall keep out of the way of the sailing vessel except in the following situations:

1. When a sailing vessel is overtaking a power vessel, the overtaken vessel has the right-of-way and the sailing vessel shall keep out of the way

2. In a narrow channel, a sailing vessel shall not hamper the safe passage of a power-driven vessel which can navigate only inside such channel.

Sailing vessels do not exchange whistle signals with each other, nor do they exchange such signals with power vessels. Sailboat skippers should realize that, even though power boats are far more maneuverable than sail vessels, power boats do not have power brakes. It is foolhardy to defy fate by tacking immediately under the bow of a power vessel in the comforting assurance that you have the right-of-way. The power vessel's transmission could fail to engage in full reverse and an accident could very likely result. Having the right-of-way is small comfort when viewed in the light of a damaged hull and possible injury to those aboard.

Sound Signals

On the Great Lakes, sound signals are given in all weathers, regardless of visibility. Every power vessel which receives a signal shall promptly answer such signal with the same signal or sound the danger signal. Passing signals are required to be given and answered regardless of whether or not a change of course is to be made. Signals must be sounded at about the time the vessels are within one-half mile of one another. "Cross signals" such as answering one blast with two, or two blasts with one, are forbidden under the rules. If a signal is not understood, or if the other vessel's actions are not understood or deemed unsafe, the danger signal should be sounded and both vessels should observe the rule applying thereto.

These signals shall be sounded on the whistle, and are as follows:

One distinct blast—"I am altering my course to starboard."

Two distinct blasts—"I am altering my course to port."

Five or more rapid blasts—The danger signal.

One long blast of at least 8 seconds—Used by a vessel within one-half mile of a bend in a channel, or by a vessel leaving her berth.

NOTE: Under Great Lakes Rules, "distinct blasts" should not be confused with "short blasts" of one second's duration. The one second blast is considered too short and, although the length of the blast is not specified, a blast of from two to three seconds would appear to satisfy the requirements.

Conduct in Restricted Visibility

Fog Signals
In restricted visibility, whether by day or night, fog signals shall be sounded on the whistle as follows:

A power vessel underway shall sound three successive distinct blasts on the whistle at intervals of not more than one minute.

A vessel in tow shall, at intervals of one minute, sound "four bells" on the bell in the same manner as "four bells" is struck indicating time. Strike the bell twice in quick succession, wait a short interval, and strike the bell twice again in quick succession.

A sailing vessel underway shall sound, at intervals of not more than one minute, the following signals on the fog horn:

If on the starboard tack with wind forward of the beam—one blast

If on the port tack with wind forward of the beam—two blasts

If the wind is abaft the beam on either side—three blasts

The rules do not describe the length of these blasts.

Vessels at Anchor
When at anchor or aground in or near a channel or fairway, a vessel shall ring the bell rapidly for three to five seconds at intervals of not more than two minutes. In addition, such vessel shall sound one short blast, two long blasts and one short blast in quick succession on the whistle at intervals of not more then three minutes.

Speed in Fog
Every vessel shall, in thick weather by reason of fog, mist, falling snow, heavy rain or other causes, proceed at a moderate speed. If a fog signal of another vessel is heard from a direction apparently not more than four points from right ahead, the vessel hearing such signal shall at once reduce speed to bare steerageway and navigate with caution until the vessels have passed one another. In reduced visibility, it would appear logical to give one-half of the visible distance to the other vessel. Under this assumption, if two vessels are coming directly at one another, each would be able to stop in half of the visible distance. "Moderate speed" under Great Lakes Rules would appear to be satisfied under these conditions.

Western Rivers Rules of the Road

Power Vessels Meeting End-on
When two power vessels are meeting end-on, or nearly so, so as to involve risk of collision, it shall be the duty of each to alter course to starboard sufficiently to pass each on the port side of the other, if this can be done in safety. This maneuver shall require an exchange of one-blast whistle signals when the vessels are no less than one-half mile apart. Either vessel may blow the first signal and the other vessel shall promptly answer.

Power Vessels Meeting at the Confluence of two Rivers
When two power vessels meet at the confluence of two rivers, the vessel which has the other to port shall give the first signal. In no case shall the vessels attempt to pass each other until there has been a thorough understanding as to the side each vessel shall take.

Power Vessels Meeting in Narrow Channels or Rivers
When an ascending vessel is approaching a descending vessel on a river, the ascending vessel shall give the first signal by one blast of the whistle if she desires to pass on the port side of the descending vessel. The ascending vessel shall give two blasts if she desires to pass on the starboard side of the descending vessel. These signals shall be promptly answered by the descending vessel if the maneuver is considered safe. Each shall be governed accordingly. If the descending vessel deems

it dangerous to do so, she shall signify the fact by giving the danger signal, a series of rapid blasts (not less than four) on the whistle. It then shall be the duty of the ascending vessel to answer by a similar danger signal. Engines of both vessels shall then be stopped and backed if necessary until signals for passing are given, answered and understood, with the descending vessel having the right-of-way. After the danger signals have been mutually given, the descending vessel must then indicate, by whistle, the side which she desires for passing and the ascending vessel shall govern herself accordingly.

Power Vessels Crossing

When power vessels are crossing so as to involve risk of collision, the vessel on the port side of the other shall keep out of the way of the other. Both vessels shall exchange one-blast signals (either blowing first) to signify intentions to comply with the Rules.

If conditions are such as to prevent compliance with these signals, the misunderstanding or objection shall be made apparent by the danger signal, four or more short and rapid blasts of the whistle, and both vessels shall be stopped and backed if necessary until signals for passing in safety are given, answered and understood.

Every steam vessel when approaching another vessel so as to involve risk of collision shall slacken her speed, or, if necessary, stop and reverse.

Power Vessels Overtaking

Any vessel overtaking another shall keep out of the way of the overtaken vessel, until she is past and clear, and no subsequent altering of course shall make the overtaken vessel a crossing vessel. A vessel being overtaken shall in no way attempt to cross the bow or the head of the tow of an overtaking vessel.

A vessel approaching from the stern shall be considered to be an overtaking vessel and, if desiring to pass on the overtaken vessel's starboard side, shall indicate her intentions by one blast on the whistle. If she desires to pass on the port side, she shall indicate her intentions by two blasts on the whistle. In no case shall she attempt to pass until the overtaken vessel has answered her signals to show she understands and that the way ahead is clear. If the overtaken vessel answers the passing request with a danger signal, the overtaking vessel shall blow acknowledgement (the danger signal) and wait for the overtaken vessel to signal a safe side.

Vessel Leaving a Berth or Anchorage

A vessel leaving her berth or anchorage shall give three distinct blasts on her whistle and approaching vessels shall take care to ascertain her course and, at that time, exchange the proper signals for passing. Keep in mind that this is a special circumstance covered by the General Prudential Rule (Rule 25) and the Rule of Good Seamanship (Rule 26) until the undocking vessel has cleared the dock and set her course.

Power Vessels in River Bends

Whenever a power vessel ascending or descending a river approaches a bend she shall, when the head of her tow is 600 yards from such bend, give three distinct blasts on the whistle, which shall be answered by vessels approaching from the other side of the bend. Upon hearing such an answer, she shall proceed with caution until the vessels are in sight of each other and the proper signals for passing have been exchanged.

Special circumstances may render a departure from these rules necessary to avoid immediate danger and in such case neither vessel shall have the right-of-way and both shall navigate with caution until such danger is over.

Special Whistle Light

Most vessels shall carry, in addition to regular running lights, an amber light high enough above the pilot house to have an uninterrupted view from approaching vessels, which will light in conjunction with the blowing of the whistle.

Special Caution for Small Craft

In presenting this material concerning Rules of the Road for Western Rivers, much information has been necessarily omitted principally because of the fact that great emphasis is placed on rules governing commercial craft. This omission in no way implies that the operators of pleasure vessels should attempt to play "Rules of the Road" with heavily laden vessels or large tows and force their will upon such commercial craft, regardless of which vessel may have the right-of-way.

Burden and Privilege on Western Rivers

On Western Rivers, burdened vessels are as follows:

Any vessel (sail or power) which is overtaking another.

Any power vessel crossing a river.

Any power vessel approaching another from the other vessel's port side.

Any ascending power vessel when meeting another vessel in a narrow channel or confined space such as a bridge; the ascending vessel shall hold her position at slow or stop, permitting the descending vessel a clear passage. (It's easier to hold a vessel against the current.) Vessels ascending a river will, unless a clear understanding by an exchange of whistle signals is reached, give the choice of passing side to the descending vessel.

Any vessel (sail or power) of 65 feet or less in length that can maneuver easily shall not hamper the passage of a large vessel or vessel with tow that is ascending or descending a river.

A sailing vessel does not have the right to hamper the safe passage of a large vessel or vessel with tow that is ascending or descending a river.

Sound Signals

On the Western Rivers, the following sound signals shall be used:

One blast—"I intend to alter my course to starboard."

Two blasts—"I intend to alter my course to port."

NOTE: The duration of the blasts is not specified. These are signals of intent and assent. Each signal

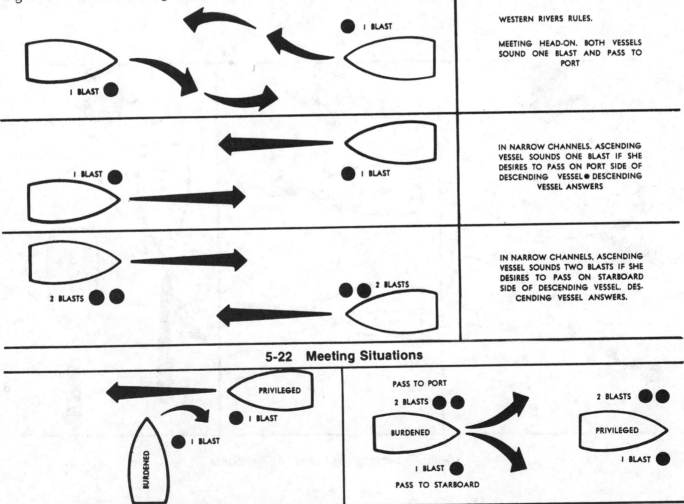

5-22 Meeting Situations

5-23 Crossing Situation   5-24 Overtaking Situation

5-25

must be answered with a similar signal or the danger signal.

However, a vessel descending a river and meeting another vessel may sound the danger signal (four or more short rapid blasts) in reply to an ascending vessel's one or two-blast signal and then indicate by a whistle signal on which side she wishes to pass.

Four or more short, rapid blasts—The danger signal. Any vessel, upon hearing the danger signal, shall make all efforts to hold her position and not proceed until she has a clear understanding of what danger exists, and act accordingly.

Vessels approaching a bend in a river shall, when 600 yards distant, sound three distinct blasts on the whistle, to be answered by any other vessel approaching from the other direction.

Conduct in Restricted Visibility

Fog Signals

In fog, mist, falling snow or heavy rainstorm or any other condition of restricted visibility, whether by day or night, the fog signals to be used shall be as follows:

A vessel underway and towing another vessel or vessels shall sound at intervals of not more than one minute, three distinct blasts of the whistle of approximate equal length.

A vessel underway *without* a tow shall sound at intervals of not more than one minute, three blasts of the whistle, the first two of equal length and the last blast to be longer (two short, 1 long).

A vessel with or without a tow, lying to, meaning to hold her position near or against the bank by using her engines, or temporarily moored to the

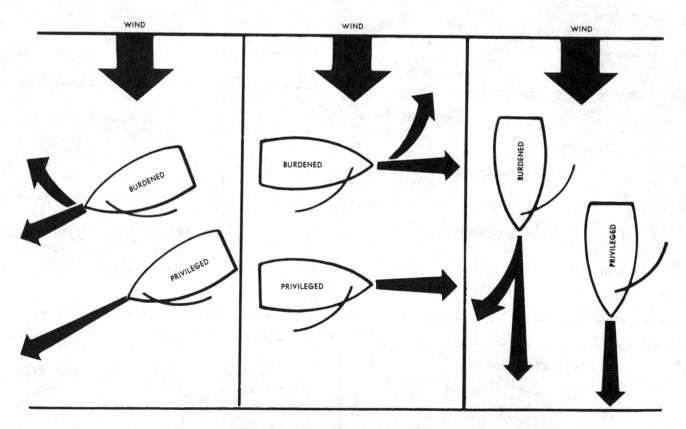

5-25 International Rules for Sailboats

5-26

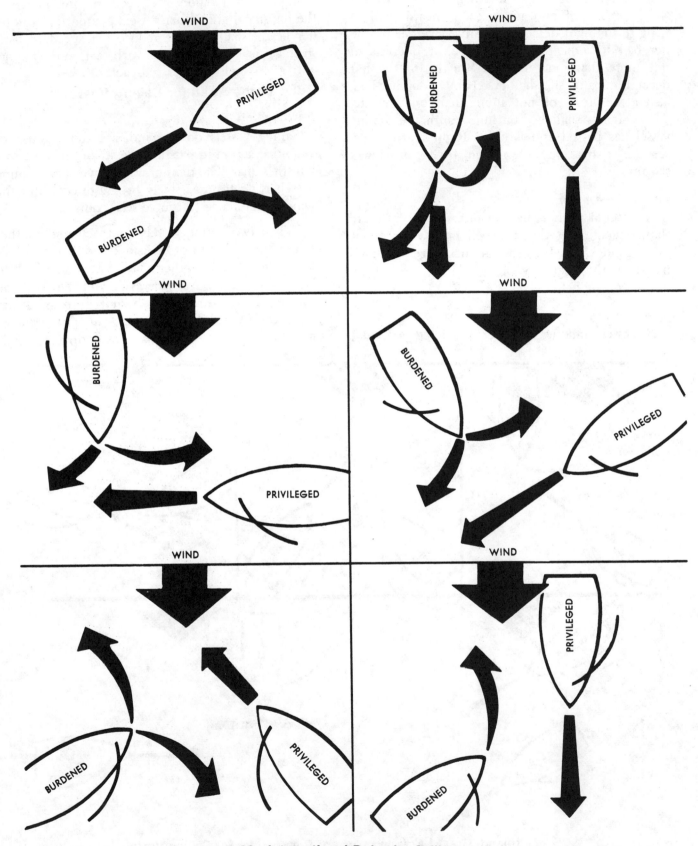

5-26 International Rules for Sailboats

5-27

bank, when a fog signal or other sound indicating the approach of another vessel is heard shall, if lying to the right descending bank, give one tap on her bell to indicate her presence, at intervals of not more than one minute. If lying to the left decending bank, she shall give two taps on her bell, also at intervals of not more than one minute. These signals shall be continued until the passing vessel has passed and is clear. Right and left descending bank are determined by facing downstream.

Vessels at Anchor

A vessel at anchor shall, at intervals of not more than one minute, ring the bell rapidly for about five seconds. Vessels in special anchorages, as designated by the Secretary of the Army, are not required to ring bells.

Speed in Fog

A vessel underway, under restricted visibility, shall proceed at a moderate speed and, upon hearing the fog signal of another vessel apparently ahead of her beam, shall at once reduce her speed to bare steerageway and navigate with extreme caution until the vessels have passed each other.

Rules of the Road for Sailing Vessels

Introduction

Sailing vessels do not indicate their course or intended action in passing a vessel of any type by a whistle signal. The right-of-way between two sailing vessels is determined solely by the direction of the wind in reference to the vessels' courses.

When two sailing vessels approach one another so as to involve risk of collision, one of them shall keep clear of the other. The vessel required to keep clear is the burdened vessel, and the other the privileged vessel which is required to hold her course and speed. Sailing vessels (under sail alone) have the right-of-way over power-driven vessels

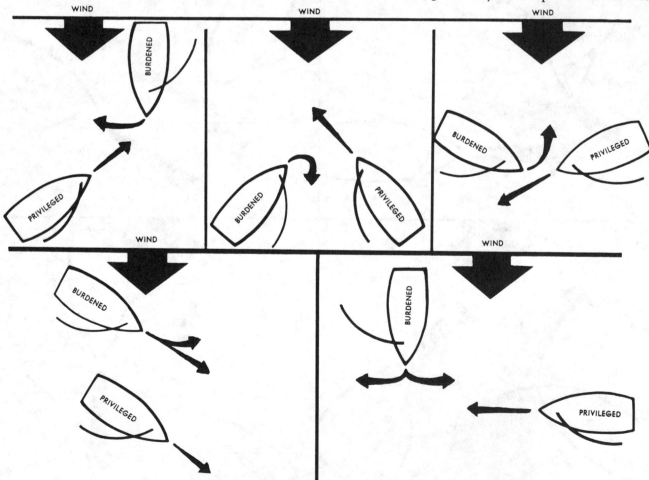

5-27 Inland, Great Lakes and Western Rivers Rules for Sailing Vessels.

5-28

except: (1) when the sailing vessel is overtaking a power vessel, or (2) in a narrow channel where a sailing vessel shall not have the right to hamper the safe passage of any vessel which can navigate safely only within such channel, and (3) sailing vessels shall keep clear of any vessels engaged in fishing with nets, lines or trawls.

International Rules for Sailing Vessels

When two sailing vessels are approaching one another so as to involve risk of collision, one of them shall keep out of the way of the other as follows:

1. When each has the wind on a different side, the vessel which has the wind to the port side shall keep out of the way of the other.

2. When both have the wind on the same side, the vessel which is to windward shall keep out of the way of the vessel which is to leeward.

3. For the purposes of these rules the windward side shall be deemed to be the side opposite to that on which the mainsail is carried. On square-rigged vessels, it shall be deemed to be the side opposite to that on which the largest fore-and-aft sail is carried.

Inland, Great Lakes and Western Rivers Rules for Sailing Vessels

When two sailing vessels are approaching one another so as to involve risk of collision, one of them shall keep out of the way of the other as follows:

1. A vessel which is running free shall keep out of the way of a vessel that is close hauled.

2. A vessel which is close hauled on the port tack shall keep clear of a vessel which is close hauled on the starboard tack.

3. When both vessels are running free, with the wind on different sides, the vessel which has the wind on the port side shall keep out of the way of the other.

4. When both vessels are running free with the wind on the same side, the vessel which is to windward shall keep out of the way of the vessel which is to leeward.

5. A vessel which has the wind aft shall keep out of the way of the other vessel. NOTE: *This rules does not apply to the Great Lakes.*

CHAPTER 6

Aids to Navigation

Introduction

Along the coasts and navigable waters of the United States and its possessions, there are thousands of devices to give a mariner his exact position at all times, in any weather, in relation to the land and to hidden dangers. These devices range from steel and concrete structures, such as buoys and lighthouses, to invisible beacons of an electronic nature such as radiobeacons, RACONS and LORAN. They are all designed for one purpose — aiding seamen.

Aids to navigation assist mariners in making landfalls when approaching from overseas, mark isolated dangers, make it possible for vessels to follow the natural and improved channels, and provide a continuous chain of charted marks for coastal piloting. As all aids to navigation serve the same general purpose, such structural differences as those between an unlighted buoy and a lightship, or a lighthouse and a radiobeacon, are solely for the purpose of meeting the conditions and requirements for the particular location at which the aid is to be established.

All aids to navigation (except private aids) in the waters over which the United States has jurisdiction are designed, built and maintained by the United States Coast Guard. It is a tremendous job. There are more than 40,000 aids to navigation in U.S. waters alone. This responsibility has been executed well; and today the United States has the best system of aids to navigation in the world.

The Lateral System

The waters of the United States are marked for safe navigation by the lateral system of buoyage.

This system employs a simple arrangement of colors, shapes, numbers and light characteristics to show the side on which a buoy should be passed when proceeding in a given direction. The characteristics are determined by the position of the buoy with respect to the navigable channels as the channels are entered from seaward toward the head of navigation.

As all channels do not lead from seaward, arbitrary assumptions must at times be made in order that the system may be consistently applied. The characteristics of buoys are based on the assumption that proceeding in a southerly direction along the Atlantic coast, in a northerly and westerly direction along the Gulf coast, in a northerly direction on the Pacific coast, and in a westerly and northerly direction on the Great Lakes (except Lake Michigan) and in a southerly direction in Lake Michigan is proceeding from seaward. On the Intracoastal Waterway, proceeding in a general southerly direction along the Atlantic coast, and in a general westerly direction along the Gulf coast is considered as proceeding from seaward. On the

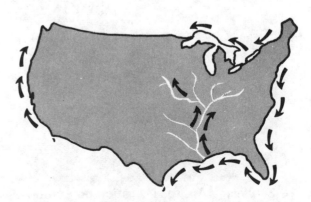

6-1 Arbitrary Direction Under Lateral System

6-1

Mississippi and Ohio Rivers and their tributaries, the aids to navigation characteristics are determined as proceeding from sea towards the head of navigation although local terminolgy describes "left bank" and "right bank" as proceeding with the flow of the river.

In addition to the lateral system of buoyage, several special purpose buoyage characteristics, which have no lateral significance, are utilized to mark dredging areas, quarantine areas, fish net areas, anchorages, race courses, experiments or tests.

Buoys

The primary function of buoys is to warn the mariner of some danger, some obstruction or change in the contours of the sea bottom, or to delineate channels leading to various points, so that he may avoid dangers and continue his course safely. The utmost advantage is obtained from buoys when they are considered as marking definitely identified spots, for if a mariner knows his precise location at the moment and is properly equipped with charts, he can plot a safe course on which to proceed. Such features as size, shape, coloring, numbering and signaling equipment of buoys are but means to these ends of warning, guiding and orienting the navigator. However, a word of caution should be included here concerning buoys and other floating aids to

6-2 Placing Aid to Navigation on Station by Coast Guard Buoy Tender

navigation. Buoys should not be regarded as immovable objects. They may be missing, adrift, or off the charted position due to heavy storm, unusual tides, ice, and collisions. Even buoys that are on station should be passed a reasonable distance off, since they may be necessarily located close to the shoals they mark. Therefore, boatmen should not rely completely upon the position or operation of floating aids to navigation, but should utilize bearings toward fixed objects or aids to navigation on shore whenever possible. The lights on lighted buoys may be extinguished, or sound-producing devices on sound buoys may not function. Buoys fitted with bells, gongs or whistles which are activated by wave action do not produce sounds at regular intervals. Principally for this reason, their positive identification is not always possible.

Coloring of Buoys

All buoys are painted distinctive colors to indicate their purpose or, in the lateral system, the side on which they should be passed. The meaning of lateral system buoys, when proceeding from seaward, as indicated by their colors, are as follows:

BLACK BUOYS mark the left side of the channel as you proceed from seaward. Black buoys are sometimes used to mark wrecks or obstructions in the channel. In this case, these buoys must be kept on the port side of your vessel as you proceed from seaward.

RED BUOYS mark the right side of the channel as you proceed from seaward. Red buoys are also used to mark wrecks or obstructions in the channel. When red buoys are used in this manner they must be kept on the starboard side of your vessel as you proceed from seaward.

RED AND BLACK HORIZONTALLY BANDED BUOYS mark junctions in the channel, or wrecks or obstructions which may be passed on either side as you travel in the direction previously determined as "proceeding from seaward." If the topmost band is black, the preferred channel will be followed by keeping the buoy on the port side of the vessel. If the topmost band is red, the preferred channel will be followed by keeping the buoy on the starboard side of the vessel. NOTE: When approaching these red and black horizontally banded buoys from the opposite direction, as proceeding *toward* seaward, it may not be possible to pass on either side of these buoys. This is particularly true when you are following one channel downstream and another joins in from the side. Always consult the chart for the area.

PASS EITHER SIDE   **STAY FAIR DISTANCE AWAY**

6-3 Vertically and Horizontally Banded Buoys

BLACK AND WHITE VERTICALLY STRIPED BUOYS mark the fairway or midchannel.

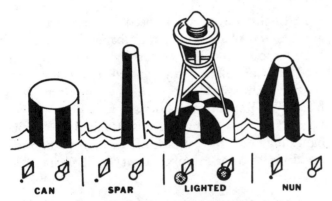

CAN   SPAR   LIGHTED   NUN

Black and white vertically striped buoys
mark the fairway or mid-channel.

6-4 Lateral System.

The meaning of special purpose buoys is indicated by their colors as follows:

WHITE BUOYS mark anchorage areas.

YELLOW BUOYS mark quarantine anchorage areas.

WHITE BUOYS WITH GREEN TOPS are used in connection with dredging and survey operations.

WHITE AND BLACK ALTERNATE HORIZONTALLY BANDED BUOYS mark fish net areas.

WHITE AND INTERNATIONAL ORANGE BUOYS ALTERNATELY BANDED, EI-

THER HORIZONTALLY OR VERTICALLY, are for special purposes to which neither the lateral-system colors nor the special-purpose colors apply.

YELLOW AND BLACK VERTICALLY STRIPED BUOYS are used for seadrome markings and have no marine significance.

Shapes of Buoys

Buoys have many shapes, from simple spars to complicated structures. Some buoys have lights on them. Lighted buoys have no shape significance but almost all lateral unlighted buoys do have shape significance. Buoys which have shape significance are usually painted solid-red or solid-black.

NUN BUOYS are conical in shape, and are painted solid red. As mentioned previously, they indicate the right hand side of the channel upon entering from seaward.

6-5 Nun Buoy

CAN BUOYS are cylindrical in shape and are painted solid-black. These indicate the left side of the channel upon entering from seaward.

On all other buoys, the shape is of no significance. Sometimes buoys of conical or cylindrical shape are used with a paint pattern other than solid-red or solid-black. These could be horizontally banded (red and black) or vertically striped

6-6 Can Buoy

(white and black). In these instances, the paint color pattern is significant, while the shape of the buoy is not.

Other buoys (other than conical or cylindrical shaped) may be painted solid-red or solid-black and used in the place of a nun or can buoy when it is desired to direct special attention to the aid.

LIGHTED BUOYS, SOUND BUOYS AND SPAR BUOYS are not differentiated by shape to indicate the side on which they should be passed. Their purpose is indicated by color, number, and light characteristics.

Numbering of Buoys

Most buoys are given numbers, letters or combinations of numbers and letters which are painted conspicuously upon them. These markings facilitate the identification and location of the buoys on the charts.

All solid colored red or black buoys, except those in the Western Rivers Aids to Navigation System, are given numbers or combinations of numbers and letters. Other colored buoys may be given letters. Numbers increase from seaward and are kept in approximate sequence on both sides of the channel by omitting numbers where required. Odd numbers are used only on solid-black buoys. Even numbers are used only on solid-red buoys. Numbers followed by letters are used on solid-colored red or black buoys when a letter is required so as not to disturb the sequence of numbering, or on important buoys, particularly those marking isolated offshore dangers. An example of the latter case would be a buoy marked "2 DR," in which

instance the number has the usual significance, while the letters "DR" indicate the place as Duxbury Reef. Letters without numbers are applied in some cases to black and white vertically striped buoys, red and black horizontally banded buoys, solid-yellow buoys, and other buoys not solid colored red or black.

In the Mississippi River System, unlighted buoys are not numbered, while the numbers on lighted buoys have no lateral significance, but indicate the number of miles from a designated point.

Lighted Buoys

Buoys of special importance must be seen at night, therefore they are equipped with lights. Lighted buoys may be used in place of either can or nun buoys. Lights are *never* used on can or nun buoys.

Lights and Reflectors

Red lights on buoys are used only on red buoys and red and black horizontally banded buoys with the topmost band red. Green lights on buoys are used only on black buoys or red and black horizontally banded buoys with the topmost band black. White lights on buoys are used on any color buoy. No special significance is attached to a white light on a buoy, the purpose of the buoy being indicated by its color, number, or its light phase characteristic.

Many unlighted buoys are fitted with optical reflectors. These greatly facilitate the locating of the buoys at night by means of a searchlight. Optical reflectors may be white, red or green, and have the same significance as lights of these colors. In addition, most modern buoys have corner radar reflectors designed into the superstructure to improve the radar response.

Light Phase Characteristics

Lights on red buoys or black buoys will always be regularly flashing or regularly occulting. A flashing light flashes at a rate of *30 or less* flashes per minute. An occulting light, on the other hand, is a steady light that is interrupted by short eclipses of darkness. The time the light is "on" is more than the time it is "off." One easy method of remembering the difference between a flashing light and an occulting light is that a flashing light "blinks on" while an occulting light "blinks off." When it is desired that a flashing light have a distinct cautionary significance, as at sharp turns or sudden constrictions in the channel, or to mark wrecks or dangerous obstructions which can be passed safely on *one side only*, the frequency of flashes will be at a rate of *60 or more* per minute. This frequency of flashes is known as a quick flashing light.

Lights on red and black horizontally banded buoys will always show an interrupted quick flashing characteristic; for example, a sequence of quick flashes for about 5 seconds followed by an eclipse of about 5 seconds, repeated 6 times per minute. These buoys are placed at points where it is desired to indicate junctions in the channel, or wrecks or obstructions which may be passed on *either side*.

Lights on black and white vertically striped buoys consist of a short flash followed by a long flash, providing the letter "A" of the Morse Code. The series (one short and one long flash) recurs at the rate of about eight per minute. These buoys are placed at points where it is desired to indicate the midchannel or fairway. These lights are always white.

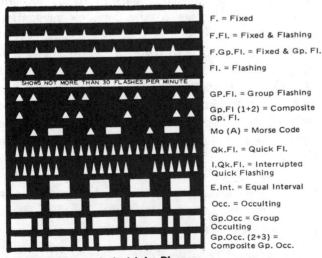

6-7 Characteristic Light Phases

F. = Fixed

F.Fl. = Fixed & Flashing

F.Gp.Fl. = Fixed & Gp. Fl.

Fl. = Flashing

GP.Fl. = Group Flashing

Gp.Fl (1+2) = Composite Gp. Fl.

Mo (A) = Morse Code

Qk.Fl. = Quick Fl.

I.Qk.Fl. = Interrupted Quick Flashing

E.Int. = Equal Interval

Occ. = Occulting

Gp.Occ = Group Occulting

Gp.Occ. (2+3) = Composite Gp. Occ.

Most lighted buoys are equipped with a special device which automatically controls the electric current to the light. This device causes the light to operate during the hours of darkness and to be extinguished during the daylight hours. These devices are not of equal sensitivity, therefore all lights do not come on or go off at the same time. Mariners should ensure correct identification of aids during twilight periods when some lighted aids to navigation are on while others are not.

Daybeacons (Daymarks)

There are many aids to navigation which are not lighted. Structures (not buoys) of this type are called daybeacons. They vary greatly in design and construction, depending upon their location, and the distance from which they must be seen. Daybeacons are colored, as are lighthouses, to distinguish them from their surroundings and to provide a means of identification. Daybeacons marking the sides of channels are colored and numbered in the same manner as buoys and minor light structures; red indicating the right side entering and black the left side entering. Red day beacons will carry an even number within a red triangle or daymark and black daybeacons will carry an odd number within a black (or green) square daymark. Many daymarks are also fitted with optical reflectors to facilitate locating them at night by means of a searchlight.

6-8   Single Pile Light with Daymark

Sound Buoys

Buoys equipped with sound signals do not lose their effectiveness during low visibility. Important buoys may be bell buoys, gong buoys, whistle buoys or horn buoys. Each type has an easily recognizable sound. Bell buoys have four clappers hung loosely about the bell so that even a slight pitching of the buoy causes the bell to ring. Gong buoys differ from bell buoys in that three or four gongs of different tones, each with a separate clapper, are rung in random order by the motion of the buoy in the sea. These signals are actuated by the motion of the sea, so one should be cautioned that they do not emit regular signal characteristics and, when the sea is calm, may emit no sound signals at all. Since the air used in whistle buoys is captured and compressed by the rising and falling of the buoy in the sea, these whistle buoys are used principally in open and exposed places where sufficient ground swell normally exists to operate the mechanism. A type of sound buoy in which a horn or sometimes a bell is sounded at regular intervals by mechanical means is also used.

6-9 Lighted, Radar Reflector, Bell Buoy

The Intracoastal Waterway System

The Intracoastal Waterway, to which is applied the system of marking about to be described, is that comparatively shallow channel lying parallel to and extending along the Atlantic and Gulf Coasts from New Jersey to the Mexican border. This special marking system is applied to the so-called "inside route" proper, and to those portions of all connecting waterways which must be crossed or followed in order to make a continuous passage.

All buoys, daybeacons and light structures marking the Intracoastal Waterway have some portion of them painted yellow. This is the distinctive coloring adopted for the waterway. Lighted buoys have a yellow band at the top. Unlighted buoys have a yellow band at approximately the midsection. Day-

marks have a yellow border. Daymarks are usually mounted on single piles. When the pile carries a daymark (or daybeacon), the daymark is either a green square with a yellow border or a red triangle with a yellow border depending on whether the pile is on the port hand or on the starboard hand, as the navigator proceeds southerly along the East Coast or westerly along the Gulf Coast channels of the Intracoastal Waterway.

The coloring and numbering of buoys and Daymarks, and the color of lights on buoys and on light structures is on the same lateral system as that prevailing in other waterways. The basic rule is that RED BUOYS and Daymarks are on the right-hand side of the channel when proceeding from New Jersey toward Mexico, and BLACK BUOYS and Daymarks are on the left-hand side of the channel when proceeding in the same direction. This rule is applied in a uniform manner from one end of the Intracoastal Waterway to the other, regardless of the widely differing compass headings of the many sections, and the fact that rivers and other waterways marked on the seacoast system are sometimes followed. When the Intracoastal Waterway route coincides with another waterway, such as a river on which aids to navigation are marked from the sea to the head of navigation according to the lateral system of buoyage, special markings are used consisting of yellow squares or yellow triangles painted on a conspicuous part of such dual-purpose aids to navigation. A yellow triangle on an aid to navigation indicates that the aid must be left on the starboard side, and a yellow square on an aid indicates that it must be left on the port side, regardless of the color or number of such aid, when traversing the Intracoastal Waterway route from north to south on the Atlantic coast and from east to west along the Gulf coast.

Numbering of Intracoastal Waterway aids follows the basic rule, numbers increasing from New Jersey to Mexico. Aids are numbered in groups, usually not exceeding 200; numbering begins again at "1" at certain natural dividing points. Lights on buoys follow the standard system of red or white lights on red buoys, or green or white lights on black buoys. The color of the lights on fixed structures also follow this general rule. Range lights, not being lateral markers, may be any of the three standard colors.

Western Rivers System

Western Rivers system includes the waters of the Mississippi River between its source and the Huey P. Long Bridge and all of the tributaries emptying thereinto and their tributaries, and that part of the Atchafalaya River above its junction with the Plaquemine—Morgan City alternate waterway, and the Red River of the North.

Aids to Navigation on all of the above rivers are arranged in a numerical order. Each aid bears a number identical to the mileage of the stream at that point, as determined from the latest chart. The mileage of the aid is determined from a reference point, generally marked zero. This point may be coincident with the river mouth, or the confluence of two rivers, or at an arbitrarily determined point. Aids are located on either the left bank or the right bank, as determined when navigating the waterway in a downstream direction. Sometimes the orientation is stated in the Light List as "the left descending" or "the right descending bank."

Characteristics of Lights

Lights on the left descending bank of all waterways in the System are either fixed white or fixed red, group flashing (2) white or red, equal interval white or red, quick flashing red, or interrupted quick flashing red. Lights on the right bank descending are either fixed white or fixed green, flashing white or green, equal interval white or green, quick flashing green, interrupted quick flashing green or fixed green.

Visibility of Lights

The majority of lights on Western Rivers are visible through 360°, that is, all around the horizon, and show approximately the same candlepower viewed from any direction. For those navigational situations where superior candlepower is required,

use is made of lanterns projecting light in one direction only. These are known as directional aids. They are used in two ways; (1) to supplement a 360° light by increasing candlepower in one direction only, and (2) used alone to show only superior candlepower in one direction. Directional aids are established with different degrees of horizontal spread; narrow spreads or beams are used to define long, narrow reaches; wider spreads are used where situations are not critical but a light of superior candlepower is needed. To assist in identification of the bank being marked, the lights vary in color and characteristic. Where confusing background lights require the showing of a distinctive light, recourse is made to color and flashing or occulting characteristics.

Placing of Lights and Daymarks

Lights are placed along river banks to afford the mariner assistance. Lights are spaced with due regard to their useful candlepower, the shape of the river, and the length of the reaches. Primarily, the lights serve as leading (or holding) lights at the head and foot of each crossing, supplemented by intervening lights where necessary. Secondarily, no crossing being involved, lights are placed along one bank or the other for use as passing lights. Where long reaches occur, directional lights of high candlepower are used either alone or in conjunction with a passing light at the same station, to provide a reliable leading light. The exact use of any light can only be determined from the chart, or from experience.

Vessels must keep well clear of fixed aids if there is sufficient channel to do so because there may be dangerous underwater obstructions present in the vicinity. All light structures are equipped with a number board showing the number of the aid in black figures, which is also the mileage of the river at that point.

Daymarks

Crossing daymarks are diamond-shaped wooden panels. Passing daymarks on the left descending bank are triangular-shaped, red and carry red reflectors. Passing daymarks on the right descending bank are square and carry white or green reflectors. Two boards painted white and fastened together to form an "X" are used as temporary crossing daymarks on the Missouri River.

Buoys

Buoys used to mark channels in the Mississippi River System conform to the standard lateral buoyage system of the United States. In addition, the tops of most unlighted buoys in the Mississippi River System, except horizontally banded buoys, are painted white for distinctive contrast against the shore background. All buoys carry reflectors. Buoys on the left descending side of the channel reflect red. Buoys in the right descending side of the channel reflect white, corresponding to the similar usage of reflectors on shore aids.

Lighted buoys marking wrecks show a quick flashing characteristic, sixty (60) flashes being shown per minute to indicate that particular caution is required. Colors of lights shown from buoys marking wrecks are white or red on the left descending side of the channel, and white or green on the right descending side of the channel.

Lighted buoys marking channel junctions or obstructions, which may be passed on either side, show an interrupted quick flashing characteristic; for example, a sequence of five equally spaced flashes repeated ten times per minute. The color of light shown may be white, red or green; preferably white if about midchannel, red if toward the left descending and green if toward the right descending side of the channel. However, white may be used for any situation to preclude confusion with other lighted aids or background lights.

Special attention is invited to buoys, both lighted and unlighted, painted with red and black horizontal bands. These buoys mark junctions or obstructions which may be passed on either side, the preferred side being indicated by the color of the topmost band. If such a buoy should be encountered near the apparent channel limit, it should be passed only after soundings indicate which is the proper side to pass.

In pooled rivers, buoys are normally set to mark the nine-foot contour at normal pool elevations. In open rivers, buoys are placed to mark project depths with consideration being given to the prevailing river stage.

Buoys should always be given as wide a berth as possible in passing, consistent with the size of the vessel, and the width, length and sharpness of the crossing. Buoys should always be used with caution. They may be carried off station by high water, accumulation of drift, ice, or sunk by collision or other causes. When carried off station, destroyed or removed to prevent loss, buoys are replaced on station at the earliest opportunity. Unlighted buoys may be constantly shifted with the changes in the channels. While they mark isolated dangers on the right and left descending banks, their principal use is to outline bars and shoals at the "crossings" and hence mark the channel.

Radar Reflectors

Certain aids to navigation may be fitted with special fixtures, called Radar Reflectors, which are designed to enhance their ability to reflect radar energy. In general, these fixtures materially improve the aids for use by vessels equipped with radar.

Safety Harbor and Safety Landing Markers

In the pools of the Tennessee River, safety harbors and safety landings have been provided. Safety harbors are usually deep coves or inlets adjacent to and extending back from the navigable channel. Entrance markers, on shore, consist of a direction board, about three feet by six feet. The upper limits of such harbors are marked by cross of boards. Safety landings are areas where the banks have been prepared by carefully clearing all stumps and boulders so that vessels may land safely. The upper and lower limits of these areas are marked by direction boards. White direction boards indicate first class harbors, providing nine-foot depth at all pool stages. Orange direction boards indicate second-class harbors, providing depths of nine feet except at extreme drawn-down pool stages.

Emergency Lights or Sirens

When a rotating amber light is noted or a siren is heard on a waterfront facility, an emergency situation shall be considered to exist at that facility. Mariners should stand well clear of any facilities giving such signals and report the occurrence immediately to the nearest Coast Guard unit. These warning signals are required to be installed at all facilities which handle hazardous chemicals.

Uniform State Waterway Marking System

Many bodies of water used by boatmen are located entirely within the boundaries of a state and are subject to regulation by the state. These waters do not connect to the sea. Since the concept of proceeding from seaward cannot be applied to these self-contained bodies of water, the lateral system of buoyage cannot be used. Thus, the individual states are left with no choice except to mark their waters with a different aids to navigation system.

The Uniform State Waterways Marking System has been devised for these lakes, ponds and rivers; and most states have adopted its use. However, some states deviate from this system to a certain extent in order to suit local conditions. Boatmen are well advised to determine in advance the aids to navigation system in use before embarking on these inland waters.

The Uniform State Waterways Marking System employs two categories of waterway markers—regulatory markers and aids to navigation.

Regulatory Markers

These consist of buoys and signs which indicate information pertaining to rules and regulations. All regulatory markers have white backgrounds and orange borders. They may be circular, diamond or rectangular in shape. In most instances the nature of the danger or regulation is indicated in black letters or figures within the shape or adjacent to it.

6-10 A dangerous area is indicated by an open diamond shape, as shown below.

6-11 A prohibited area is marked by a diamond with a cross inside, as shown below.

6-12 A controlled area, such as one which excludes water skiing or fishing, is indicated by a circle, as shown below.

6-13 General information and directions are shown on a square or rectangular marker, as shown below.

Aids to Navigation

Aids to navigation on state waterways use red and black buoys to mark channel limits. Red and black buoys are generally used in pairs. The vessel should pass between the red buoy and its companion black buoy. These buoys will be found on opposite sides of the channel, with the red buoy on the left descending side and the black buoy on the right descending side of the river or stream.

Buoys that are not placed in pairs have distinctive colors which indicate the direction of the dangerous water from the position of the buoy.

VERTICAL RED AND WHITE STRIPED BUOYS indicate that vessels should not pass between the buoy and the nearest shore. Danger lies inshore of the buoy.

WHITE BUOYS WITH RED TOPS should be passed to the south or west. Do not go to the north or east of these buoys as danger lies to the north or east, as the case may be.

WHITE BUOYS WITH BLACK TOPS should be passed to the north or east. Do not go to the south or west of these buoys as danger lies to the south or west, as the case may be.

Identification of Markers and Aids to Navigation

Uniform State Waterway Marking System aids and markers may carry numbers, letters or words. Odd numbers are used on solid-black buoys and black-topped buoys. Even numbers are used on solid-red buoys and red-topped buoys. All numbers increase in an upstream direction, or toward the head of navigation.

Lighted buoys display regularly flashing, occulting or equal-interval light characteristics. Red lights are used on solid-red buoys; green lights are used on solid-black buoys; and white lights are used on all other buoys and regulatory markers.

Other Aids to Navigation

Lighthouses

Lighthouses are found on all coasts of the United States, on the Great Lakes, and along some of the interior waterways of the country. These structures are so well known that they require little description. Lighthouses are placed where they will be of most use, on prominent headlands, at entrances, on isolated dangers, or at other points where it is necessary that mariners be warned or guided. Their principal purpose is to support a light a considerable height above the water. The same structure may also house a fog signal and radiobeacon equipment, and also contain quarters for the keepers.

The terms, "secondary lights," "minor lights," and "automatic lights" indicate in a general way

6-14 Lighthouse

a wide variety of lights. These lights may be displayed from towers resembling the important seacoast lighthouses, or may be shown from almost any type of inexpensive structure. The number of lights with keepers in residence is gradually being reduced. The ultimate goal is to have all lights operate automatically, or nearly so. The essentials of lights where keepers are not in residence are: best possible location dependent on the physical conditions of the site, sufficient height for the location, a rugged support for the lantern, and a housing for the electric batteries from which the light is operated. Many types of structures meet these essentials—small tank houses surmounted by a short skeleton structure or tower, a cluster of piles supporting a battery box and the lens, and countless other forms.

Lights are used as a means of conveying certain definite information, and are given distinctive characteristics so that one light may be distinguished from another. This distinctiveness is obtained by employing lights of varying colors, by having lights that burn steadily, and others that flash at intervals of great variety.

By varying the length of the periods of light and darkness of any of the flashing or occulting characteristics, a great variety of characteristics may be obtained. Advantage is taken of this to secure the necessary distinctiveness between aids of a given area.

Fog Signals

Fog signals form an important part of the equipment of many lighthouses situated in sections of the country where fog or low visibility is prevalent. Fog signals may also be found on floating aids to navigation. The function of the fog signal in the system of aids to navigation is to warn of danger, and to provide the mariner with a practical means of determining his position with relation to the fog signal at such times as the station or any visual signal which it displays is obscured from view by fog, snow, rain, smoke or thick weather. Among the devices in common use as fog signals are:

DIAPHONES, which produce sound by means of a slotted reciprocating piston actuated by compressed air. Blasts may consist of two tones of different pitch, in which case the first part of the blast is high and the last of a low pitch. These alternate pitch signals are called "two tone."

DIAPHRAGM HORNS, which produce sound by means of a diaphragm vibrated by compressed air, steam or electricity. Duplex or triplex horn units of differing pitch produce a chime signal.

SIRENS, which produce sound by means of either a disk or a cup-shaped rotor actuated by compressed air or by electricity.

WHISTLES, which produce sound by compressed air emitted through a circumferential slot into a cylindrical bell chamber.

BELLS, which are sounded by means of a hammer actuated by hand, by a descending weight, compressed gas or electricity.

Fog signals are distinguished by their characteristics as specified for each aid. The characteristic of a fog signal is described by its tone and signal characteristics. Its tone is determined by the device used to create the sound, such as diaphragm horn, diaphone, siren, bell or whistle. Fog signals on fixed stations or lightships produce a specific number of blasts and silent periods each minute, when oper-

ating, to provide positive identification. Fog signals on buoys are generally activated by the motion of the sea, and may emit no sound signals at all when the sea is calm. Fog signals at stations where a continuous watch is maintained are sounded when the visibility decreases to five miles, and also whenever the fog whistle of a passing vessel is heard. Fog signals at locations where no continuous watch is maintained may not always be sounded promptly when fog conditions exist or may operate erratically due to mechanical difficulties.

Range Lights

Two lights, located some distance apart, visible usually in one direction only, are known as range lights. They are so located that the mariner, by bringing his vessel into line with them, when they will appear one over the other, places his vessel

6-15 Open Range — Not in Channel

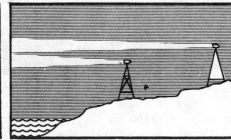

6-16 Closed Range — in Channel

on the axis (or in the center line) of the channel. If he steers his vessel so that the lights remain constantly in line vertically, he will remain within the confines of the channel. Entrance channels are frequently marked by range lights. The Delaware River and the St. John's River on the Atlantic coast, and the Columbia River on the Pacific coast are examples of successive straight reaches marked in this manner. The lights of ranges may be any of the three standard colors, and may also be fixed, flashing or occulting; the principal requirement being that they stand out distinctly from their surroundings and from the background. Most range lights lose brilliance rapidly as the vessel moves off the channel center line.

Ranges should be used only after a careful examination of the chart. It is particularly important to determine the distance the range can be safely followed. This information is not obtainable from a visual inspection of the lights.

Lightships

Lightships serve the same purposes as lighthouses, being equipped with lights, fog signals and radiobeacons. They take the form of ships only because they are placed at points where it would be impracticable to build lighthouses. Lightships mark the entrances to important harbors and estuaries, dangerous shoals lying in much frequented water, and also serve as leading marks for both transoceanic and coastwise traffic.

6-17 Lightship

The masthead lights, the fog signals, and the radiobeacon signals of lightships all have definite characteristics, so that each lightship may be distinguished from the others and also from nearby lighthouses. As with lighthouses, details regarding these signals are shown briefly on charts and more completely in the light lists.

A lightship underway or off station will fly the International Code Signal flags "LO" signifying the lightship is not at anchor on her station. While underway (and not on station), the lightship will not show or sound any of the signals displayed or sounded while on station as a lightship, but will display the lights prescribed by the International or Inland Rules of the Road for a vessel of its class. While on station, a lightship shows the masthead light only, and a less brilliant light on the forestay, the latter serving to indicate the direction in which the ship is heading. By day, the lightship will display the International Code signal of the station, whenever it appears that an approaching vessel does not recognize the lightship or requests the information. As lightships ride to a single anchor, the light on the forestay also indicates the direction of the current. Lights on lightships are displayed from one hour before sunset until one hour after sunrise and at all times when the sound signal is in operation.

Relief lightships may be placed at any of the lightship stations and, when practicable, exhibit light, sound and radiobeacon signals having the same characteristics as the station. All lightships are

6-18 Off Shore Light Structure (Texas Tower)

painted red with the name of the station in white on both sides. Relief lightships are painted the same color as the regular station ships, with the word "RELIEF" in white letters on both sides.

When the Coast Guard's modernization program is complete, it is anticipated that offshore light stations (Texas tower type structures) and large navigation buoys (LNB) will replace most lightships. Of the original 24, only Oregon's Columbia River and the Nantucket Shoals Lightships will remain. They will maintain stations where it would be impractical to build offshore stations.

Maritime Radiobeacons

Radiobeacons are valuable aids during fog and are also available for navigation in clear weather. In order to use this system, the mariner needs a radio direction finder, which is a specifically designed radio receiver with a directional antenna. This receiver is used to determine the direction of the signal being emitted by the shore station, relative to his vessel.

The basic value of the radiobeacon system lies in its simplicity of operation and its relatively low cost even though the results obtained may be somewhat limited. The general problems and practices of navigation when using radiobeacons are very similar to those encountered when using visual bearings of lighthouses or other charted objects.

Most United States and Canadian radiobeacons must share a group frequency with other radiobeacons. Normally, the stations operate in groups of six, each station in a group using the same frequency and transmitting for one minute in its proper sequence. A few radiobeacons transmit for one minute with two minutes of silence, and some radiobeacons transmit continuously without interruption.

Radiobeacons operate during all periods, either sequenced or continuously, regardless of weather conditions.

For station identification, simple characteristics consisting of combinations of dots and dashes are used. These combinations, and the lengths of the dots, dashes and spaces are chosen for ease of identification. It is not necessary to be skilled in the art of radiotelegraphy to identify the stations. The combinations are not transmitted as Morse Code and are not referred to as such.

They are referred to by dots and dashes depending on the combinations used. For example, Cape Henlopen's characteristic is ···· ·-·- and Portland's is ·- ·· ····· All radiobeacons superimpose the characteristic on a carrier which is "on" continuously during the period of transmission. This extends the usefulness of the marine radiobeacons to aircraft and vessels which employ automatic radio direction finders.

The service range is determined by the strength of the radiated signal. The actual useful range may vary considerably from the service range with different types of radio direction finders and during various atmospheric conditions.

The accuracy of radiodirection finders is dependent upon the skill of the operator, the equipment used, and the radio wave interference. Skill in using a manually operated radio direction finder can be acquired only through practice and by following exactly the operating instructions provided with the equipment. An understanding of adverse conditions and direction finding limitations must be achieved before the navigator can use the equipment with confidence.

As an operator obtains bearings with a manually revolving loop type direction finder, he can estimate the bearing by the arc of silence (null) or minimum strength of the radiated signal. He should, however, be cognizant of the possibility of errors and should evaluate the circumstances under which the bearing was taken. Bearings taken on inland stations could contain error due to refraction or reflection, and such bearings should be used cautiously. Bearings taken around the periods of morning and evening twilight should be considered of doubtful validity due to "night effect." Erroneous readings could be caused by currents induced in the direction finder antenna by re-radiation from structural features aboard the vessel, such as masts, davits, radio antennas and other vertical metallic objects. Lateral deviation of the radio wave can occur when the great circle route between the transmitter and the receiver is roughly parallel to a coastline. Also, bearings taken when a land mass is between the transmitter and the receiver should be used with caution. Whenever possible, the mariner should check his radio bearings against visual sightings in clear weather to determine the degree of accuracy that is to be expected in periods of reduced visibility.

Loran

The term "Loran" is derived by combining the first letters of the words "LOng RAnge Navigation." Loran is an electronic system by means of which a navigator can determine position or a line of position accurately and quickly, unaffected by weather. It consists of loran transmitting stations on shore, specially designed receivers with an electronic time measuring device (loran receiver indicator), and special loran charts and tables. There are two loran systems in use today, Loran-A (previously known as "standard loran") and Loran-C.

Loran-A

Basically, Loran-A operates on the principle that since the velocity of radio waves is very nearly constant, measurement of difference in arrival times of radio pulses from two synchronized transmitting stations can provide a hyperbolic line of position (LOP). Two or more such lines of position intersect to provide a position fix.

Loran-A receiving equipment is commonly used aboard both aircraft and ships. The equipment is reliable and requires no special calibration.

The use of Loran-A has steadily increased in the last 25 years. It is the least expensive area navigation system for the user. Investment cost has steadily decreased and the recreational boating community has shown a steadily increasing interest. The system has a proven reliability of 99% time on air.

As of 1 January 1974 Loran-A groundwave fix coverage was available over 10% of the northern hemisphere and skywave fix was available over 74% of the same area. Almost the entire U. S. Gulf and East Coasts are within prime coverage areas. The U. S. West Coast seaward fix coverage is limited to some degree by the curvature of the coast.

Loran-C

Loran-C is a hyperbolic system of radio navigation similar to Loran-A and is available throughout a large area of the world. Ships and aircraft can use it in all weather conditions over land and sea to obtain higher accuracy position information at greater distances than those obtained in the Loran-A system.

Previously Loran-C has not been in wide use by the general navigating public due to the relatively high cost of the receiving equipment. However, recent industry developments have resulted in a downward cost breakthrough and now Loran-C receivers costs are approaching that of Loran-A equipment.

Racon

A radar transponder beacon which emits a characteristic signal when triggered by the emissions of ship's radars. This will appear approximately every 1½ minutes on the radar PPI as an International Morse Code character extending radially away from the position of the racon.

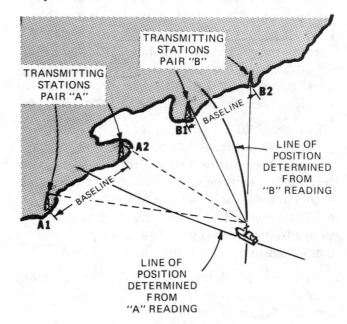

6-19 Loran Transmitting Stations

Chart Symbols for Aids to Navigation

All aids to navigation are depicted on charts by the use of symbols. These symbols make no attempt at accuracy in scale or detail. Chart No. 1, published in booklet form, lists each symbol in use on charts issued by the U.S. Lake Survey, National Ocean Survey (NOS) and the U.S. Navy Oceanographic Office. The student is well advised to procure a copy of this booklet and become familiar with the symbols for the more commonly used aids to navigation, and marine hazards relative to the operation of small craft.

Symbols for Buoys

The basic symbol for a buoy is a diamond and a small circle (a dot will be shown instead of the circle on older charts). The circle denotes the position of the buoy. The diamond is used primarily to draw attention to the position of the circle, and it also may partially describe the aid in question.

The position of the diamond with reference to the circle is of no significance. The diamond may be placed in any attitude relative to the circle to suit the situation and to afford the least amount of interference with other local features or conditions on the chart. (If the diamond is below the circle on the chart, it does not mean that the buoy is upside down!)

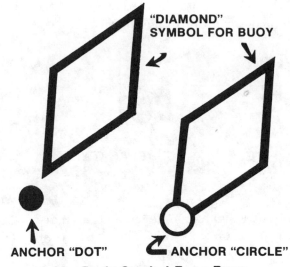

6-20 Basic Symbol For a Buoy

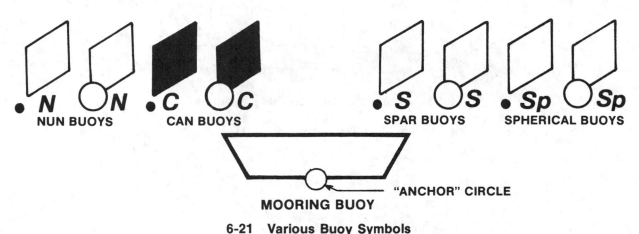

6-21 Various Buoy Symbols

The shape of the buoy will be indicated by initials if the shape is of significance.

A mooring buoy is the only buoy that is depicted by a symbol other than the diamond and circle.

This symbol is a quadrangle with the circle at the bottom.

If the aid is painted red, the diamond will generally be colored red; and if the aid is painted black, the diamond will be black. If the aid is red and black horizontally banded, the diamond will be red and black. If the aid is white and black vertically striped, the diamond will have a line drawn through its long dimension.

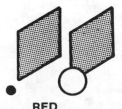

6-22 Red and Black Buoy Symbols

6-23 Banded Buoy Symbols

The five color patterns used on buoys which have no lateral significance are shown as follows:

(In each case below, the buoy is cylindrical in shape.)

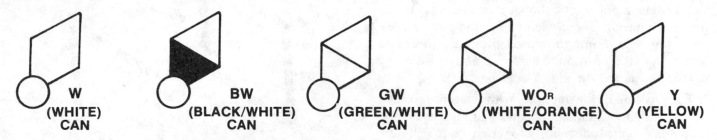

W
(WHITE)
CAN

BW
(BLACK/WHITE)
CAN

GW
(GREEN/WHITE)
CAN

WOr
(WHITE/ORANGE)
CAN

Y
(YELLOW)
CAN

6-24 Buoys with No Lateral Significance

If a buoy is lighted, a magenta colored disc will be overprinted on the circle. The characteristic of the light will be described briefly. This is done by the use of abbreviations. These are as follows:

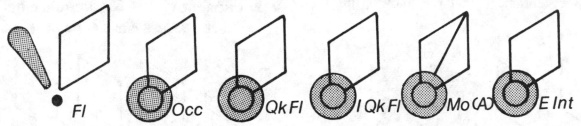

Fl   Occ   Qk Fl   I Qk Fl   Mo (A)   E Int

6-25 Example of Lighted Buoy Symbols

Flashing lights may be further identified according to their timed characteristics.

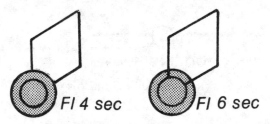

Fl 4 sec   Fl 6 sec

6-26 Time Characteristics of Flashing Light Buoys

The color of the light is also indicated on the chart. Colors of lights on buoys are either red, green or white. For red or green lights, the initials R or G are used. If the color of the light is not identified on the chart, it is assumed that the light is white.

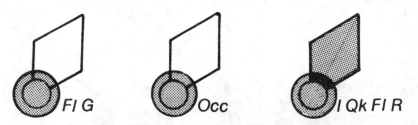

Fl G   Occ   I Qk Fl R

6-27 Colored Lights on Buoys

Other features may also be on the buoy. These are sound signals, radar reflectors, numbers or letters, or any combination of these features. Bells and horns are spelled out; radar reflectors are abbreviated; and numbers or letters which are painted on the aid are shown in quotation marks.

6-16

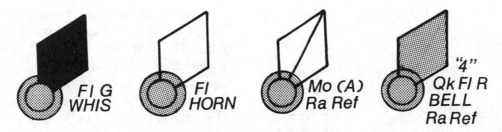

6-28 Other Features on Buoys

The Rule of Lettering

On all charts, lettering is printed in both vertical and slanted type. The basic rule is that if an object is afloat, or if it covers and uncovers with tidal action of the water, the descriptive wording or abbreviation is printed in *SLANTED TYPE*. If the object is not afloat, or if it does not cover and uncover with the tide, the descriptive wording is printed in VERTICAL TYPE. Thus a mariner can tell at a glance if ALPHA ROCK is an islet or a reef. If the wording is printed in slanted type, it can at times be under water and thus may not be seen. All descriptive lettering for floating aids to navigation is found in slanted type, while descriptions of lighthouses, ranges and other objects not afloat are found in vertical type.

Symbols for Lighthouses

The basic symbol for a lighthouse is a circle with an overprinted magenta disc. Major lights are named and described while minor lights are described only. The characteristics of the light are shown; the height of the focal plane of the lantern above mean high water is also shown. The geographic or nominal range is shown (approximately) in miles, and other equipment on the station is listed.

The symbol shown below describes a minor light (not named). The light is fixed white and the lantern is 20 feet above mean high water and visible nine miles. (Height of eye of the observer is assumed to be 15 feet above mean sea level.)

**FW
20 Ft. 9M**

6-29 Symbol for a Minor Light

If the lighthouse has a radiobeacon, the magenta disc is surrounded by a magenta circle and the radio frequency and identifying signal are described.

If the radiobeacon shared a frequency with other stations, the sequence within the group would be indicated by a Roman Numeral. Each station is assigned a minute in its proper sequence. If this station were fourth in its group, the Roman Numeral IV would appear behind the RBN frequency. (Normally, the stations operate in groups of six.)

Certain lights are not visible through the 360° arc of the horizon, because of interference by land masses. When a light is observed through a portion of its arc, the symbol for the light on the chart is shown with an obscured sector.

Some lights contain a red sector to warn of special dangers within the arc of visibility of the sector. When a light contains such a sector, it is shown on the chart.

Symbols for Lightships

Symbols for lightships include a brief description of the vessel's signaling capabilities.

Columbia River Lightship has a diaphone and

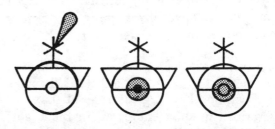

6-30 Symbols for Lightships

Radiobeacon in addition to the light. The Radiobeacon shares frequency 304 KHz with five other lights in the vicinity, and is second in the regular sequence of six one-minute transmissions.

This sequence, which is typical of the shared sequence system, is as follows:

Minute

I	Cape Arago Lt	— • — —
II	Columbia River LS	— — • •
III	Willapa Bay Lt	• • — —
IV	Cape Disappointment Lt	— — —
V	Cape Blanco Lt	— — — •
VI	Yaquina Head Lt	• — —

All on frequency 304 KHz

Symbols for Ranges and Daybeacons

Ranges are depicted on charts by the symbols for the lights (if lighted) and a dashed line indicating the direction of the range.

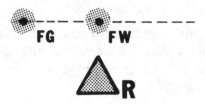

6-31   Symbols for Ranges and Daybeacons

Since the far light is higher than the near light, this range is followed by keeping the fixed green light directly above the fixed white light.

Daybeacons are depicted by small triangles, sometimes colored to match the aid itself. Beacons are never afloat, and have a great array of shapes. They are described in sufficient detail in the Light List to make identification possible.

Distance of Visibility at Sea

This chapter on Aids to Navigation would not be complete without some comment concerning the distance of visibility of objects at sea.

Distance of visibility is dependent on many factors. For all objects, atmospheric conditions become the first limiting factor. Dense fog could reduce the visible distance to zero. The height of the object increases the distance from which it can be seen. Similarly, if one increases the height of the eye, objects may be seen at a greater distance. Thus height of the object and height of eye become the second limiting factor. On lighthouses (and other lighted aids) the intensity of the light becomes the third limiting factor. Regardless of how high a light is placed above water level, it will not be seen as far away in the case of a weak light as it would be if it were a more powerful light.

Atmospheric Conditions

When listening to weather reports before putting out to sea, one often hears terms such as "thick fog" or "haze." These terms are not mere generalities, but are determined according to values which have been agreed upon by all maritime nations and are listed in the "International Visibility Code." A part of the table of *Meteorological Optical Range* is reproduced below. By reference to this table, the navigator may determine the approximate distance from which objects (headlands, breakwaters, etc.) may be expected to be seen in the circumstances.

METEOROLOGICAL OPTICAL RANGE

Code No.	Weather	Statute Miles	Yards
0	Dense Fog	0.0 to 0.03	0 to 50
1	Thick Fog	0.03 to 0.12	50 to 200
3	Moderate Fog	0.12 to 0.31	200 to 500
3	Light Fog	0.31 to 0.62	500 to 1,000
			Nautical Miles
4	Thin Fog	0.62 to 1.2	0.5 to 1.0
5	Haze	1.2 to 2.5	1.0 to 2.0
6	Light Haze	2.5 to 6.2	2.0 to 5.5
7	Clear	6.2 to 12.0	5.5 to 11.0
8	Very Clear	12.0 to 31.0	11.0 to 27.0
9	Exceptionally Clear	over 31.0	over 27.0

NOTE: On Coastal Waters, the Nautical Mile is employed. On the Great Lakes (and on all inland waters) the Statute Mile is used.

Nominal Range

Nominal Range is the maximum distance at which a light may be seen in clear weather (Visibility Code 7 above) expressed in nautical miles on coastal waters and statute miles on the Great Lakes. Nominal range is listed in the Light List for lights having a computed nominal range of five nautical miles (or statute miles) or more.

Luminous Range

Luminous range is the maximum distance at which a light may be seen under existing visibility conditions. The luminous range varies considerably with atmospheric conditions and the intensity of the light. The luminous range may be determined by Luminous Range Diagrams included in the various Light Lists published by the Coast Guard. The student is referred to these publications for further study, if interested.

Geographic Range

Geographic range is the maximum distance at which a light may be seen under conditions of perfect visibility, limited by the curvature of the earth only. This is expressed in nautical miles for coastal waters and in statute miles for the Great Lakes. This distance may be found on some charts with a brief description of the light, and assumes the eye of the observer to be at a height of fifteen feet above sea (or lake) level. In cases of lights with moderate candlepower, the nominal range (again in conditions of perfect visibility) may be shown on the charts in place of the geographic range. The National Ocean Survey will chart only the nominal range of all lights.

The following tables give the approximate geographic range of visibility of an object which may be seen by an observer whose eye is at sea level. In practice, it is necessary to add to these a distance of visibility corresponding to the height of the observer's eye above sea level.

DISTANCE OF VISIBILITY OF OBJECTS AT SEA COASTAL WATERS
(Nautical Miles)

Height (feet)	Distance (nautical miles)	Height (feet)	Distance (nautical miles)	Height (feet)	Distance (nautical miles)
5	2.6	70	9.6	250	18.1
10	3.6	75	9.9	300	19.8
15	4.4	80	10.2	350	21.4
20	5.1	85	10.5	400	22.9
25	5.7	90	10.9	450	24.3
30	6.3	95	11.2	500	25.6
35	6.8	100	11.4	550	26.8
40	7.2	110	12.0	600	28.0
45	7.7	120	12.5	650	29.1
50	8.1	130	13.0	700	30.3
55	8.5	140	11.5	800	32.4
60	8.9	150	14.0	900	34.3
65	9.2	200	16.2	1,000	36.2

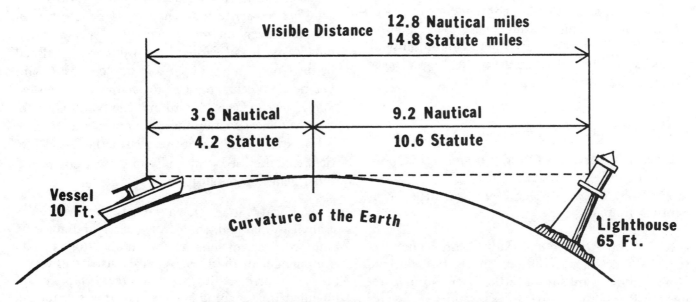

Visible Distance **12.8 Nautical miles**
14.8 Statute miles

3.6 Nautical **9.2 Nautical**
4.2 Statute **10.6 Statute**

Vessel 10 Ft. Curvature of the Earth **Lighthouse 65 Ft.**

6-32 Example of Geographic Range of Visibility

Height (feet)	Distance (statute miles)	Height (feet)	Distance (statute miles)	Height (feet)	Distance (statute miles)
5	2.9	70	11.0	250	20.9
10	4.2	75	11.4	300	22.9
15	5.1	80	11.8	350	24.7
20	5.9	85	12.2	400	26.4
25	6.6	90	12.5	450	28.0
30	7.2	95	12.9	500	29.5
35	7.8	100	13.2	550	31.0
40	8.3	110	13.8	600	32.3
45	8.9	120	14.5	650	33.6
50	9.3	130	15.1	700	34.7
55	9.8	140	15.6	800	37.3
60	10.2	150	16.2	900	39.6
65	10.6	200	18.7	1,000	41.7

Useful Navigational Publications

Light Lists

In order to keep mariners informed concerning the status of various aids to navigation, which change almost daily, the Coast Guard and the Navy Oceanographic Office issue certain informative publications. One series is the *Coast Guard Light Lists*, which are complete compilations of all aids to navigation maintained by the Coast Guard, geographically listed. The Light Lists give supplementary information on aids to navigation which cannot be included on the charts. Copies of the Light Lists are available from the Superintendent of Documents, Government Printing Office, Washington, D.C., 20402, at a nominal fee, and from local sales agents, who are listed annually in the *Weekly Notice to Mariners*.

The following Lists are available:

Light List, Atlantic Coast, Volume I (CG-158) describing aids to navigation in the United States waters from St. Croix River, Maine, to Little River, South Carolina.

Light List, Atlantic and Gulf Coast, Volume II (CG-160) describing aids to navigation in the United States waters from Little River, South Carolina, to Rio Grande River, Texas, and the Greater Antilles.

Light List, Pacific Coast and Pacific Islands, Volume III (CG-162) describing aids to navigation in United States waters off the Pacific Coast and outlying Pacific Islands. For the convenience of mariners, there are included also the lighted aids on the coast of British Columbia, maintained by the Canadian government.

Light List, Great Lakes, Volume IV (CG-157) describing aids to navigation maintained by the United States Coast Guard, and the lighted side maintained by the Dominion of Canada on the Great Lakes and the St. Lawrence River, above the St. Regis River.

Light List, Mississippi River System, Volume V (CG-161) describing the aids to navigation on the Mississippi and Ohio Rivers and navigable tributaries.

Notice to Mariners

The *Notice to Mariners* announces items of importance to the safety of marine navigation concerning aids to navigation, channel conditions, menaces to navigation and all special conditions of interest to mariners. There are three methods by which this information is disseminated—Broadcast Notices, Local Notices and Weekly Notices. Urgent notices concerning changes or deficiencies in aids to navigation are issued by means of radio broadcasts. *Local Notices to Mariners* are issued by the Commanders of the applicable Coast Guard Districts. Weekly notices to mariners, published jointly by the Coast Guard and the Naval Oceanographic Office, contain information on aids to navigation over much wider areas than the Local Notices, and are used principally to correct charts and other nautical publications.

The Local Notices are valuable to the boatmen as a navigational aid to local waters, and may be obtained free of charge by application to the Commander of the Coast Guard District in which the boat is principally operated. Weekly Notices are intended for seagoing vessels and others requiring information covering wide areas.

CHAPTER 7

Piloting

Introduction

All navigation, from the most elementary to the most complex, involves two things — determining the present position of one's ship or plane, and directing that vehicle from one known position to another. Navigation is frequently described as both an art and a science; it's an *art* because of the skills and techniques required, and a *science* because it's based on the systematic application of physical laws.

In a basic text like this, we only have space to deal with the essentials of one branch of the larger subject — *coastal navigation,* often referred to as *piloting.* As the name suggests, this subject involves directing the movements of a ship or boat along the coast, by using visible landmarks ashore, navigational aids, and soundings (measurements of the sea bottom's depth and composition). Although piloting isn't generally considered as complex or demanding as the two other kinds of navigation, *electronic* and *celestial,* it isn't necessarily easier, if only because there is less elbow room for mistakes in shallow, rock-strewn coastal waters.

This chapter is addressed to that sometime navigator, to the skipper or crewmember who merely wants to be able to find his or her way from place to place with tolerable accuracy, if not with pinpoint precision. Having mastered the material in this section, one must then go out on the water and use it. If there is any key to offhand navigation, it's practice.

The tools required are minimal, and one should avoid heavy investments in equipment until the basic techniques are well in hand. What you will need aboard your boat will vary according to your stowage space and the conditions under which you'll

be working, but here is a list of the initial gear, most of which is described in fuller detail later in the chapter:

Charts of the area in which you sail;
A good-quality magnetic compass;
Binoculars, 7x35 or, if you have room, 7x50;
Parallel rules or course protractor;
Dividers, for measuring off distance;
Pencils, preferably medium-soft #2.

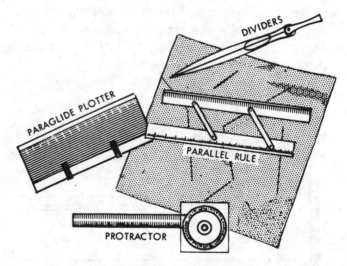

7-1 Plotting Instruments

The Nautical Chart

Maps are what make serious navigation possible, and a map has been defined as "a symbolic picture of a portion of the earth drawn to scale." A nautical chart is only a map that emphasizes features useful to the mariner — the shape of the coastline, landmarks visible from the sea, manmade aids to navigation, and depths.

Today's chart is a technological marvel, containing as much information as several large books. This compression is possible in part because of the use of symbols that stand for various objects that can't be represented on a chart in a scaled-down version of their true shapes. We'll come back to the symbols used on a chart in a while, but first let's consider the kinds of charts available to the American coastal sailor.

Charts of U.S. waters are prepared and published by the National Ocean Survey (NOS), and free catalogs are available directly from that organization; these catalogs are also provided by authorized chart sales outlets, which include map stores, major boatyards and marine dealers. Charts are only as good as the information on them, and because that information changes, you should be sure to buy and use up-to-date charts. It pays to get new charts every couple of years, and when an area is subject to frequent change because of soft bottom, strong tides and the like, to check at the local chart outlet every year to see if a new edition of your local chart has been issued. The "Notice to Mariners" will give information on changes which apply to charts as they occur. This information can be used to keep your charts current at all times. Even when you buy a new chart, some chart correction work will probably be required.

Generally speaking, charts are classified according to *scale*. This term simply refers to the size of an object on the chart relative to its size in reality: A

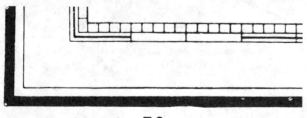

29th Ed., Sept. 4/76

12273

(formerly C&GS 1226)

7-2   Date of Issue

harbor may be one inch wide on your chart. If the chart's scale is 1:20,000, the harbor's actual width is 20,000 times charted size, or nearly 1,700 feet; but if the chart scale is 1:40,000, the same inch-wide representation stands for a harbor that's well over 3,000 feet in width.

Charts of harbors or inlets are unusually rendered in 1:20,000 scale, and sometimes 1:10,000. Coastwise charts, embracing stretches of shoreline that contain several harbors, are 1:80,000. The name of the chart gives the area it covers — *Long Island Sound - Eastern Part,* for instance, or *Tampa Bay*.

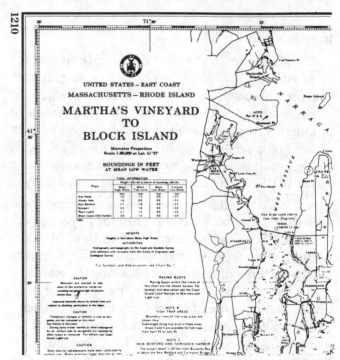

7-3   Descriptive Portion of Chart 1210

Special folio-style charts, known as Small Craft Charts, are published for areas having much small-boat traffic, the theory being that the format — several fold-out segments stapled together in protective covers, with tidal and facility information — is easier to use in the confined space of a small vessel. Small Craft Charts are 1:40,000 in scale.

Obviously, high-seas craft use charts that are much smaller in scale than the ones described here, over 1:1,000,000 in some cases. (A *small*-scale chart is one in which features are presented in smaller size and less detail than on a *large*-scale chart.) As a rule of thumb, the casual navigator should carry a chart on which the entire projected voyage can be encompassed, as well as larger-scale charts for any bays or

7-4 Small Craft Chart

On a nautical chart, water depth is measured downward from sea level, while the heights of landmarks are given in feet above sea level. But because of *tide,* which changes sea level in salt-water areas on a regular basis, some allowance must be made on the chart for the fact that the depth isn't always the same.

Tidal rise and fall is reasonably predictable, so chartmakers have selected a given point in the tidal cycle as the one at which heights and depths are measured. For safety's sake, depth measurements (called *soundings*) are noted on the chart as of *low water* (or low tide) — the point in the tide's cycle when there will be the *least* depth at a given point. On the East and Gulf Coasts of the United States, the tidal datum is *Mean* (or normal) *Low Water;* the actual low water depth on any given day in a month will vary somewhat from this figure according to a number of factors.

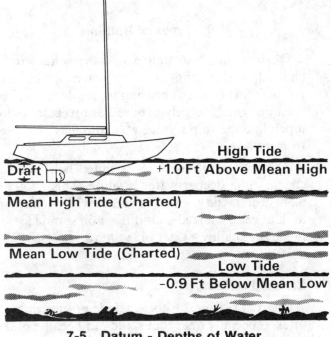

7-5 Datum - Depths of Water

harbors he might have to enter. In practical terms, an afternoon's cruise will seldom require more than one large-scale chart, and even a harbor chart will usually be quite comprehensive enough for serious piloting.

If yours is a largely open boat, you will want to protect your chart by encasing it in a transparent plastic cover that will allow you to lay the chart out flat in the open, without fear of its being damaged by spray or rain. Although charts are printed on specially-treated paper, they are not improved by being wetted.

Datum and sea level

One technical term requires definition for you to get the most from your chart: *Datum* refers to the base line from which a map's vertical measurements are made — heights of land or landmarks or, in the case of a chart, depths of water. Most landsman's maps use sea level as a datum, and that's quite good enough for them. But to a sailor, the depth of the water is vitally important, and that depth is constantly changing.

On the Pacific Coast, there are two high tides and two low tides each day, as on the Atlantic and Gulf of Mexico, but on the West Coast one set of daily tides is markedly higher than the other. Thus, the datum on Pacific Coast is *Mean Lower Low Water,* or the lower of two average low tides.

Depths of water are usually given in feet on U.S. charts, but some older, small-scale charts show soundings in *fathoms* (1 fathom = 6 feet). The kind of measurement, the scale and the datum are prominently noted on each chart. Besides depths, charts also note the type of bottom, using any of a number of abbreviations, the more common of which are shown here. This information is especially useful when trying to select a place to anchor, as good holding ground — sand or hard mud — is an essential aspect of a safe anchorage.

1	_1_	Ground
2	S	Sand
3	M	Mud; Muddy
4	Oz	Ooze
5	Ml	Marl
6	Cl	Clay
7	G	Gravel
8	Sn	Shingle
9	P	Pebbles
10	St	Stones

7-6   Types of Bottoms

Obstructions and dangers in the water are also charted, and symbols tell the mariner what to be ready for. It is worth bearing in mind that a wreck, even one that's largely exposed, soon ceases to look much like the ship it once was, and may be difficult to recognize.

As a rule, shallow water is tinted light blue on a chart, while deeper water is white. This allows the navigator a ready, visual reference without having to look at each charted sounding. You should learn to relate the shallow-water blue tint to your own boat's draft.

Charted details

Charted features ashore include prominent structures, especially ones that stand out because of their recognizable shape (such as churches and water towers); land contours are frequently charted;

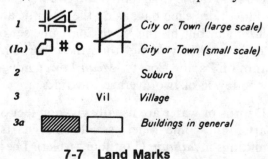

1		City or Town (large scale)
(1a)		City or Town (small scale)
2		Suburb
3	Vil	Village
3a		Buildings in general

7-7   Land Marks

bridges of all types are listed in detail. The vertical clearance of a bridge, by the way, is based on mean high water to allow a factor of safety. The navigator should remember that buildings only appear on the chart when someone tells the chartmaker to put them there; conversely, a structure that was once prominent enough to chart may have been destroyed or screened by a larger building while it still appears on a chart. That's why aids to navigation are far more reliable to use as landmarks.

The actual shoreline contour itself is one of the chart's most important features. Usually tinted pale yellow, or _buff,_ land sometimes appears as light _green,_ if it's swampy or if it covers and uncovers with changes in water level.

Aids to navigation

Manmade structures, both fixed and floating, serve as signposts, beacons, direction signals and warnings of dangers to the mariner. Aids to navigation, placed and serviced by the U.S. Coast Guard, occur either in patterned groups that indicate a channel, or path of deep water, or as individual aids that serve as warnings of isolated dangers or points of special significance.

The small-boat operator will normally find himself using aids to navigation as individual

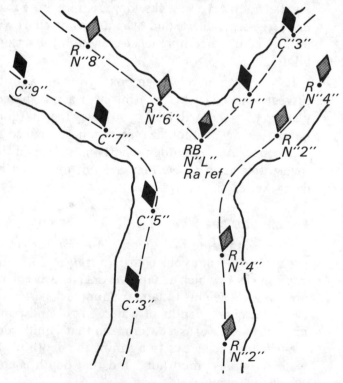

7-8   Channel System

recognition or reference points, but owners of larger vessels will often need to keep within a channel's boundaries in order to stay afloat. Even if you don't regularly use the channels for their intended purpose, you ought to know what the various floating aids (collectively called *buoys)* and fixed markers mean.

The accompanying diagrams illustrate a simplified channel system. Some points about it should be emphasized.

1. There is no functional difference between lighted and unlighted buoys or between buoys and fixed aids, although simpler and less costly aids are used where they are adequate for the purpose.

2. The only significant buoy shapes are the cylindrical *cans* and the cone-topped *nuns:* The former mark the left-hand side of a channel going from open water toward an anchorage or smaller body of water; nuns mark the right-hand side.

3. Significant buoy colors are *red* and *black*. Although cans are generally black and nuns red, buoys of varied shape may be either color. The thing to remember is that red aids mark the right side of inbound channels, black the left. Red-and-black horizontally striped buoys mark obstructions in the channel or channel junctions. Black-and-white vertically striped buoys mark inlet entrances or mid-channel.

4. Red lights go with red aids; green lights appear on black aids. White lights may be placed on aids of any color.

5. Light patterns tell you, in some cases, not only which buoy you're looking at, but what it does. Most aids use very simple flashing patterns; the more complex, multi-colored patterns identify major lighthouses.

6. Aids are numbered from open water toward sheltered water, with "1" or "2" the first buoy in a channel series. A new channel branching off a main channel will begin a new series of buoy numbers. Red-and-black and black-and-white buoys are not numbered at all.

7. Sound-producing aids — horn, bell and gong buoys, among others — are employed where sound will presumably aid navigators in re-

stricted visibility; the sound itself has no particular meaning.

Obviously, aids to navigation — except for major lighthouses — are far too small to appear on the chart in their true shape. Instead, symbols are used to indicate the position, type, number and color of aids. A chart on these pages shows how the more common symbols relate to the buoys for which they stand.

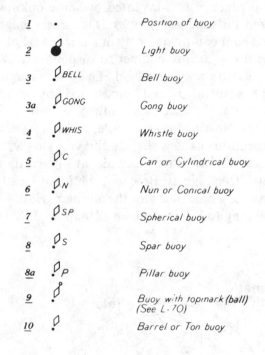

7-9 Buoy Symbols

The actual location of an aid to navigation is the small circle at the bottom of the diamond (when it's a buoy), or the isolated circle that indicates a fixed aid. Lighted buoys are distinguished by light-purple circles overprinted around the position circle. Lighted fixed aids have a light-purple exclamation mark with its sharp end pointing toward the position circle.

In practical piloting, you should remember that buoys are anchored in place, and at low tide they may move off their charted position — may even wind up outside the channel they mark. They may also be sunk or displaced by ice, collision or vandalism. Fixed aids, on the other hand, stay put. Even if their lights are extinguished, they are usually recognizable.

The Magnetic Compass

Many centuries ago, mariners oriented themselves by the sun's place of rising and setting or by the direction of prevailing winds. This was less than precise (especially on windless, cloudy days), and the magnetic compass, slowly perfected over the ages, became the sailor's most common and reliable direction-indicating instrument.

In principle, the magnetic compass remains as simple as when it was invented by some unknown traveler in early medieval times. It is a linear magnet balanced so it can pivot freely in a horizontal plane and line up — as any magnet so suspended will — with the earth's magnetic field. The linear magnet, properly suspended and unaffected by nearby ferrous metal or electrical influence, will point toward the North Magnetic Pole, an area on earth whose location changes slightly and very slowly, but which lies in far northern Canada, at some distance from the "true" North Pole — a fictional location that serves as a base point for the familiar grid of latitude and longitude lines seen on all maps and charts.

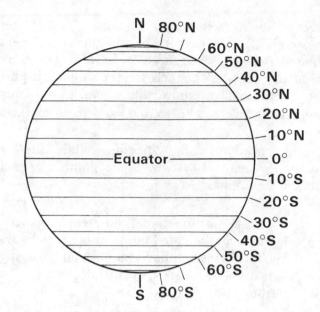

7-11   Parallels of Latitude

Latitude and longitude

Parallels of latitude are numbered north and south from 0° at the Equator to 90° North and 90° South at the true North and South Poles respectively. Each degree is subdivided into 60 equal segments called *minutes,* and each minute into either 60 seconds or 10 tenths of minutes, according to the notational system one prefers. On charts, true North is usually located at the top, and the parallels are indicated along the side margins by divisions in the black-and-white border, as well as by actual lines running across the chart surface at stated intervals that depend on the chart scale. It's handy to remember that one minute of latitude (but not longitude) equals one nautical mile, 6080 feet. Each chart also contains at least one printed scale, in nautical miles, kilometers, statute miles and/or yards. (Small Craft Charts are sometimes printed to show a maximum stretch of shoreline per sheet, and when this is the case, the top edge of the chart may not be North.)

Meridans of longitude run north and south between the true poles. By an ancient convention, meridians are numbered east and west from Green-

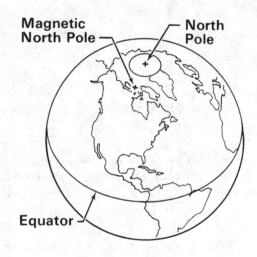

7-10   Relative Position of Poles

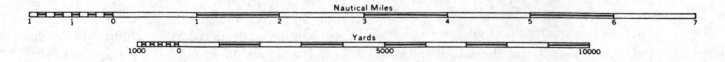

7-12   Printed Scale on Chart

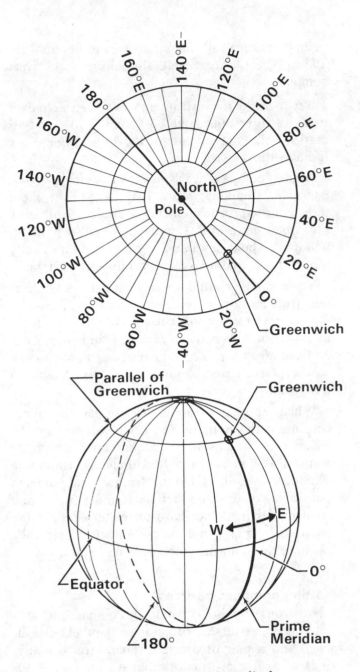

7-13 **Meridians of Longitude**

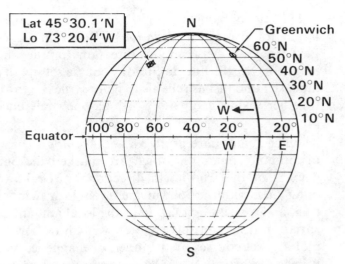

7-14 **Grid System of Longitude and Latitude**

73° 20.4'West, there is only one place it can be This grid system of positioning is not too useful or meaningful to the small boat operator, however, and a grid based on true North does make it difficult for the mariner whose compass points to magnetic North. For obvious reasons, charts can only accommodate one reference grid. The navigator with a magnetic compass is left with two choices — "correct" his compass reading to the true North equivalent of its magnetic direction, or use an angular measuring device or system that reads out in magnetic degrees.

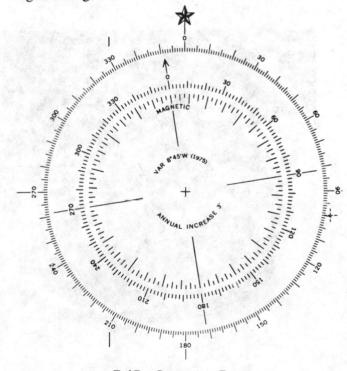

7-15 **Compass Rose**

wich, England. West and East Longitude meet at 180° in the Pacific Ocean, down most of which the International Date Line runs. The entire United States is thus in West Longitude — from about 60° West on the East Coast to about 130° West in California or 150° West in Hawaii.

The grid system of latitude and longitude, so essential for celestial navigation, is also useful for pinpointing position without reference to navigational aids or landmarks. If, for instance, a boat's position is given as 45° 30.1'North,

Traditional navigators make an arithmetic calculation to correct for *variation* — local difference East or West between the direction of true and magnetic North. For day-to-day course setting, it's far easier and just as reliable to ignore true North altogether, using magnetic North as one's reference point.

On each chart are printed several *compass roses,* directional circles on which are marked the 360 degrees of the true north directional circle in an outer ring, with the 360° magnetic circle in an inner ring, and a written notation of the local amount of variation. Later in this chapter we'll show how to plot and set courses by the inner, or magnetic, rose using either parallel rules or a course protractor; for the moment, merely bear in mind that any *course* — the direction from one point to another — can be expressed equally well in degrees true, related to true north, or degrees magnetic, based on the direction of magnetic north.

Selecting a compass

A magnetic compass should be chosen to suit the boat you will use it on. A 2 inch or 2½ inch diameter compass card might be suitable for most boats less than 26 feet in length. The popular 3½ inch diameter compass card is ideal for most boats in the 23

7-16 Magnetic Compass

to 26 foot range and is adequate for most boats up to about 35 feet. Larger boats should use a still larger compass.

Try to locate the instrument so you can sight over it in all directions, and be sure the fore-and-aft marks — the center pivot and the *lubber's line* — are in line with the keel.

A good compass nearly always has *internal compensators,* small magnets that allow the instrument to be adjusted for local metal or electrical influence (known as *deviation*). If you plan to cruise at night, and if your boat has an electrical system, it's handy also to have a compass with a built-in red light.

The compass should also be located at least three feet from radios, other electronic instruments or masses of ferrous metal. This may be hard to achieve in a small boat. When you've done your best, sail out and anchor at a place in the harbor where you can see several charted landmarks or fixed aids to navigation.

When the boat is riding steadily, face north according to the compass and orient yourself on the chart. Pick out as many natural and manmade features as you can and find their corresponding symbols on the chart. Do this from several points in your home waters and then try it underway. You'll soon find that it's not hard to relate reality to the chart, as long as you don't commit the navigator's cardinal sin — losing track of where you are.

Plotting compass courses

Now you're ready to try plotting compass courses. You'll need a course protractor or parallel rules, a pencil and a pair of dividers. There are so many kinds of course protractors that it's impossible to give instructions for each type. For that reason, this book will show course plotting with parallel rules — after you've mastered their use, you may want to try something different.

To set a course on the chart, first pick start and finish points. While learning, it's a good idea to use buoys that are well within sight of each other. Draw a straight line between the two points and lay one edge of the parallel rules along it.

Now "walk" the rules to the nearest compass rose. This involves moving one rule while firmly holding the other in place, being careful not to lose the direction of the original line. It takes practice, and

7-17 Parallel Rules

you will have to do it over several times until you get the hang of it. You'll also need a flat, smooth surface under your chart, the larger the better, but no smaller than about two by two feet. When one edge of the rules has been walked to the compass rose, move it slowly and carefully until it intersects the small + that marks the rose's center.

From the *inner* degree circle, read out the course where the rule's edge intersects the circle, on the side in which you are heading. This is your *magnetic* course. Write it along the top edge of the penciled course line as three digits followed by the letter "M" (for magnetic): a course of 90° would thus be *090 M.*

Checking the compass

Having plotted a buoy-to-buoy course, take your boat out and carefully put her on that course. It's a good idea to plot several possible courses in directions that are at least 45° different one from the other. Using the course noted above, your compass should read 90° or East, the same thing. When you arrive at the mark for the other end of the charted course, reverse your heading and run back. Your compass should now read 180° different from the first heading, or 270°. (This 180° reverse is called the *reciprocal*).

If your original compass course and its reciprocal are the same as what you've plotted on the chart, or within 2-3 degrees either way, your compass is adequately free from deviation, the error caused by magnetic influences within the boat. If on the other hand, you have an error of 5° or more on any heading, first check the accuracy of your plotting, then try running the courses again. If the error persists, check for a mass of ferrous metal, an electronic de-

vice or wiring near the compass. Presuming you find no removable source of interference, you must either move the compass, compensate the instrument according to the manufacturer's instructions, or make a *deviation table,* a record that indicates the amount of compass error on various evenly-spaced headings. Both compensation and making a deviation table are beyond the scope of this book, but are seldom necessary on small craft.

Positioning Your Boat

Assuming, however, that your compass is reasonably accurate, you can now employ it for positioning your boat. To do this, pick out two identifiable landmarks or (preferably) navigational aids that form a more or less 90° angle with your boat as the apex. Now locate the two markers on your chart.

Head the boat directly at one mark and note the compass course. As soon as you've written it down, head for the other mark and make a note of the compass heading to it.

For the sake of argument, let's assume your first direction (called a *bearing*) was 095 M and the second was 195 M. Calculate the reciprocals of each bearing: 095 + 180 = 275; and 195 + 180 = 375, or 015 (when you pass 360°, of course, you have to begin over with 001).

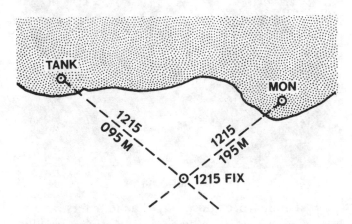

7-18 Cross Bearings—Two Landmarks

Next, plot these reciprocals — 275° and 015° — *from* the charted positions of the respective marks. Each of these plotted lines is called a *Line of Position,* and your boat must be somewhere along it. Where two lines of position cross is obviously where you are.

To double-check your work, try three lines of position, In theory, they should intersect at one point, but they most probably won't. Practice doing the same thing over and over until they come reasonably close together.

Speed-Time-Distance

In setting course, it's important to know how long it'll take you to get from place to place. Unfortunately, it's hard to figure such times with much precision in the average small boat, for several reasons.

Even if your boat has a speedometer these instruments are not terribly accurate or reliable at slow speeds. Finally, your boat's speed over the bottom — her real speed — will be invisibly affected by the current, the movement of the water in which you're floating.

If you're attempting to pilot accurately, you just have to do the best you can.

7-19   Tachometer

Most inboard engines have tachometers, and a boat's speed at a given tachometer setting is usually quite predictable. Use a stopwatch to time yourself while running between buoys. Be sure to run both ways at the same speed to cancel out the effect of current. Make the runs at several different tachometer settings and then calculate your speeds after you return home. (Caution: always calculate the speed each way and average the two speeds — never average the times).

From the data you have accumulated you can make up a speed-tachometer table, commonly referred to as an RPM table.

The basic formula for calculating speed, time and distance when two of the three are known is: $60D = ST$ (or $60 \times D = S \times T$) where D is distance in nautical miles, S is speed in knots and T is time in minutes. One simple and versatile way to use this relationship is by use of the illustration shown here.

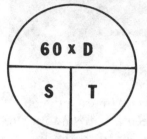

Cover the symbol for the answer you need. The formula for the answer remains uncovered. Example: For SPEED: cover the letter S. The formula is $\frac{60 \times D}{T}$

For DISTANCE: Cover 60xD. The formula is SxT. Divide the result by 60.

For TIME: Cover T. The formula is $\frac{60 \times D}{S}$

7-20   Speed, Time and Distance Relationship

Measuring Distance on a Mercator Chart

Distance on a Mercator chart is always measured on the latitude scale. This is the scale appearing on the left and right sides of the chart. One nautical mile equals one minute (1') of latitude (a mile a minute). Since there are 60 minutes in one degree, one degree of latitude equals 60 nautical miles. Since there are 360° in a circle, the circumference of the earth is 21,600 nautical miles. By dividing this figure into the circumference of the earth established by international agreement, we find that the nautical mile is

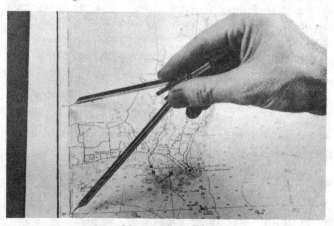

7-21   Measuring Distance

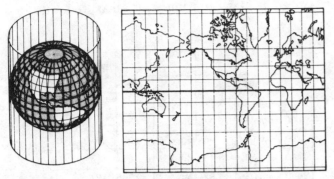

- Angles are correctly represented • Great circle appears curved
- Rhumb line appears as straight line
- Distortion in BOTH directions

7-22 Mercator Projection

6076.1 feet long. This is approximately 1/8 longer than the 5280 foot statute mile.

One characteristic of a Mercator chart is that the size of areas is distorted. Because of this distortion, one minute of latitude will appear to get larger when moving away from the equator. On large scale charts, up to about 1:80,000, it makes very little practical difference where we measure along the latitude scale, for the change in scale from top to bottom of the chart is very slight. However, for smaller scale charts covering larger areas, the difference in the length of a minute of latitude is easy to find from top to bottom of the chart, and it becomes a factor in accurate chart work. Therefore, it is good practice to make it a habit to always measure at about the mid latitude of the course line on all charts.

Plotting

To complete our study of piloting we need to take the things we have learned about charts, compasses, and piloting instruments and put them together in

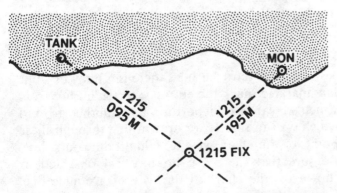

7-23 Cross Bearings—Two Landmarks

actual practice. In any piloting situation, the answers to be determined are usually concerned with either establishing a course line or determining position. The determination of position may be the whole problem, but most of the time position is only a point necessary to the fixing of a course line to another destination.

Time

Time is displayed on a chart by using the 24 hour system. In this system the first two digits tell the hour (00 to 23) and the last two digits give the minutes (00 to 59). Midnight is 0000. Thus 9:45 AM is written as 0945, while 9:45 PM is written 2145.

Plotting Symbols

There are several terms and symbols which are used in piloting. You should be completely familiar with these before proceeding.

— A *"line of position"* (LOP) is a line, from a known position, along which a vessel is presumed to be located. LOP's are commonly obtained by taking a bearing on a charted object. A line of position is labelled with the time and bearing *to the object.*

It is indicated on a chart as:

$$\frac{0930}{100}$$

When an LOP is obtained by sight along a range only the time is shown, as: 0930

— A *"fix"* is an accurate position, usually obtained by crossing 2 or more LOP's. A fix is indicated on a chart as:

0945 FIX

— A *"DR Position"* is a position determined by applying a vessel's course(s) and speed(s) to the last accurate position. A DR position is indicated on a chart as:

0945 DR

— An *"estimated position"* is the most probable position for a vessel, determined from bearings of questionable accuracy. It is often a DR position modified by the best information possible. An estimated position is indicated on a chart as:

0945 EP

The "DR" Plot — The Dead Reckoned Plot

If our cruise is to be of considerable length, it is customary practice to set up our DR track. This is simply a plot of our course marked with hourly positions, determined purely from speed based on engine RPM and our speed curve. For sailing craft, this would have to be speed as estimated by some form of log or speedometer.

7-24 Speedometer

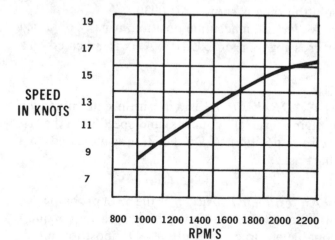

7-25 A Typical Speed Curve

Speed Trial Tabulation Over Measured Mile

RPM	N-S		S-N		Average Speed	Current
	Time	Speed	Time	Speed		
800	6m 47s	8.85	8m 32s	7.03	7.94	.91
1000	5m 46s	10.41	7m 31s	7.98	9.18	1.23
1200	5m 01s	11.96	6m 46s	8.87	10.41	1.55
1400	4m 28s	13.43	6m 13s	9.65	11.54	1.89
1600	4m 03s	14.82	5m 47s	10.38	12.6	2.22
1800	3m 42s	16.22	5m 01s	11.96	14.09	2.13
2000	3m 31s	17.06	4m 53s	12.29	14.67	2.39
2200	3m 24s	17.64	4m 41s	12.81	15.22	2.42

7-26 Speed Table

If along our course, there are certain landmarks from which we can accurately determine our position, this would be done and these positions would be plotted and compared with our DR position for the same time. This will tell us much about our progress.

The comparison of the DR positions with the actual positions will help us arrive at some very valuable conslusions regarding the effect of wind, current, and steering error on our progress. Naturally, one fix will not answer any question except whether or not we are on course, but a series of positions compared with the DR plot will provide these answers. However, these calculations are beyond the scope of this text. As we have indicated previously, this type of piloting is more practical in cruising than in day sailing.

Plotting DR

Outside of most harbors there is a buoy or some landmark to mark the entrance to the harbor from which we can take departure, and another, toward which we can sail. If we draw a line through these points on our chart, we have laid off our course line. Be sure that there are no physical obstructions shown on the chart in the way of a course line. Changes in course are sometimes necessary to avoid these obstructions.

If we are using parallel rules, we can walk the course line up to the nearest compass rose and read our magnetic direction on the inner ring of the rose.

The magnetic course is indicated on the chart.

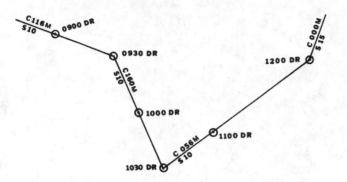

7-27 Typical DR Plot

After your course has been set it should be standard operating procedure for you to mark off the distance to be run with your dividers. Estimating the speed of your boat from your speed curve, and knowing the distance to be run, it will be very easy to estimate your time of arrival at your next reference point. This procedure is a must in periods of low visibility, such as fog.

The "rules" for when to update a DR are:
1. Every hour on the hour
2. Whenever there is a course and/or speed change
3. Whenever a FIX or an EP is obtained

Additionally, a new course line is started from every FIX. Also, much more frequent plotting is appropriate when in channels or other restricted waters.

Visual Ranges

A more accurate way of obtaining an LOP is to observe a range. If two charted objects are in line, at that moment your position must lie along the line extended between them. Any two such objects, when in line, constitute a range.

Summary

As noted at the beginning of this chapter, the navigation of the average small boat is a seat-of-the-pants procedure. Having mastered the simple techniques discussed here, you should have no great trouble getting where you want to go, provided you do keep practicing what you've learned. For longer voyages, it pays to take more serious instruction in piloting technique.

CHAPTER 8

Marine Engines

Introduction

The gasoline powered marine engine has been used as a propulsion unit for many years; in fact, history records its use in the 6000 mile voyage of a 35' craft in 1911, only eight years after the Wright brothers first engine powered heavier than air flight. In the ensuing years, the gasoline engine has become the source of power used most by small craft. In 1972, statistics indicate that there were more than 700,000 inboard boats in use, including auxiliary powered sailboats and documented boats; some 800,000 diesel and gasoline engines, including those converted from automotive engines; 7,400,000 outboard engines; and some 300,000 inboard-outdrive units. The estimated cost of these engines in use in 1972 exceeds the original cost of the Pentagon.

This chapter will be devoted to the care and maintenance of the brute that powers the small craft fleet. No part of a boat is more important than the engine and a good skipper will be sure that the engine is properly maintained and cared for at all times. If it is neglected, many long hours of hard work will inevitably result. To properly maintain the engine, a place should be set aside on the boat for tools and spare parts. These should be replenished as needed and every spare part should be in good working order.

The engine and engine compartment should be kept clean at all times. Regular cleaning requires little effort, but if this care is neglected, a difficult job will follow. Never leave oily rags or papers lying around - they will create a hazard. Keep the engine compartment clean and well ventilated to minimize the possibility of fire or explosion. For boating safety, ventilation of engine and fuel compartments is most important.

One other word on safety: NEVER leave the keys in the ignition switch after the engine has been stopped. There is always the possibility of accidental ignition (such as that caused by a child or adult falling against the key). The boat might also be stolen if someone can get in quickly and crank the engine.

Almost all of today's pleasure craft are powered by engines. This is as true of sailboats as of powerboats since, except for sailing dinghys and small class sailboats, most are equipped with auxiliary engines.

Engines on pleasure craft may be inboard or outboard. An inboard engine is installed within the hull while an outboard engine is installed on the transom (outboard of the hull) or mounted within an engine well. But, regardless of the mounting method, all marine engines have a great deal in common. All are intended to do the same job - provide power to turn the propeller, which moves the boat.

This chapter deals with internal combustion engines and covers the theory of operation of four-cycle and two-cycle diesel and gasoline engines. Routine maintenance and trouble shooting are reviewed.

All engines, except ramjets and rockets, are designed to convert an expanding gas into a rotating force. Let's look at the basic operation of reciprocating engines. A reciprocating engine has a piston that moves up and down. All reciprocating engines have three basic parts. The first is a cylinder which acts like a bottle to hold the expanding gas. The second is the piston which slides snugly into the cylinder and is pushed by the expanding gas. The third part is the crankshaft which connects to the piston by a connecting rod and converts the reciprocating, or up and down motion of the piston, into rotary motion. The crankshaft works like the pedals on a bicycle which convert the up and down motion of your knees to the rotary motion of the sprocket.

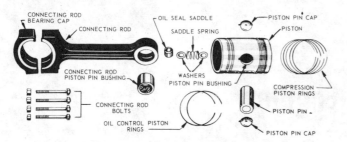

8-1 Piston and Connecting Rod Parts

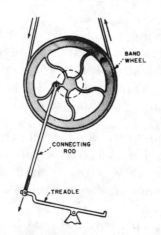

8-2 The Crankshaft Action of a Treadle and Bandwheel

Gasoline, when mixed in the right proportions with air, will explode. An electrical spark can ignite this explosive mixture and the resulting explosion creates an expanding gas. Oil, when sprayed into hot air, will also explode. Diesel, when he designed his engine, used compression to generate enough heat (1,000° F) to cause an explosion when oil was sprayed into the hot air at the proper moment. The term "internal combustion engine" is used whenever expanding gases are generated and contained in an engine's cylinder.

Internal combustion reciprocating engines require a proper mixture of fuel and air in order to run.

Before we study the theory of operation, we should first know what is meant by the terms "two-cycle" and "four-cycle." An engine runs by repeating a series of explosions over and over again. A cycle includes all the steps required to create one explosion in a cylinder. In a two-cycle engine, the piston moves two strokes - one down and one up - to complete one cycle. In a four-cycle engine, the piston moves four strokes - down, up, down, and up.

The Four-Cycle Engine

The following steps are required to complete the cycle of a four stroke (four-cycle) gasoline engine.

1. As the piston moves down in the cylinder for the first stroke, a vacuum is created in the space above the piston. A valve (the intake valve) is timed to open at this instant, allowing an explosive mixture of gasoline and air to be drawn into the cylinder. This is the intake stroke.

2. As the piston starts up on the second stroke, the intake valve closes, the cylinder is sealed, and the mixture in the space above the piston is compressed. This is the compression stroke.

3. Just before the piston starts down for the third stroke, an electrical spark at the spark plug ignites the explosive gas. The expansion of gas from the resulting explosion pushes the piston down. This is the power stroke.

4. As the piston starts up in the fourth stroke, another valve (the exhaust valve) opens and the piston pushes the burnt gases out. This is the exhaust stroke. At the top of the exhaust stroke, the exhaust valve closes, the piston and cylinder are now ready for the next four-stroke cycle.

Four-cycle diesels are similar to gasoline engines except as follows: the diesel intake stroke does not draw in a gas/air mixture, only air. The air is compressed in the second stroke, but at a much higher compression ratio, creating an intense heat. The heat (1,000° F) is much higher than the ignition point of the diesel fuel. When the diesel oil is sprayed into the hot air, by injectors which atomize the oil into a fine mist, the oil explodes forcing the piston down for the third stroke, the power stroke. The fourth stroke is the exhaust stroke.

The Two Cycle Engine

In the two-cycle machine, the functions of intake, compression, power, and exhaust are not marked by individual and distinct strokes. The four functions blend together in two strokes. The first stroke combines power and exhaust; the second combines intake and compression.

The two-cycle diesel incorporates a valve in the head or combustion chamber; this is for exhaust. Intake is via a set of holes or ports located near the bottom of the cylinder. The two-cycle diesel, typified by the well known Detroit Diesel (GM) functions as follows:

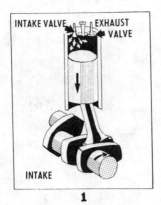
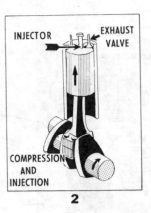

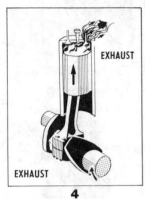

8-3 Four Cycle Diesel Engine

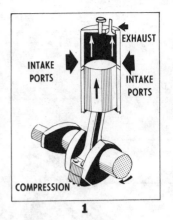
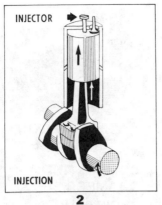

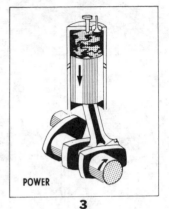
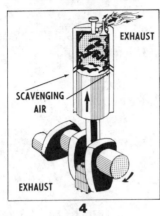

8-4 Two Cycle Diesel Engine

1. Starting with highly compressed very hot air in the top of the cylinder, fuel oil is sprayed into the combustion space. The oil bursts into flame, and the combustion pressure is terrific.

2. High pressure expanding gases push down the piston on its power stroke.

3. When the piston is down about three-quarters of the way on its power stroke, exhaust valves in the cylinder head open. Out rushes the pressurized, burned gas.

4. Continuing its travel, the piston next uncovers a series of intake ports at the bottom of its stroke. Through these ports rush compressed air, filling the cylinder and driving residual exhaust gas out the still-open exhaust valve. The piston now rises, covering the intake ports. Immediately, the exhaust valve closes, and the ascending piston compresses the trapped air in preparation for the next series of events.

We see that in the two-cycle engine there is a power pulse for each downward stroke of the piston. In the four-cycle engine there is a power pulse only every other downward stroke.

We saw that in the four-cycle engine, mixture or air was sucked into the cylinder by a down stroke of the piston. By comparison, in the two-cycle engine, working matter must be forced into the cylinder at the completion of exhaust. The diesel incorporates a high pressure rotary blower to force air into the cylinder. The two-cycle gasoline engine uses "crank-case compression" to do the job. Here, the crank-case is sealed, and the piston's downward motion creates positive crankcase pressure.

Think of the gasoline two-cycle engine (typified by the outboard) as having two working chambers. One is the cylinder we have already described; this is the upper chamber. The other is the crankcase below the piston; this is the lower chamber: It acts as a pump delivering fuel-air mixture to the working cylinder.

The lower chamber is connected directly to the carburetor through a one-way spring or reed valve which allows the gas/air mixture to be drawn into the chamber, but does not allow it to be pushed back.

These two chambers operate simultaneously but will have to be considered individually as we trace

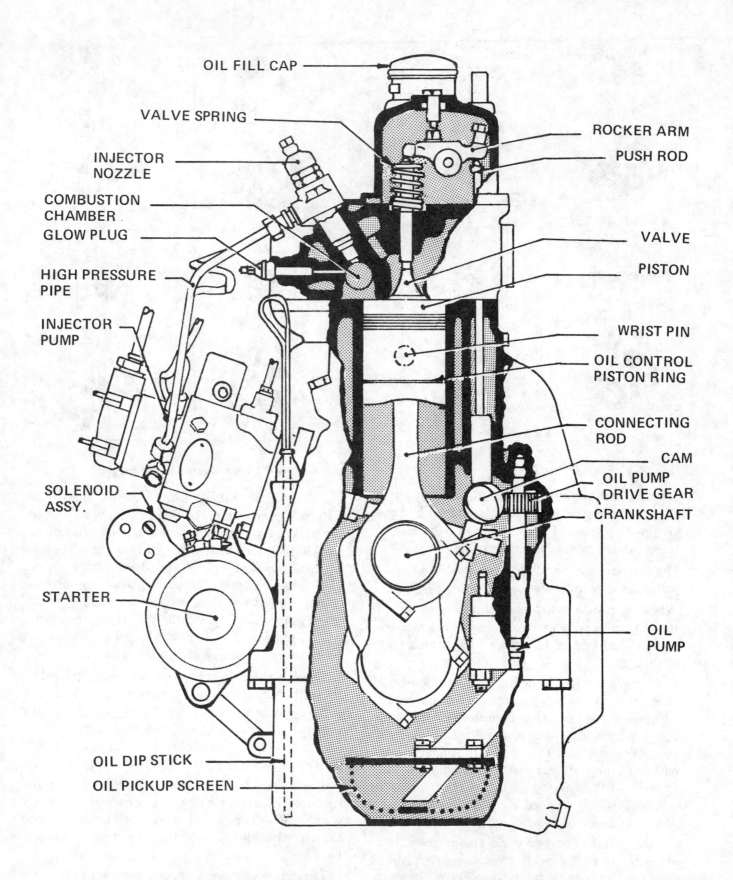

OIL FILL CAP

VALVE SPRING

INJECTOR NOZZLE

COMBUSTION CHAMBER

GLOW PLUG

HIGH PRESSURE PIPE

INJECTOR PUMP

SOLENOID ASSY.

STARTER

OIL DIP STICK

OIL PICKUP SCREEN

ROCKER ARM

PUSH ROD

VALVE

PISTON

WRIST PIN

OIL CONTROL PISTON RING

CONNECTING ROD

CAM

OIL PUMP DRIVE GEAR

CRANKSHAFT

OIL PUMP

8-5   Diesel Engine — Transverse Section

8-4

the flow path. We will consider the cycle of only one piston. When an engine has more than one piston, each lower chamber is separate and sealed from the other chambers. The other new thing to consider is that the two-cycle gasoline engine does not have valves, as we saw on the previous engines, but ports. These ports are holes located in the sides of the upper chamber or cylinder and are covered by the piston. They are covered until the piston is almost at the bottom of the stroke.

Let's trace the flow of working matter through the two-cycle gasoline engine.

As the piston moves up, the lower chamber becomes a vacuum, drawing an explosive gas/air mixture from the carburetor. At the same time, an explosive charge of gas/air is being compressed in the upper chamber. At the top of the stroke, the compressed gas in the upper chamber is exploded, forcing the piston down. As the piston starts down, the mixture which is now trapped in the lower chamber is pressurized. Near the bottom of the stroke, the intake and exhaust ports are uncovered. Exhaust gases are forced out and are replaced by the incoming pressurized explosive mixture. As the piston starts up, it covers the ports and a new cycle begins.

Supplementary Accessories

Internal combustion engines generate heat and, because they have moving parts, require lubrication. This means supplementary systems are required to run the engine efficiently.

Lubrication Systems

Any surface which rubs or slides against another surface will generate friction and heat. Naturally, friction can never be eliminated entirely; however, there are many ways to reduce the friction. One of the most common ways is to provide a thin liquid film between the two sliding parts. In engines, the fluid used for this film is lubricating oil.

There are many complex methods used to lubricate bearing surfaces, but we shall cover only the most common found in marine engines. Engines are provided with channels or ducts which carry the oil to all internal moving parts. A pump forces the oil through these ducts. A reservoir of oil is located in a crankcase pan fastened beneath the engine. Oil is pumped from the lowest spot in the reservoir, the sump, through a screen that removes large particles

or metal chips. Placed downstream of the pump may be an oil cooler to remove excess heat and a filter to remove fine particles of dirt. On most engines, oil is ducted through the connecting rods and runs down the cylinder walls from the piston skirt.

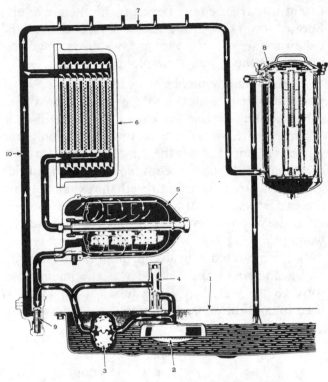

1. OIL PAN
2. SCREEN—OIL PUMP INTAKE
3. PRESSURE OIL PUMP
4. VALVE—PRESSURE RELIEF
5. OIL STRAINER
6. OIL COOLER
7. OIL MANIFOLD IN CYLINDER BLOCK
8. OIL FILTER
9. BY-PASS VALVE
10. BY-PASS AROUND STRAINER AND COOLER

8-6 Lubrication System

In two-cycle gasoline engines, there is no oil reservoir, so oil is mixed with the gasoline. The oil is suspended in the mixture as tiny droplets. When the gas/oil mixture is drawn into the crankcase, the gasoline, being more volatile, vaporizes, thus leaving some of the oil droplets to condense on the metallic surfaces. New oil is being supplied constantly; therefore, no filtering or cooling is required.

Two-cycle diesel engines are lubricated in the conventional manner, the same as four-cycle marine and automobile engines. There is no need to mix lubricating oil in diesel fuel since the fuel is directly injected; it is not drawn through the crankcase. Remember that crankcase compression is not used in the modern two-cycle diesel: A separate high pressure blower furnishes combustion air. This was described earlier.

Cooling Systems

Water is the common agent used to cool marine engines. Some small outboards of two or three horsepower use air cooling and are provided with fins to help dissipate the heat. Air-cooling is not efficient for larger engines except with the use of elaborate blowers requiring additional space and, if the exhaust system is run inboard, water cooling is required for the exhaust manifolds and ducts.

Marine engines may be cooled with raw sea water pumped from outside the boat, or with a closed fresh water cooling system similar to that used in cars. When raw sea water is used for cooling, only one pump is required. After the sea water passes through the engine, it is used to cool the exhaust manifolds and is discharged overboard with the exhaust. There are two ways to cool a closed fresh-water system. After the water is circulated through the engine by a water pump, it passes through a keel cooler, a type of radiator mounted outside on the hull of the boat, and is cooled by the sea water as the boat moves through the water. A separate sea-water pump is used to cool the exhaust manifolds and this water is

discharged with the exhaust in the same duct. Keel coolers create a drag on the hull of the boat and may reduce the boat speed as much as two or three knots. If this loss of speed is a disadvantage, a heat exchanger may be used.

Many modern gasoline inboards and the great majority of diesels are equipped with closed circuit, fresh water cooling incorporating a heat exchanger mounted directly on the engine. A marine version of the automobile's radiator, the heat exchanger cools water (or water & anti-rust solution) which is pumped rapidly through the engine.

The pump used to circulate coolant through the heat exchanger and engine is the centrifugal variety, the same kind as used on car and truck engines. It pumps an enormous volume of water, assuring even temperatures throughout the system.

A second pump, usually a vane or gear type, pumps a smaller volume of cold seawater through the heat exchanger and back to the sea. Cold seawater in the heat exchanger performs the same function as cool air blowing through the automobile's radiator. The beauty of the system is that the

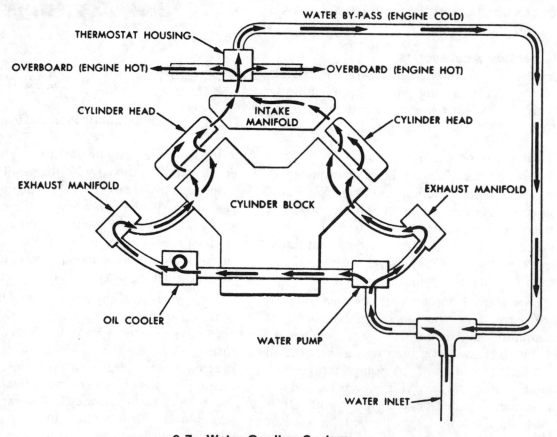

8-7 Water Cooling System

engine's interior is never exposed to the corrosive effects of seawater. (Even most lake and river water is less than pristine.)

Exhaust manifolds on engines having closed circuit heat exchanger cooling may be cooled either by the fresh water or expended seawater. The preferred method is, of course, by fresh. In either case, the exhaust pipe, the pipe running to the transom, is cooled by expended seawater except in very special cases where the pipe running to the transom may be jacketed.

Fuel Systems

We have discussed explosive mixtures, but not how they are made. We will start with the simpler diesel system. The fuel is pumped from the fuel tank through a coarse filter to remove large particles, then through a final filter, before entering the injector system. Each injector has a valve that not only passes the fuel to the injector, but also meters the amount to control engine speed. In order to achieve a fine mist spray for complete combustion, the oil passes through an extremely fine hole in the injector at a very high pressure. The injectors are easily clogged, which means that extremely clean fuel and clean filters are essential.

Filtering is also essential for gasoline engines; for, after the fuel is pumped from the fuel tank into the carburetor, it passes through jets with fine holes to atomize the fuel before it is mixed with air. The carburetor not only atomizes the fuel to ensure a complete mix, but also meters the proper amount of gasoline - for the amount of air available - to maintain an explosive mixture.

Electrical System and Accessories

If an engine could be started with a hand crank, the only accessories required would be a belt to drive the cooling water pump, and for a gasoline engine,

an electrical source to fire the spark plugs. The high voltage required to arc across the spark plug gaps is supplied by either magneto or battery ignition. In either system, low voltage is momentarily converted to high voltage at the proper instant. A magneto utilizes the rotating motion of a flywheel to generate and deliver to the spark plugs a high voltage pulse of electric current at the proper instant.

On outboards with one or two cylinders, a magneto is the electrical source, with separate circuits for each plug. Outboards with additional cylinders have a more complicated magneto or a battery ignition system. Large outboards require a starter motor and a battery for power. Some outboards have a generator or alternator to recharge the battery.

Inboard engines have a battery ignition system or a magneto system. The battery supplies current for the spark plugs and also powers the starter motor. A generator or alternator is provided to recharge the battery at a rate determined by the regulator.

Because the cooling, lubrication, and electrical charging functions are so essential to proper operation, gauges are provided to monitor these functions. Make it a part of your underway routine to periodically check the gauges.

Routine Check List

When preparing to leave the dock, before casting off the lines, check the oil pressure and be sure the cooling water is circulating. If water is not circulating, determine the cause immediately, otherwise overheating may develop and substantial damage could result.

To ensure reliable operation of the engine after leaving the dock, the following check list is provided to be used before leaving dock.

1. **FUEL.** Top off the fuel tank; don't run out of fuel at sea.
2. **OIL.** Dipstick should indicate oil level is within proper operating range. Don't overfill beyond the top level indicator.
3. **HYDRAULIC DRIVE TRANSMISSION.** Check the oil level on the dipstick. Again, don't overfill beyond the top level indicator.
4. **ALTERNATOR AND PUMP BELTS.** Replace if frayed; tighten if loose. Belts should not be too tight as excessive belt and bearing wear may result.

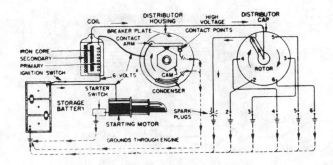

8-8 Battery Ignition System

5. **WATER.** Closed cooling systems - top off or fill to proper level.

6. **BATTERIES.** Fill with distilled water to proper level. Check to see if they are fully charged. If a hydrometer is available, the cells should be checked for proper gravity.

7. **BILGE BLOWERS.** Ventilate at least 5 minutes before starting the engine.

8. **ALARM SYSTEMS.** There are many alarm systems available for monitoring the items above; however, these systems do not eliminate the need to check the gauges.

9. **GREASE CUPS.** Keep clean and filled.

10. **FILTERS.** Keep clean and change at frequency recommended by manufacturer's operating manual.

11. **ENGINE.** Permit the engine to warm up slowly. Don't get underway with a cold engine. The result may soon be a breakdown of valves, pistons, bearings, etc. It is mandatory that the proper warm-up period be followed so that oil reaches all the moving parts. It is better to warm the engine "in gear" with propeller loading rather than by prolonged idling.

12. **FUEL PUMP.** Some engines are equipped with double diaphragm fuel pumps with a small sight glass indicator. If the sight glass contains fuel, one of the diaphragms has ruptured. The second diaphragm should continue to operate, supplying fuel to the engine, as this is a back-up feature intended for emergency situations. If a ruptured diaphragm is indicated, the fuel pump should be replaced or repaired prior to the boat getting underway.

Inboard Marine Engine Trouble Shooting

THE GOLDEN RULE to follow in locating engine trouble is not to make more than one adjustment at a time, and to attempt to crank the engine after each adjustment is completed. Consider how the engine operates, and attempt to determine the probable cause of any irregular operation, locating the trouble by the process of elimination. Remember that the cause is usually a simple one, rather than a mysterious and complicated one.

ENGINE WILL NOT TURN OVER - check the battery with a hydrometer or voltmeter. A hydrometer reading of 1.275, or a voltmeter reading of 12-13 volts, will indicate a fully charged battery. If these are not available at the moment, make a test lamp. **DO NOT** short across battery terminals with tools, or solid wire, under any circumstances. A simple test lamp may be made from a double contact 12 volt socket with pigtails or a 110 volt pigtail socket and 25 watt 12 volt bulb. A good battery will produce a bright light. Try to start the engine and observe. If the light does not dim at all, the starter is not being energized. If light goes out instantly, a loose or corroded battery terminal is indicated. If light dims and stays dim after starter switch is released, a weak battery is indicated. **NEVER** do anything that would cause a spark at the battery posts as an explosion could follow by igniting gas that occurs in battery cells under certain conditions.

If the engine doesn't start after the battery has been checked, the trouble may be in the starter switch. Inspect all the electrical connections to ensure that they are tightly secured. Test starter solenoid with a starter jumper, or listen for a clicking sound when starter switch is activated. A test lamp may also be placed across the small terminal and ground of the solenoid. It should light when starter switch is activated. If it does not light, check starter switch by placing a test lamp across the switch terminal and ground. If the test lamp lights, check for broken, loose, or corroded wire between switch and starter solenoid. Check all wiring on solenoid for tightness and condition.

Next, check the pinion gear on the starter motor to see if it is jammed. If the pinion is jammed against the flywheel, it may be freed by loosening the bolts which hold the starter motor to the flywheel housing. Reinstall the starter motor and try to start the engine again.

If the battery is supplying sufficient power to the starter and the engine is turning but will not start, then perhaps there is insufficient fuel. Simple; how-

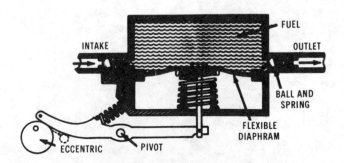

8-9 Gasoline Engine Fuel Pump

ever, lack of fuel is one of the main reasons that most engines won't start - BELIEVE IT OR NOT! If an ample supply of fuel is found, then check the fuel line to make sure that it isn't clogged.

Look at the sediment bowl on the fuel line. It should be filled with gasoline. If it isn't, the fuel line or tank vent may be clogged. Or, the valve on the fuel line may have been closed. Check to see if the valve is in the open position. If the valve is in the open position and the fuel line is clogged, disconnect the fuel line at the fuel pump and blow through the line. If the line is clear, then reconnect it to the fuel pump. Be very careful when performing any function which might allow fuel to spill.

Determine whether or not fuel is reaching the carburetor. Remove the sediment bowl (again, be cautious) from the fuel pump. The screen should be clean so that fuel can pass through it. Reconnect the sediment bowl and try the engine again. If your battery is still holding out (along with your patience), make another test.

been left out too long. Dry the engine out by putting the choke in the "OFF" position and opening the throttle wide; then, with the ignition on, turn the engine over several times. Let's hope that this is the final test and the engine starts.

Before the following tests are started, be absolutely sure there are no fumes present. SAFETY is of prime importance, and the electric shock hazard, particularly in the normally damp environment of an engine compartment, is extremely dangerous. Some engines are now being equipped with capacitor discharge (C-D) ignition systems which raise the secondary voltage as high as 60,000 volts. Since each lead must placed a certain distance from the engine block during these tests, it would not be unreasonable to expect one unaware of the dangers to use his hand in positioning and holding the leads. A simple, inexpensive wooden clothespin which may be hand held or clipped to a bracket is one solution to this problem. It is very important that at least this improvised holder be used if no better protection is

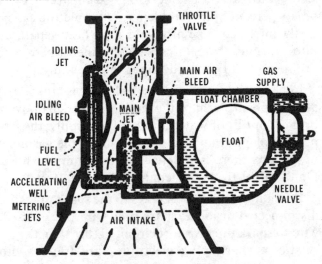

8-10   Float-Type Carburetor

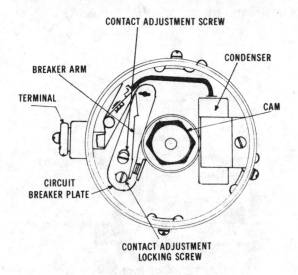

8-11   Distributor

This test is harder. Remove the spark plugs. Note if they are fouled with deposits and feel them to determine if they are wet. If there is no trace of gasoline in the cylinders and the plugs are dry, the carburetor may be out of adjustment, the float level may be too low, the choke may be inoperative, or the jets may be clogged with dirt or gum. Clean out the carburetor with "gunk" or "gum-out". Put it back together again and see if it works. However, if the plugs are wet, the engine is flooded. The automatic choke may need adjustment or the manual choke has

available. Since some engines are equipped with C-D ignition, it should be mentioned that they involve solid state circuits, and correction of a faulty C-D system is best accomplished by replacement of the "black box".

The following tests are for suspected ignition trouble. Ignition trouble is generally suspected when the battery is fully charged and the starter motor is functioning properly but the engine will not start or is running irregularly. WATCH OUT FOR HIGH VOLTAGE.

Remove the wire leading from the high tension terminal of the coil to the distributor. Hold the end of the wire 3/16" from the cylinder head. Turn the engine over, and test for spark. If there is a weak spark or no spark, the trouble might be in the coil or in the distributor. If the spark from the coil is weak after the distributor has been checked, the coil may be defective.

Examine the distributor cap and the breaker points. Check the breaker points, they may be stuck together or even welded together. In an emergency, points can be pried apart with a knife or screwdriver. A weak spark or no spark may be caused by a bad condenser which could result in the points being pitted or welded together from arcing. Again, if the points are replaced, the condenser should also be replaced. While the distributor cap is off, examine it to see if any hairline cracks can be detected. If cracks are found, replace the cap with a new one. This is one of the real starting problem areas. Also check the inside of the distributor cap and the rotor for moisture. Dry them out, as moisture can cause a short.

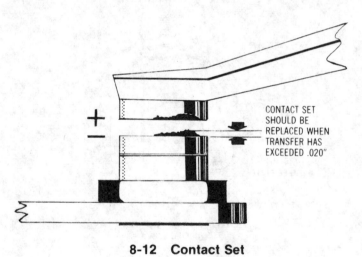

CONTACT SET SHOULD BE REPLACED WHEN TRANSFER HAS EXCEEDED .020"

8-12 Contact Set

If the distributor and coil are found to be satisfactory, individual spark plugs should be tested. Starting with one cylinder at a time, disconnect the spark plug cable and hold the end of the cable about 3/16" from the cylinder head. Turn the ignition on. A starter jumper may be used if there is no emergency switch. A good strong spark should be evident as the engine turns over. If the spark is good, the plug may be cracked or fouled. Check each plug carefully and, if necessary, replace it.

Outboard Marine Engine Trouble Shooting

There are three basic requirements for an outboard engine to function properly:

1. A good mixture of fuel and air;
2. Good compression of this mixture; and
3. A good ignition spark.

If any one of these is not satisfactory, trouble will result. A correct mixture of fuel and air requires that the fuel must be clean and free from sediment and mixed with oil in the correct proportion. The air vent, shut-off valve, and mixture needle valve must all be opened. Be sure the motor is primed and the carburetor is functioning properly. Rings, bearings, etc., will not be discussed, but check the engine carefully to see if there are any leaking gaskets. Check the coil, distributor, spark plugs, distributor cap, breaker points, and wires carefully. Follow the steps given in the check-off list under "Inboard Marine Engine Trouble Shooting."

Complete each step in sequence and, after each step, try to start the engine. Don't be impatient. Over ninety percent of the problems are simple and can be easily corrected. The problems have been separated into various categories. Determine where the problem is and proceed under that heading.

Fuel or mixture trouble - check the gas tank; is the air vent open? Perhaps the engine is flooded or over-primed, or dirt or water is in the fuel supply; the jets may be plugged up; too much oil is in the gasoline; or, finally, there is a defective fuel pump or hose. Don't forget to try the engine after each test.

Ignition trouble - see if wires to the spark plugs are disconnected or loose; spark plug wires are crossed; wire to spark plug is short circuited (break in the insulation); spark plug electrodes are fouled with excess oil or moisture; plugs are improperly gapped; plugs have a break or crack in the jacket or insulator; plugs are dirty; breaker points are improperly gapped; breaker points are fouled with oil; or there are broken or loose wires to the coil or condenser.

If the engine misses, check for a plug shorting on the motor frame or hood, water or oil on wire terminals or spark plug exterior, or badly deteriorated insulation on the wires. Again, try the engine. If it doesn't start, examine the magneto system. Check the setting on the points; look carefully to see if they are pitted or fouled. If they are, replace the points and the condenser. Don't try to save money by not

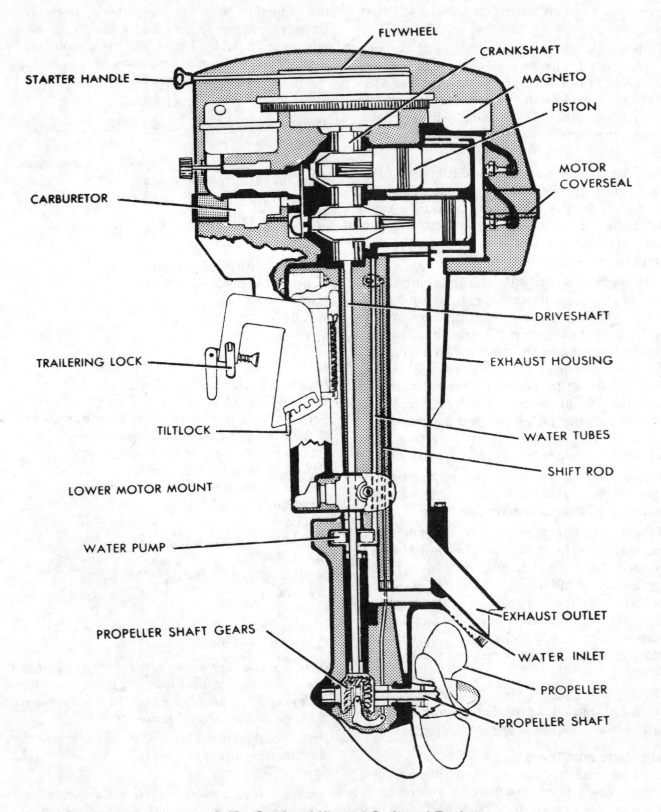

FLYWHEEL

CRANKSHAFT

MAGNETO

PISTON

STARTER HANDLE

MOTOR COVERSEAL

CARBURETOR

DRIVESHAFT

TRAILERING LOCK

EXHAUST HOUSING

TILTLOCK

WATER TUBES

SHIFT ROD

LOWER MOTOR MOUNT

WATER PUMP

EXHAUST OUTLET

PROPELLER SHAFT GEARS

WATER INLET

PROPELLER

PROPELLER SHAFT

8-13 Sectional View of Outboard Engine

replacing the condenser. If the points are bad, the odds are that the condenser is also bad. Examine all wires carefully as a broken or cracked wire will short the engine out.

If the engine will not start, thoroughly examine the carburetor. If there is any dirt in the carburetor, it may result in a fuel mixture which is too lean. Dismantle the carburetor and make sure that the ports are clean, free from dirt, and tight fitting. After checking the carburetor, try starting the engine again.

If the engine will not speed up, it may be overheated. This may be caused by lean mixture or not enough oil in the gas. Check the operator's manual to determine the correct carburetor settings. Follow the manufacturer's instructions carefully and then attempt to crank the engine again.

If the engine still overheats, one or a combination of the following conditions may exist: the lower unit is not deep enough in the water; water circulation is obstructed; or the thermostat is defective. Examine the intake opening or the water pipe connections. Check the water inlet and outlet pipes or jackets carefully to see if they may be obstructed with scale or dirt. How about the propeller? Read the specifications in the operator's manual. If the propeller is too large, it will cause the engine to overheat. One that is too small will cause the engine to overspeed.

If the engine knocks, the spark may be advanced too far or it may be the result of using low-grade gasoline in a high compression engine.

If the engine vibrates excessively, one or more cylinders may not be firing. This may be caused by poor ignition or mechanical failure. A bent or fouled propeller, loose mounting bracket, or loose flywheel will have the same effect. If the engine vibrates and emits large amounts of smoke, the trouble may be in the fuel system. Improper fuel mixture or defective choke operation may be the problem.

Finally, if the engine is hard to turn over, check the oil, determine if the propeller is fouled or if there are parts that are broken or binding.

Spare Parts and Tools

A lot of space has been spent reviewing trouble shooting. Now you must prepare for an emergency by carrying the proper spare parts and tools with which to follow up on the trouble shooting. There are many marine "service stations" now available for the boatman; however, there is always the chance that something will go wrong while you are in an isolated spot or some place where there is no mechanic available. Therefore, it is a good rule to have aboard a few spare parts and some simple tools. We recommend the following:

PARTS

Inboards	Outboards
Spark plugs	Spark plugs
Coil	Starter cord
Fuel filter element and gasket	Shear pins
Fuel pump	Cotter pins
Points and condenser	Propeller
C-D circuit assembly (if applicable)	
Propeller	
Complete distributor or parts	
Generator and starter brushes	
Fuses	
V-belts	
Spare oil	

TOOLS

Standard 6″ screwdriver
Phillips Head 6″ screwdriver
Set of Allen-screw (hexagonal) keys or wrenches
6″ or 8″ open-end adjustable wrench
Pair of common slip-joint pliers
Pair of locking Vice Grip pliers
Pair of electricians pliers with wire cutter
Spark plug wrench
Hammer
Test light, 12-volt
Scout knife
Ignition tools with feeler gauge
Hydrometer
Clothespins
Clean rags and paper towels
Oil can with clean oil

NOTE: The boatman, handy with tools and a pretty respectable mechanic, will do well to add the following tools to his on-board kit. These are in addition to those listed above:

Set of combination open-end and box wrenches in the following sizes: 1/4″, 5/16″, 3/8″, 7/16″, 1/2″, 9/16″, 5/8″, 11/16″.

Socket wrench set with sockets of the same sizes as listed above, and having 3/8″ drive including a ratchet handle.

GENERAL SUPPLIES

In addition to the listed parts, it's a good idea to carry a supply of general materials, often referred to as a "good junk box." With this kind of supplies, you can often improvise some kind of "jury rig" to get a dead engine going, or keep it limping until you reach port without calling for help. In the junk box can be included such items as: tape, cotter-pins, hair-pins, lengths of copper and steel wire, copper tubing, neoprene tubing, electric motor brushes, fuses, nuts, bolts, screws, nails, washers, epoxy cement, jumper cables, small C-clamps, nylon cord, elastic bands, pump packing, Permatex gasket compound.

NOTE: Every boatman should carry operating or manufacturer's manuals for his particular engine and the other equipment aboard.

Fueling

Extremely hazardous conditions are encountered when fueling. Safety rules should be rigidly observed. When taking on gasoline, all engines should be stopped, galley flames extinguished, hatches, windows and ports secured, and electrical devices shut off. Smoking must be forbidden. Diesel fuel, being less flammable, is not as hazardous as gasoline; however, observing the same safety rules is advisable and should contribute to development of "the safety habit."

The gasoline nozzle must contact the filler-pipe deck flange at all times during fueling. This prevents the possibility of explosion caused by the discharge of static electricity. (Similar precautions should be observed when fueling tanks used with outboards.) The filler-pipe deck flange must be connected to the boat's ground system. Static electricity is generated internally throughout the length of the gas hose by the flow of gasoline and by atmospheric conditions. Modern fuel pump equipment has been designed to prevent such discharge and the danger is, therefore, less than in the past. However, safety precautions are still an absolute necessity.

Space must be allowed for fuel expansion; the tank should not be filled to capacity. Approximately five percent should be allowed, based on the average coefficient of fuel expansion. It is not necessary to mathematically compute the fuel expansion; experience can be the controlling factor.

When the fueling operation has been completed, any spillage should be wiped up immediately. Exhaust blowers should be operated for a minimum

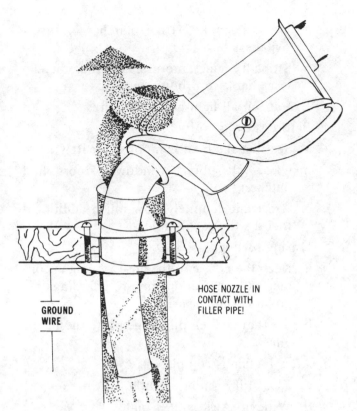

**8-14 Filler-Pipe Deck Flange
with Hose Nozzle**

GROUND WIRE

HOSE NOZZLE IN CONTACT WITH FILLER PIPE!

of five minutes before starting engines. This is sometimes difficult to accomplish when the dock is crowded and other boats are waiting to fuel.

Be thoroughly familiar with the dangers of handling gasoline and the necessary precautions to reduce the risk of fire. Become acquainted with the most effective means of extinguishing a gasoline fire. Gasoline explosions and fires are the leading cause of property damage and one of the significant causes of loss of life and injury on small boats. Gasoline is used as fuel on the majority of boats now in operation, and the boat operator constantly faces the hazards of gasoline fire or explosion.

The following Rules for Fueling are reprinted from a publication of the National Fire Protection Association and should be thoroughly learned by every boat operator:

1. Fuel tanks should be properly installed and vented overboard.

2. Fueling should be completed before dark except in emergencies.

3. Whenever a boat is moored at service dock for fueling:

a. Do not smoke, strike matches or throw switches;

b. Stop all engines, motors, fans and other devices liable to produce sparks;

c. Put out all light and galley fires.

4. Before starting to fuel:

a. See that the boat is moored securely;

b. Close all ports, windows, doors and hatches;

c. Ascertain definitely how much additional fuel the tanks will hold.

5. During fueling:

a. Keep the nozzle of the hose, or can, in contact with the fill opening to guard against possible static spark;

b. See that no fuel spillage gets into the hull or bilges.

6. After fueling is completed:

a. Close fill openings tightly;

b. Wipe up ALL spilled fuel;

c. Open all ports, windows, doors and hatches;

d. Permit boat to ventilate for at least five minutes;

e. See that there is no odor of gasoline in the engine room or below decks before starting machinery or lighting fire. Dangerous vapors will settle to the lowest level of the bilges;

f. Be prepared to cast off mooring lines as soon as engine starts.

NOTE: Portable fuel tanks should never be filled in the boat. Do this on the dock.

Pre-Season Routine Maintenance Outboards

1. IGNITION SYSTEM. Go over the spark plugs and points. Regap, clean, install, and replace if badly worn or pitted. Check the battery with a hydrometer to ensure that it has a full charge. Clean and inspect the battery cables. Check the polarity before connecting the cables to the terminals. Clean and lubricate electric starter drive mechanisms.

2. LUBE OIL SYSTEM. Remove the oil level plug on the lower unit gear case and check for the proper oil level. If the oil is dirty, change it. Remove and clean fuel filter. Clean the carburetor's exterior.

3. METAL SURFACES. Wipe off all surfaces with a clean cloth. Check surfaces for water leaks. When run for the first time, check the operation of the engine's cooling system.

Post-Season Routine Maintenance — Outboards

1. FUEL SYSTEM. With engine operating in fresh water, put oil into the carburetor air intake(s) until the engine starts to smoke heavily. As soon as this happens, stop the engine. Drain the float chamber on the carburetor. Remove and clean the fuel filter bowl. Drain and clean the filter elements. Check all gaskets carefully for wear, breaks, or enlarged cutouts. If in doubt, replace the gasket. Empty and clean the fuel tank.

2. IGNITION SYSTEM. Remove the spark plugs; push the throttle all the way to the stop position. Turn the flywheel over a couple of times manually to pump out any residual water in the cooling system. Clean and lubricate the electric starter. It is recommended that the battery be removed and stored in a dry place. During lay-up, the battery should be charged about once a month. Don't leave it on a constant trickle charge. If the battery is not removed, leave the spark plug terminals disconnected for the winter; this may avoid someone accidently trying to start the engine. Go over the points; if badly worn, replace them. If they are not too badly pitted or worn, then file even, regap, and secure.

3. METAL SURFACES. Wipe all metal surfaces with a lightly oiled rag. This will keep the surfaces from rusting during the winter months. Remove the propeller and lubricate the propeller shaft.

4. LUBRICATION. Drain the lower unit gear case and refill with the lubricant specified by the manufacturer. Consult the owner's manual for other required lubrication.

Pre-Season Routine Maintenance — Inboards

1. FUSE SYSTEMS. Prior to putting the boat in the water, go over the electrical system very carefully. Trace each circuit and develop a wiring diagram. Determine the fuse rating and store several spare fuses of each size in the parts kit. Don't overlook the spare fuses; the fuse box can't be "jury rigged" without the possibility of starting a fire. Put the wiring diagram in a wax sandwich bag so it won't be ruined by moisture.

2. BREAKER POINTS AND CONDENSER. There are special ignition wrenches used to adjust and set the points. These wrenches aren't too expensive and represent a good investment. Before the season starts, check the points carefully for sharp points or pitting. A fine file is needed to smooth off the points and then regap the points. Don't use emery boards or sandpaper on the points; emery dust or sandpaper dust or grit may contribute to difficulties in the electrical circuit. If the contact points are badly worn, replace the points and the condenser. Using the manufacturer's operating manual, set the proper gap. Then test the engine.

3. SPARK PLUGS. Before the season starts, go over the plugs carefully, clean and regap. Replace if badly worn. Refer to the trouble shooting section and follow instructions.

4. CARBURETOR. If the boat has been laid up for the winter and all fuel was not drained, there may be a gum residue in the carburetor. There are numerous commercial carburetor cleaners in spray cans on the market that will help. Check all parts very carefully. Replace worn or broken gaskets.

5. HOLD-DOWN BOLTS. Go over the base of the engine carefully to determine if any of the bolts are loose. This can result in vibration and cause the engine to run improperly. While checking the hold-down bolts, make sure the bolts on the propeller shaft flange coupling are tight. If the boat has been out of water, this coupling was probably loosened to avoid strain. Check stuffing boxes for the propeller shaft and rudder post.

6. FLAME ARRESTERS. Clean and inspect the flame arresters.

7. GENERATOR BELTS. Check the generator belt carefully. If it is frayed or worn, replace it. If loose or too tight, adjust it according to the operator's manual.

8. COOLING SYSTEM. Inspect the water hoses thoroughly. Remove cork plugs and store for use again next winter. Check all clamps; make sure they are tight. Check for leaks. If the hoses are limp or soft, replace them. They may be about to rupture. If water pump is belt-driven, give the belt the same check as generator belt. Check the coolant level in a closed system.

9. BATTERY. Check with a hydrometer to make sure it has the proper specific gravity - that all the cells are good. Clean the terminals and cover with grease. Before connecting the battery cables, check the polarity. The cable lugs and battery terminals are marked (+) and (–) or (POS) and (NEG). Just match them.

10. LUBRICATION. If oil was changed before storage, check the oil level only. If oil was not changed, do so now. Perform all other engine lubrication specified by the manufacturer. Check transmission or gear case for lubricant.

Post-Season Routine Maintenance — Inboards

1. LUBE OIL SYSTEM. Allow the engine to operate in fresh water until it is warm; then drain the oil and replace it with new oil. If the engine has a filter, change and replace it with a new one. Start the engine again and pour engine oil slowly into the carburetor air intake until the engine stalls. Fill all grease cups and lubricate all points specified by the manufacturer.

2. COOLING SYSTEM. Next, drain the water cooling system and, if equipped with a closed system, replace with a half and half mixture of permanent automotive type anti-freeze and water. If raw water cooled, flush with fresh water and drain. Check the water pump carefully for worn gaskets, leaks, cable breaks,

worn hoses, etc. Use cork plugs to drive into the exhaust and cooling water lines.

3. IGNITION SYSTEM. Remove the spark plugs. While they are out for cleaning, regapping, or replacing, squirt a little oil into each cylinder and proceed to turn the engine over a few times. Replace the plugs but don't cinch them down tightly. Don't turn the engine over again until next spring. Use the manufacturer's recommended lubricant on the distributor, starter, and generator. Examine the breaker points and condenser. Check the points for pitting or excess wear. Replace if badly worn or, if not worn too badly, file points until even. As previously mentioned, the points and condenser should be replaced concurrently. Remove the battery and store.

4. FUEL SYSTEM. Drain all fuel from the carburetor and fuel lines. The removal of fuel cuts down the possibility of a fire hazard and the formation of gum or varnish in the fuel system.

5. DRIVE SYSTEM. Drain the transmission and fill it with the proper lubricant. Disconnect the propeller shaft flange. An outdrive gear box should be drained, flushed, and filled with the manufacturer's recommended lubricant.

6. GENERAL. Wipe all the exposed metal surfaces with a lightly oiled rag. This should inhibit rusting during the winter. If the engine has a hood or cover, it should remain on the engine. But don't seal off the engine; it is mandatory that air be allowed to circulate around the engine. Do seal securely the opening at the carburetor intake with strong plastic film or other moisture proof material. On overhead valve engines. remove valve cover and give the entire valve assembly a good oiling.

CHAPTER 9

Marlinspike Seamanship

Introduction

Marlinspike seamanship is the art of handling and working all kinds of fiber, synthetic and wire rope. It includes every variety of knotting, splicing, worming, parceling, serving and fancywork. Marlinspike seamanship has been developed to such an extent that intricate and complicated work in rope can be done to the amazement of the landlubber. Although this is but one of a boatman's skills, excellence in handling line is usually a sign of accomplishment in all fields of boating.

The use of rope aboard vessels has greatly diminished since the days of the clipper ships, but the uses that remain play an important part in the safety of ships and the men who sail them. Think of the damage and injury to a boat and the people on board that could result if the anchor rope were to part on a stormy night because the line had deteriorated through improper stowage. Or, think of the damage that could result if a boat were to be cast adrift during the night because the mooring lines were improperly secured to the cleats. In this chapter, the composition, use and care of rope will be discussed, together with an explanation of some of the more important knots and splices.

Composition of Rope

Rope is manufactured from natural fiber, synthetic materials or wire. Wire rope is little used aboard small craft, therefore this discussion will be confined to natural fiber and synthetic rope. Natural fibers used may be of many types, such as Manila, sisal, hemp, jute, cotton or flax. Of the natural fiber ropes, the best for all around use is Manila. It is used for mooring lines, anchor lines and running rigging such as sheets and halyards. Manila is noted for its strength and durability with a minimum of stretch.

Since Manila fiber is obtained mainly from the Philippine Islands, it is more expensive than many other fibers. A more readily available fiber, sisal, is widely used in place of Manila, although it is inferior to Manila in many ways. The other fibers are used mostly for small lines, lead lines and flag halyards. In recent years, many boatmen have switched from the use of natural fibers to rope manufactured from synthetic materials. These synthetics include nylon, dacron, polyethylene and polypropylene.

Size-for-size, nylon and dacron rope are much stronger than comparable size Manila rope. For this reason, you can use smaller diameter rope in nylon or dacron than can be used in Manila to get the same strength. Both types can be stored when wet without any loss of strength. Nylon and dacron are also resistant to rot, mildew, sunlight and salt water. The use of nylon is desired when strength and stretch go together, such as mooring lines and pendants, anchor lines, towing lines and spring lines. Nylon elongates about 10% at normal working loads, and over 40% up to its breaking strength.

Strength Tables

In the table shown, the weight and strength of the three most popular ropes are listed according to their diameter. In each case, the weight is approximate and the breaking strength is conservative. One should keep in mind that "breaking strength" loads should never be applied deliberately to any rope. Yachtsmen use a safety factor of 5 to 1 to provide maximum safety where lives and property are at stake. To be on the safe side, you should use a rope with a rated breaking strength of FIVE TIMES THE WEIGHT which you intend to lift or pull.

YACHTING ROPES – WEIGHT AND STRENGTH COMPARISON

SIZE Diameter	NYLON (lbs) Weight per 100 ft	lbs Breaking Strength	"DACRON" (lbs) Weight per 100 ft	Lbs Breaking Strength	MANILA (lbs) Weight per 100 ft	Lbs Breaking Strength
¼"	1.7	1,750	2.2	1,300	2.0	600
⅜"	3.5	3,200	4.5	2,850	4.0	1,350
½"	6.6	6,600	7.6	4,900	6.1	2,650
⅝"	10.5	10,200	12.4	7,800	13.1	4,400
¾"	15.0	13,500	19.3	10,780	16.3	5,400
⅞"	20.5	18,500	23.5	14,000	22.0	7,700
1"	27.0	24,000	31.3	17,500	26.5	9,000
1⅛"	34.5	32,000	40.4	23,500	35.2	12,000

Polyethylene and polypropylene ropes have become more and more popular with boatmen. They are characterized by exceptionally good strength both wet and dry, low elasticity and strong resistance to acids, alkalis, water, mildew and rot. Polypropylene is used often as a water-ski tow rope because it floats on the water.

How Rope is Made and Measured

In the manufacture of rope, the fibers are twisted together in one direction to form yarns, and the yarns are twisted together in the opposite direction to form strands. The strands are then twisted together in the original direction to form the finished rope. Occasionally, cable rope will be made, which consists of three or four ropes twisted together in the opposite direction. The final direction of the rope is known as the lay of the rope, and is described as either right-laid or left-laid.

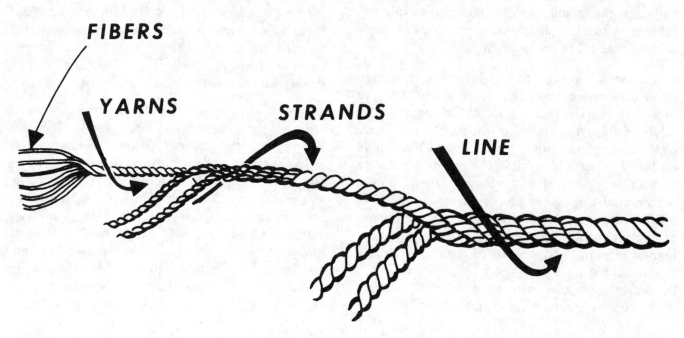

FIBERS
YARNS
STRANDS
LINE

9-1 Composition of a Line

The general term for cordage is *rope*. It becomes line only when it is put to use on a boat. However, there are a few exceptions where it is in use on a vessel and is still called rope. Such variances include bell ropes, bolt ropes, man ropes and dip ropes, among others. To call a sailor's mooring lines "ropes" is to immediately brand yourself as a landlubber of the worst order.

Fiber rope is correctly measured by its circumference. However, most marine suppliers prefer to measure it by its diameter. Most pleasure boatmen have also followed this practice. On the other hand, wire rope is always measured by its diameter. Small diameter fiber rope is known as small stuff, and is designated by size according to the number of yarns it contains. Yarns are called threads when referring

9-2

to small stuff. For example, 6 thread small stuff is made up of six yarns of fiber twisted together. Small stuff is frequently used for seizing when whipping line.

Care of Fiber Line

Your efforts in caring for fiber line aboard your boat will be repaid in greater safety and longer life. Whenever natural fiber rope is uncoiled from a new coil or when a quantity of rope is taken off a coil, there is a procedure you can follow that will avoid making kinks in the rope. The coil is placed upright so that the end of the rope inside the hole in the coil is at the bottom of the hole. The end is then taken up through the hole and the desired quantity of rope is drawn off. New synthetic fiber rope is handled in a different manner. Normally, synthetic rope is received on a reel and should be rolled off, not uncoiled. If these procedures are not followed, there will be a kink in the rope for each turn taken off the coil or reel. Kinks should always be taken out of a rope whenever they occur. By putting a strain on the rope, a kink can be made to disappear but the rope will be badly weakened by the breaking down of the fibers at the point where the kink occurred.

For easy, seaman-like handling, each length of rope should be taped temporarily at both ends with marine tape when cut from the original coil or reel and permanently whipped with nylon whipping cord at the earliest opportunity.

Rope that is not being used should be stowed in a dry well-ventilated place to prevent accumulation of moisture and resultant rot. Lines should be stowed on shelves or gratings off the deck and other material should not be stowed on top of them. Natural fiber lines are most susceptible to damage from moisture. Manila line, for instance, should be washed off with fresh water after salt water use and thoroughly dried before being stowed. Synthetic fiber lines such as nylon may be stowed when wet but this practice introduces unpleasant dampness below. All lines should be kept away from exhaust pipes and battery acids.

A fiber line should never be overworked or overstrained. Although it may not show it, the line may be seriously weakened due to breakdown of the fibers. A good way of checking for deterioration of a line is to look at the inside of the line. If there is a noticeable accumulation of grayish powdery material the line should be replaced. Another indication is a decrease in the diameter of a weakened line. Natural fiber lines will contract if they become wet or damp. A line secured at both ends will become taut during rainy weather and may become badly overstrained unless the line is loosened. This is particularly true of mooring lines and flag halyards, which should be slacked off if they become taut because of rain or dampness. It is good practice to wrap your mooring lines with canvas chafing gear where they pass through the chocks. Anchor line, too, should be protected from chafing and rubbing.

To obtain the maximum use of a line and at the same time maintain safety, it is a good idea to turn a line end-for-end periodically. Anchor ropes or boat falls, where one end of the line usually has all the strain put on it, are good examples of lines

Uncoiling Fiber Rope

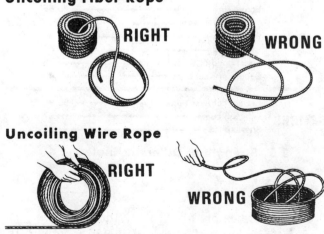

RIGHT WRONG

Uncoiling Wire Rope

RIGHT WRONG

9-2 Uncoiling Rope

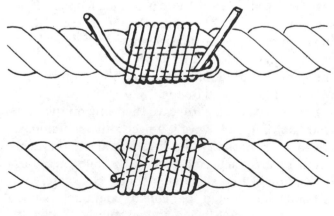

9-3 Temporary Whipping

9-3

which should be reversed from time to time. Never leave the end of a line dangling loose without a whipping to prevent it from unlaying. Unless protected, it will begin to unlay of its own accord. To prevent fraying, a temporary plain whipping can be put on with anything, even a rope yarn or a piece of friction tape.

Making Up Line

All line on board your boat should be stowed neatly when not in use. How you stow the line depends on its ultimate use. There are three methods of making up line—coiling, faking and flemishing. Line that is to be stowed in a compartment or locker should be coiled and made up, or stopped off with small stuff. Right-laid rope should be coiled right-handed (clockwise) and left-laid rope should be coiled left-handed (counterclockwise).

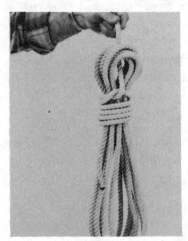

9-4   Line Ready for Stowing

Lines that are made up for a fast runoff such as mooring lines, heaving lines, and running rigging, may be faked down if there is sufficient room. Faking down consists of laying the line in coils either in a figure eight fashion or with each fake lying clear of the next. Faking down leaves the line in the most advantageous position for running out without fouling or kinking.

Some boatmen like to leave their line on the deck when not in use. To give it a neat, ornamental look, it can be flemished. The line is laid on the deck like a spring, each coil circling the one preceding it. Right-laid line should be coiled clockwise, and left-laid line should be coiled counterclockwise. To tighten the coils when you are finished, lay both hands flat on the line at the center and twist in the

direction the coils are laid, thus forming a tight mat. It should be noted here that a beautifully flemished line should not be left on a varnished surface for any length of time, especially overnight. The trapped moisture will spoil a good varnished finish.

Knots, Bends and Hitches

Among boatmen, the landsman's all-inclusive term "knot" gives way to provide more specific meaning, and includes bends and hitches. Each knot, bend or hitch serves best in a particular circumstance and is practically worthless in other situations. To meet your needs a good knot must display certain characteristics. It must hold well without slipping. If it is to be used for practical purposes and not serve as an ornament, it should be easy to tie. The superior knot is one that possesses these advantages and is easy to untie as well.

Most of the knots, bends and hitches that you will need to know in the normal operation of your craft are listed and illustrated below. While we could have added many more, they would seldom be used. It is far better to have a good knowledge of a few commonly used knots than to have a superficial knowledge of a great number of seldom used knots. Those illustrated here are functional, will serve almost every purpose, and are as easy to untie as they are to tie.

How Knots and Splices reduce strength of rope

		%EFF
	Normal rope	100%
	Anchor or Fisherman's bend	76
	Timber hitch	70-65
	Round turn	70-65
KNOTS	Two half-hitches	70-65
	Bowline	60
	Clove hitch	60
	Sheet bend or Weaver's knot	55
	Square or Reef knot	45
SPLICES	Eye splice (over thimble)	95-90
	Long splice	87
	Short splice	85

9-5   Strength of Different Knots

Square Knot (Reef Knot)

The square knot, also called the reef knot, is used to join lines of equal diameter together. It should never be used to join unequal lines as it will slip. The square knot is employed for a multitude of purposes, and is so versatile on boats that it is sometimes referred to as the sailor's knot. We should, however, include the caution that the square knot should not be used to tie lines which will be subjected to heavy loads. The square knot has a serious disadvantage in that it will "tumble" when placed under heavy strain and, in this condition, is almost impossible to untie.

9-6 Square Knot

9-7 Becket

Sheet Bend (Becket Bend)

The sheet bend, also known as the becket bend, is used for tying two lines together. This bend will securely hold two lines together even if the lines are of unequal sizes. It is comparatively easy to untie even after having been subjected to heavy strain for long periods of time. When used on a tow line, the free ends should be stopped down with twine for maximum security. The lighter line should be "bent" around the heavier line. An extra turn can be taken around the heavier line for extra security. When this is done, the bend is known as a double sheet bend, or double becket bend. The double sheet bend is also suitable for attaching a line to an eye.

Clove Hitch

The clove hitch is used to tie a line temporarily to a pile or bollard. It is easy to tie and is reasonably secure for short periods of time. Many boat-

AROUND ONCE,   **AND OVER AND AROUND AGAIN,**   **BACK DOWN AND THRU**

DROP OVER BITT

9-8 Clove Hitch

men make doubly sure by adding a half hitch to the standing part. When wet, the clove hitch may be difficult to untie.

Anchor Bend (Fisherman's Bend)

The anchor bend, also called the fisherman's bend, is simple to tie and is extremely strong. It will not slip or jamb and is easily untied, even if it has been subjected to a great strain. It is used to tie a line to an anchor ring, a buoy or a spar. To prevent the bend from working loose, a second half-hitch is sometimes taken around the standing part, or the end is seized back to the line with small stuff.

Bowline

The bowline is known as the king of knots because it is easy to tie, will not slip nor jam, and

is as easy to untie as it is to tie. Basically, the bowline forms a secure loop at the end of a line. This loop can be used in a wide variety of ways. The loop can be placed over a post or bollard as a moor-

ANCHOR BEND

ANCHOR BOWLINE

9-9 Anchor Bend and Anchor Bowline

ing line. It can be used to tie to an anchor ring. Heavy lines are often tied together by using a bowline on the end of each line, with the loops passing through each other. By passing the standing part of the line through the loop, a free running noose can be made. A bowline, properly tied, will not slip, nor does it pinch or kink the line as much as many other knots.

9-10 Bowline

Figure Eight

The figure eight is principally used as a stopper knot. It is placed at the end of a line to keep it from running through a block or other opening. The figure eight can also be used temporarily in place of whipping to keep a line from unraveling.

Two Half-hitches

Two half-hitches are very easy to tie and are used most often to secure a line to a ring, spar, post or bollard. This hitch is not as popular as the clove hitch although it displays approximately the same characteristics. It is more easily untied than the

9-11 Figure Eight Knot

clove hitch. Note that this knot consists of a turn around the fixed object and a clove hitch over the standing part of the line. Two half-hitches are better than a clove hitch when permanence is desired.

9-12   Two Half Hitches

Belaying a Cleat

Securing a line to a cleat is one of the most common procedures in docking a boat and yet it is frequently done improperly. The correct method is to lead the line in one round turn around the base of the cleat and then to form at least one figure eight around the horns of the cleat. Secure the line with a half-hitch over one horn of the cleat. One caution - be sure to have the line figure-eighting over the cleat when the half-hitch is made. Do not make the error of having the last loop come along the side of the cleat instead of crossing over. This fastening may also be referred to as a "half-hitch on a cleat" or as a "cleat-hitch".

9-13   Belaying a Cleat

Splices

Splices are used for permanently joining or marrying two lines together, making a loop in the end of a line, or finishing off the end of a line.

The Back Splice

When a line has been cut, a back splice can be woven into the end to prevent unraveling. The back splice is started with a crown knot, and finished off by tucking the left-over strands over and under the strands in the main part of the line. Be sure to burn the ends of each strand of synthetic rope before attempting any splicing to prevent unraveling of the ends. It is also a good idea to whip the ends of strands of manila or other natural fiber ropes for the same reason.

The Short Splice

Lines are short-spliced together when a slight enlargement of the diameter of the line is not a matter of importance. The only trick in short splicing is in seizing the ends together so that each strand in one end lies along the corresponding strand in the other end. After unlaying the strands, you simply butt the two ends against each other until you see that they are interlaced correctly. Once your seizing is on, tuck over and under the same way you finish off an eyesplice. Three tucks on either side of the seizing are enough.

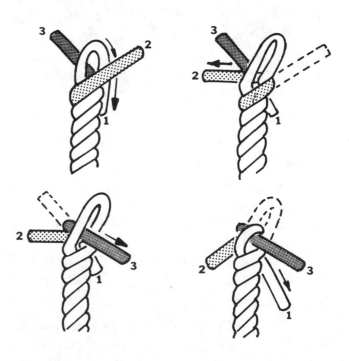

9-14   Crown Knot

9-15 Splices

The Eye Splice

When a permanent loop in the end of a line is desired, such as a mooring line, an eyesplice is used. To make an eyesplice, unlay the strands of the line and splice them into the standing part of the line by tucking the unlaid strands from the end of the line into the standing part. An original round of tucks plus two more complete rounds is enough for any ordinary eye splice in natural fiber line such as Manila. An extra tuck should be made when splicing nylon line because of its smoothness and stretch.

Illustration 9-16 shows the proper steps in making an eye splice.

The Lead Line

A lead line is a line which has been marked in such a manner that it can be used to measure the depth of the water. The line is weighted with a "lead" which should weigh at least five pounds for depths of 100 feet. Ideally, the line should be braided cotton, 150 to 200 feet long. Seamen have a system of marking the line with strips of leather or cloth, or by knots. These markings are as follows:

2 fathoms	2 strips of leather
3 fathoms	3 strips of leather
5 fathoms	strip of white cottonrag
7 fathoms	strip of red woolen rag
10 fathoms	strip of leather with a hole in it
13 fathoms	same as 3 fathoms
15 fathoms	same as 5 fathoms
17 fathoms	same as 7 fathoms
20 fathoms	2 knots
25 fathoms	1 knot
30 fathoms	3 knots
35 fathoms	1 knot
40 fathoms	4 knots

(and so on)

These markings are not in widespread use among recreational boatmen. Any markings used should be easily remembered and able to be read quickly. It is for this reason that many marine dealers feature lead lines with plastic strips attached, on which the depth is marked in easy-to-read figures. These lead lines require no memorizing of marks and are marked in single fathoms up to ten fathoms.

In practice, the lead is cast forward with an underhand swing while the boat is proceeding under very slow headway. The speed should be slow enough that the lead will reach the bottom by the time the line stands vertically. The vertical distance from the waterline to the hand of the person casting the lead should be known. The mark which is

A.—First step is to unlay the end of the rope for a short distance.

B.—Form the desired size loop. Take middle strand of unlayed end and tuck through any strand of the "standing" part of the rope. Take adjacent strand marked "**B**" in picture. Pass over strand under which "**A**" is tucked, then pass under adjacent strand of the "standing" part.

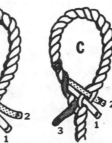

C.—Tuck remaining strand through last strand of the "standing" part of the rope, on other side.

D.—Tuck each strand alternately over and under, working against the lay of the rope. Taper off by halving the yarns on the last two tucks.

E.—Pound and roll. Then cut off remaining strands close to the rope.

9-16 Making an Eye Splice

held in the hand is read and the distance to the water is deducted from this figure.

9-17 Lead Line

The Armed Lead

Some leads have a hollowed-out portion on the bottom of the lead which can be "armed" with a quantity of tallow or bedding compound. In a pinch, a wad of chewing gum can be used although you may have difficulty in getting it to stick to the lead. Using this procedure, a sample of the bottom can be brought up. In most cases the character of the bottom is shown on your chart. By having a sample of the bottom, you may be able to further identify your position, especially in conditions of reduced visibility when no landmarks are in sight.

The Heaving Line

On small craft, a heaving line will seldom be used. Nevertheless, the well found boat will always have a heaving line aboard. A heaving line is made up of a small line (50 to 60 ft long) with a weight at one end. This weight can be a "monkey's fist" (an intricate woven knot which surrounds a weight), a soft rubber ball which has been drilled and the end of the line pulled through it, or a small chamois or canvas sand bag. The purpose of the weight is to enable the end of the heaving line to be heaved out to its full length. A heaving line is not a weapon, although, if not carefully used, it can sometimes cause as much damage as a weapon. It is for this reason that the weight should not be any heavier than necessary to carry the line out to its full length. The heaving line is made up in loose coils, arranged for free running. The line is carried in both hands with approximately half of the line in each hand. It is thrown with a strong underhand swing.

In practice the heaving line is used as a messenger to send a heavier line ashore or to another boat. It is seldom necessary to use a heaving line when approaching a pier or float. There may be instances when circumstances will not permit a boat to approach a pier close enough to heave a mooring line ashore. In these cases the necessary extra distance can generally be spanned by using a heaving line. On small craft the heaving line is most often used when passing a line from one boat to another when sea conditions make a close approach dangerous. The heaving line is heaved *over* the deck of the other craft. The weighted end of the heaving line should splash into the water on the far side of the other boat. All too many heaving lines have been thrown through the windshield or through the side window of other craft. This is not only dangerous but it seldom, if ever, favorably impresses the owner of the other boat. Do not attempt to cast a heaving line directly at another person. It could strike him and injure him although, if thrown directly at another person, it will generally fall short. To repeat, heave the line completely over the other boat. In this way it will not matter if it is thrown too far, and it will be relatively simple for the operator of the other boat to grasp.

Dipping the Eye

Sometimes two lines, with eye splices, are to be placed on one bollard. If the two eyes are simply dropped over the bollard, it may not be possible to remove the first line until the second one has been taken off. To avoid this problem, bring the end of the eye of the second line up through the eye of the first line and then drop it over the bollard. By doing this either line may be removed first with no problem developing.

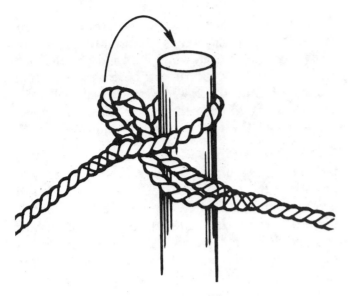

9-18 Dipping the Eye

Tow Lines

It is a tradition among seamen that a vessel in distress is not left to fend for herself. If you encounter a vessel in trouble afloat, you are morally bound to render all possible assistance without placing your boat or your crew in danger by doing so. This assistance may be limited to standing by until other help arrives but, in most cases, it involves towing the other boat to a safe mooring or anchorage.

The business of towing another boat is relatively simple if a few precautions are observed. The often-heard statement that you should insist on using the other fellow's towline is absurd. "Sea lawyers" who insist on using a towline of unknown capabilities are generally asking for trouble. You know (or should know) the condition of your lines, and you are usually well advised to use equipment you can trust. Remember that *when you take another boat in tow you assume full responsibility for this boat and all hands aboard.* If, as the result of your "assistance," the other boat is left in worse condition than it was before you touched it, you could be held legally liable. For this reason, it is simply not wise to ever tie a line to a sinking boat. Take the persons off but don't tie a line to it. If this boat sinks on the end of your towline, you might not be held responsible, but then again, you might be.

Towing equipment consists of a towline, a bridle, a short length of smaller line, and a heaving line.

A bridle is a short line (usually three times the width of your transom) with an eye splice on both ends. If possible, the bridle should be attached to the boat forward of the rudder post. In practice, the eyes of the bridle are generally placed over the stern cleats. The towline is made fast to the bridle. This centers the tow and makes it much easier to control.

The diameter of line used for the bridle will depend on what your cleats can accommodate. Needless to say, the cleats should be sturdy enough to handle a considerable strain without breaking or pulling out from the deck. If you doubt the strength of your cleats, don't use them for towing. Attach the line to something you can trust.

The size of the towline will depend on a variety of conditions. Your choice is limited to what you have aboard. If you doubt the ability of a line to handle a tow, don't use it. Sea conditions and the weight of the distressed vessel are most important.

9-19 A Towing Bridle

On many small boats, the cleats and chocks are small in size and are often attached with screws without a doubler under the deck. In these circumstances, it is possible to pull out the cleats, chocks or part of the deck. If the stem ring is bolted through (not merely installed with screws), it can often be used for towing, although in some cases the ring will not stand the strain of a long tow. If you are suspicious about the condition of the cleats or stem ring on the distressed vessel, it might be well to go aboard (with their permission) and inspect these items personally. In extreme cases, it may be necessary to pass a sling completely around the other boat, with the towline attached to the sling.

A towline should be in excellent condition and large enough for the task. If you have a choice, always use the heavier line for additional safety. If the towline is too large for the cleat of the towed vessel, double up a smaller line and attach it to the end of the towline.

A nylon towline is preferred over Manila because of its higher strength and shock-absorbing elasticity. However, a word of caution concerning towlines should be inserted at this point. All lines have a rated breaking strength and will part suddenly when over-strained. If a towline parts under strain it can snap back in either direction like a whip. Because of the elasticity of nylon line, this potential danger is greater with a nylon towline than with Manila. The towline should never be over-strained deliberately, and it is good practice to keep persons clear of the stern when you have another boat in tow. This is also true of the towed boat, and persons should be advised to keep clear of the towline on the bow.

Towing

While towing, keep the boats far enough apart to allow the towline to assume a long smooth curve which can act as a spring. Adjust the length of the towline so that both boats are climbing and descending waves together. Unless this is done, the line will be alternately slack and taut, which severely strains the line. If the towed boat is descending while the towing boat is climbing a wave, the tow-line will come up with a dangerous snap when

the relative positions of the boats on the waves are reversed. This condition is almost always present when towing in a following sea. In some following seas, the only way a boat can be towed is to trail a drogue behind the towed vessel which will offer sufficient drag to keep the tow from surfing down the waves of the following sea.

Most boatmen make the mistake of towing too fast. Towing should be done at a speed which will not strain the towing gear or fastenings and still permit complete control. In many cases, the rudder of the towed boat should be placed amidships and tied down in this position since most attempts to steer a tow do more harm than good. If the towed boat begins to yaw (swinging from one side to another on the towline) it could easily capsize. Yawing *must* be stopped as soon as it develops. This can usually be controlled by either trimming the towed boat well aft by moving as much weight as possible toward the stern or trailing a good sized drogue behind the towed boat. In some cases, it will be necessary to trim the towed boat aft and rig a drogue in order to control the tendency of the tow to yaw.

Once you get the tow into sheltered waters of a marina or harbor, you should slow down and shorten up the towline. Most powerboat operators in trouble claim "engine failure" as the cause of their problem. It's amazing how often a few gallons of fuel will "cure" their troubles. Your responsibility for this tow ends when you have her safely tied to a pier or float, so your best bet is to head for the nearest fuel float. Come up to the float slowly and have one of your crew simply step off with the towline in hand. Standing on the float, he can pull the towed boat in hand-over-hand. Unless you have experience in landing with a boat in tow, do not try to be too fancy in making your landing. The method described may not impress onlookers but it will do the job with the least amount of fuss. Additionally, it is guaranteed to work—every time!

CHAPTER 10

Sailing

Large or small, old or new, simple or complicated — all sailboats respond in the same basic ways to the forces of wind and water. By learning the principles of sailing, you can take a giant step toward handling any sailboat with skill and safety. The information presented here is, however, only an introduction to the sport of sailing: Having mastered it, you'll still be a beginning sailor.

As a novice skipper, you'll be well advised to continue your sailing education, both on the water and in the classroom. By all means go sailing — it's the best way to improve your skills, the best way to put principles and theory into practical use. But bear in mind that, at this stage, you should be extra careful. Following these simple rules will help you get the most fun from sailing:

1. Always check the weather before setting out: Get a *marine* weather forecast that's up to date. If bad or even unsettled weather is predicted, don't go — there'll be another day.

2. Never sail alone: Like skindiving solo, sailing single-handed exposes you to extra hazards and difficulties. If possible, crew for a more experienced sailor; don't be afraid to ask him or her what's going on, if you don't understand. If you sail with another beginner, take turns steering and handling the sails.

3. Select a proper boat: You can learn to sail in virtually any kind of craft, but some boats are better for learning than others. The ideal boat for most beginners is a single-masted vessel of 16-20 feet in length (assuming a crew of two or three). It should have a place to stow safety and other gear (often under the forward deck), and it should be equipped with built-in flotation, so that in case of capsize or swamping it'll stay afloat and support the crew as well.

10-1   Offshore Cruiser-racers

10-2   Daysailer

4. Make sure your boat is properly equipped. The average daysailer (boat without a cabin) needs little gear, and here are the essentials: Coast Guard-approved personal flotation device for each person aboard (a buoyant vest will do, but if you're serious about your sailing, consider one of the specially-designed vests for sailors, which allow more freedom of movement than the standard model, while providing just as much buoyancy); paddles or oars, in case the wind doesn't blow; bucket and/or pump for bailing (a sponge for getting up the last drops is a good extra); waterproof packet of distress signals — orange smoke, night flares, distress flag; anchor, and line. Finally, make sure you do your practice sailing out of the main channels, away from waterskiers and fishermen. Others will appreciate your courtesy, and you'll have a better time.

Parts of the Boat

The most important element in any boat is the hull, the container that supports the crew and their gear. While most small sailboat hulls don't have the added necessity of holding up a large engine and fuel system, they do need to provide relative stability against the heeling (tipping) forces imposed by the wind on mast and sails. There are three main ways of achieving hull stability:

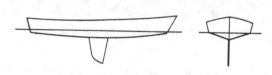

10-3   Vee-bottom Hull

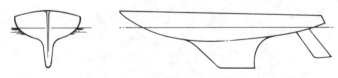

10-4   Ballast Keel Hull

1. Hull shape: a wide, flat- or vee-bottomed hull has what's called *initial stability* — its tendency is to stay on an even keel, because of its shape. To keep it from slipping sideways (called "making leeway") a fin-shaped keel is attached to the bottom. If the keel is retractable, it's called a *centerboard* or *daggerboard*.

2. Ballast counterweight: to balance the weight aloft, and the wind pressure on the sails, the keel may have cast into it a heavy metal weight, usually lead or iron. The lower the weight, the more effective the ballast keel. Heavily ballasted boats are often rounded in cross-section, as this is an easier shape to drive through the water.

3. Live ballast: In smaller boats, the crew shifts from side to side to supplement or replace ballast and/or hull shape support. Most boats sail best when heeled only slightly, and the crew *hikes out* to a greater or lesser degree to keep the boat on her feet. When not hiking out, the crew sits in the cockpit, a recess in the deck with a raised edge (the coaming) that keeps out spray.

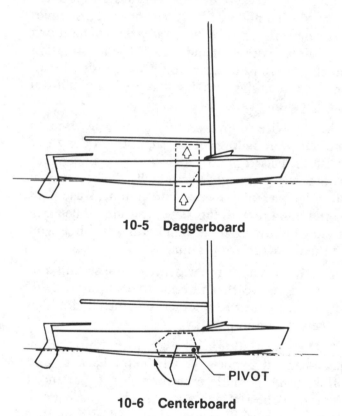

10-5   Daggerboard

10-6   Centerboard

A small sailboat's cockpit isn't very roomy, and often the crew must share it with the centerboard or daggerboard *trunk* — the watertight casing in which the board rests when raised. A centerboard is pivoted, as in the illustration, at its forward end, while the simpler daggerboard is raised up and down in its slot. Obviously, a boat with either type of board can operate in much shallower water than can a boat with a fixed keel — but with the board all the way up, a boat under sail tends to slide downwind almost out of control.

Most small sailboats are steered by a simple tiller—rudder combination. The rudder is hinged to the boat's transom (in smaller craft), and the tiller is just a lever to increase the power of the helmsman's muscles. In some boats, where the helmsman hikes out, there's a tiller extender to add inches to his reach.

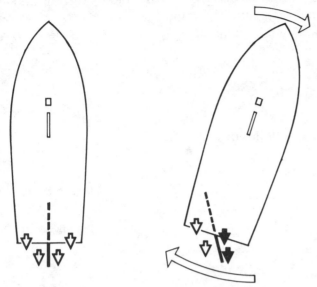

10-7   Tiller Action and Boat Heading

The tiller works as shown in the illustrations. All you need to remember is that pushing the tiller to the boat's *port* side makes the bow swing to *starboard,* and vice versa: Move the tiller away from the

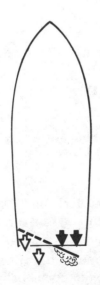

10-8   Rudder Drag Changes Heading

direction in which you want the boat to go. After an hour or two, it becomes second nature.

The Sails

A vessel can operate efficiently with anywhere from one to a couple of dozen sails. Most beginners' boats, however, have either one or two sails, the *mainsail* and the *jib.* Each, as you can see, is triangular in shape, and the main parts of each have the same names. Many sailors find it helpful to stencil *head* and *clew* on the appropriate corner of their sails.

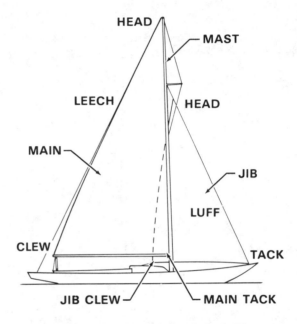

10-9   Corners of Main and Jib

While the mainsail is normally larger than the jib, this isn't the case on all boats. The mainsail's leach is extended by strips of wood or plastic — the *battens* — while the jib is normally without battens, especially if it overlaps the mast.

Both sails are raised by lines called *halyards* that run through pulleys and back down to cleats on deck. The mainsail, once raised, is controlled by another line called the *mainsheet,* usually made fast near the sail's clew. The jib has two sheets, one on each side of the mast, leading aft to cleats alongside the cockpit.

Most sails today are made of Dacron, an artificial fiber that is very strong and resists rot. Dacron sails require minimum maintenance, but it's a good idea to wash them at least once a year (in mild detergent and warm water) and have your sailmaker check them over for wear and tear once a season.

The Spars and Rigging

Obviously, cloth sails need a rigid framework to hold them up and extend them to the wind. Light wood or metal *spars* form this frame — the vertical mast and, hinged to it by a universal joint, the horizontal boom combine to extend two sides of the mainsail. While the sail itself may be fastened just at head, tack and clew, its foot and luff are usually set into grooves in the boom and mast respectively.

boat, where they are made fast to chainplates, which distribute the load to the sides of the boat.

All these wires — the stays and shrouds — are known collectively as *standing rigging*. Their purpose is to keep the mast standing straight against the many stresses imposed upon it. In complex boats, there may be many pieces of standing rigging, and in the very simplest sailing surfboards, there is no standing rigging at all — the mast is set into a

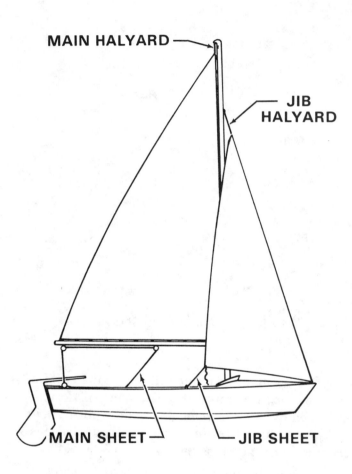

10-10   Sheets and Halyards

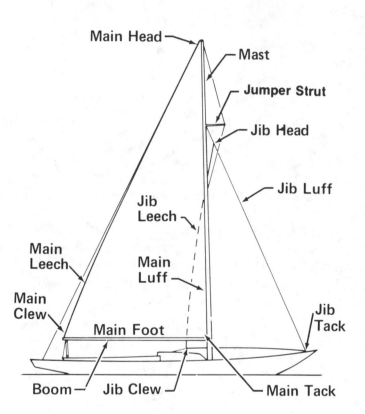

10-11   Nomenclature of a Sloop Rigged Daysailer

The jib is not attached to any spar, but is snapped with special fittings to the *forestay,* a taut wire running upward from the bow to keep the mast from falling or bending backward.

Other stainless steel wires support the mast in other directions — a backstay (not always found in smaller boats) counteracts the pull of the forestay. Shrouds run from the masthead to the sides of the

reinforced hole in the deck, and is strong enough to keep upright without stays or shrouds.

Here, then, is the complete boat, ready to sail. Most of today's popular daysailers have a fairly close resemblance to this open-cockpit *sloop* (a boat with one mast and two basic sails). Some boats are more complex in their rig, and some are markedly simpler. On the next page are a few other types of boats you may see on American waters.

10-12　Sailboard

**10-13　Catboat
Sloop in Foreground**

Essentially a surfboard with a mast and sail, this is about as simple a boat as one can find. Its type of sail is called *lateen,* and was invented by Arab sailors in the Mediterranean. While very fast and much fun to sail, boardboats like this one require very quick reactions and frequently capsize. They can be easily righted, however, often in a matter of seconds.

The native American catboat originated as a working fishing boat well over a hundred years ago. Its single sail is called a *gaff rig,* because of the extra spar — the gaff — which extends the upper edge of the sail. It is an easy boat to sail in gentle winds, but can be demanding in breezes over 10 or 15 miles per hour.

When individual sails get too big to handle, the obvious thing to do is divide them up into more sails, as on this *ketch,* a popular type of cruising boat. Other two-masted boats include the *yawl* and *schooner.*

10-14　Ketch

10-5

10-15 Catamaran

Some sailors prefer two-hulled catamarans, like this one. The rig is a variety of catboat, but the twin hulls are very narrow and easy to drive through the water, allowing high potential speeds. The crew sits in a canvas or webbing trampoline between the hulls, steering with a crossbar linked to double rudders.

Wind

Whatever the boat's shape or rig, it uses the same fuel — wind. Defined generally as *air in motion*, wind for the sailor is two different things, *true wind* and *apparent wind*.

True, or geographic, wind is what you feel when standing in one fixed place ashore. True wind direction is registered ashore on flags, on weathervanes, or on sophisticated instruments.

Apparent wind, which is what a rider feels in a moving vehicle, is a combination of true wind force and direction, and the force and direction of the wind caused by the vehicle's motion. Let's break that definition down a bit more, by use of an example or two.

On a windless day, you set out from shore in a motorboat moving at 10 miles per hour. If you put your head up over the windshield, you'll feel a 10-mile-per-hour wind blowing directly in your face — but if you throttle back, the wind drops. This is a false wind, caused by the boat moving through the air — not air moving past an unmoving boat.

Later in the day, a north wind of 5 miles per hour springs up, and you head your motorboat, at 10 MPH, directly into it. Put your head over the windshield and you'll feel a wind of 15 MPH: the true wind of 5, plus false wind of 10. Now turn and run in the opposite direction: The apparent wind drops off to 5 MPH: false wind of 10, minus true wind of 5.

So far so good, but with sailboats it's often more complicated. If you are sailing with the true wind

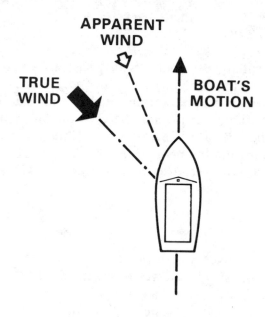

10-16 True and Apparent Wind

coming at right angles to your boat, and a false wind equal to your boat's speed coming over the bow, the apparent wind will be coming from somewhere between the two, stronger than either true or false wind.

There are ways of figuring out the exact strength and direction of apparent wind, but it's really not necessary. Just remember that what you feel in a moving boat is not the wind people are feeling

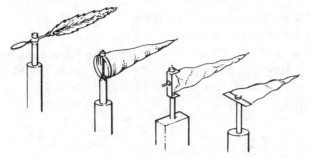

10-17 Types of Masthead Wind Vanes

ashore. To find apparent wind direction, most sailors use a masthead wind vane, like the ones shown, or a strip of light cloth about halfway up the shrouds. Be sure that your wind vane is not blanketed by the sails or by another boat.

Beating

Ancient sailing vessels nearly always sailed more or less directly before the wind, yet modern sailboats can head to within 45° of the direction from which the true wind is blowing. Because of the effect of apparent wind, it often feels as if your boat is sailing almost directly into the wind.

How is this possible? Basically, what happens is that the sail which acted like a wall when the boat was running now behaves like an airplane's wing. Looked at from above, a sail's shape is not unlike a side view of an airplane wing. As many people know, an airplane is held up — lifted — not by the air underneath its wings, but by the air passing over the curved upper surface.

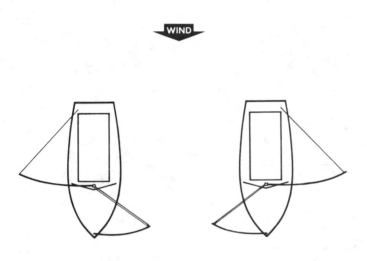

**10-18 Running:
Wind From Dead Astern**

**10-19 Air Pressure On a Sail
When Beating**

Running

It's easy to understand how a boat can sail with the wind astern, as in the diagram. With the boom fully extended to one side or the other, the sail simply obstructs the wind; the boat is pushed forward. Because of wind eddies off the mainsail, the jib often flutters helplessly when a boat is running. If the jib will stand out on the opposite side to the main (sailing *wing-and-wing,* it's called), you may be able to add a bit of speed. This kind of sailing is called *running.*

The air blowing over the convex wing or sail creates a partial vacuum (for reasons too complex to go into here), and the wing or sail is lifted up and forward — carrying the plane or boat along. The lifting force operates most strongly in the forward third of the sail's area, and the lift itself is at right angles to the sail at any given point. Therefore, only part of the lifting impetus presses the boat forward, while much of the force urges the boat sideways. Because the underwater shape of a sailboat hull is designed to take maximum advantage of forward pressure, while at the same time resisting sideways pressures, the boat moves forward — into the wind. This kind of sailing is called *beating,* or sailing *close-hauled* (because the boom is hauled as close in to the boat's centerline as possible).

Anytime a boat is not beating or running, it is said to be *reaching*. There are three kinds of reaches — a close reach, when the apparent wind is coming from forward of amidships; a beam reach, when the apparent wind is at right angles to the boat; and a broad reach, when the wind is coming from aft of amidships. In most reaching, the forces operating on the sail are a combination of push and lift, and on a beam reach, the boat often gets the most possible help from each force — which is why beam reaching is often the fastest kind of sailing.

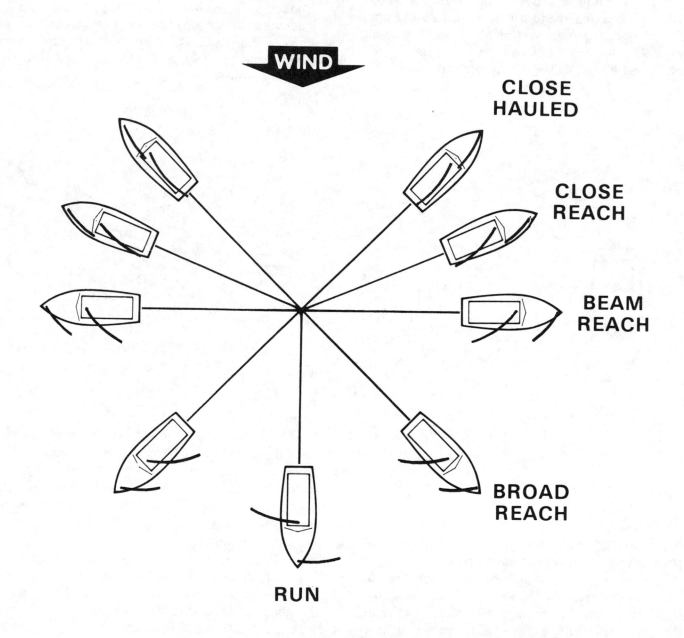

10-20 Sail and Boat Attitudes Relative to Wind When Close Hauled and Reaching

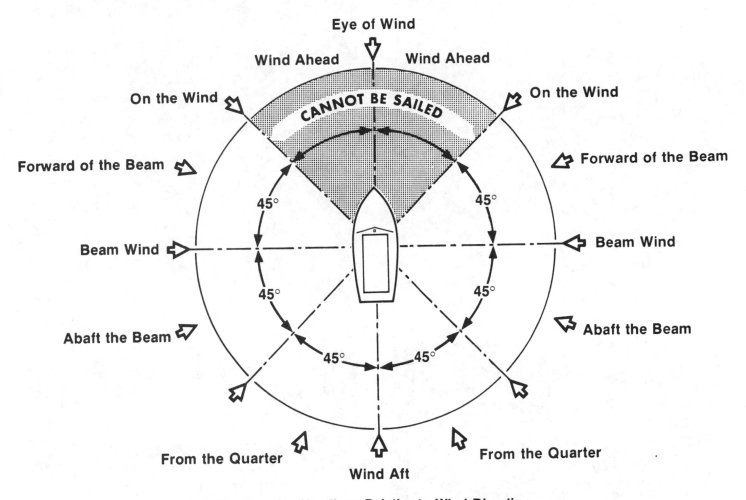

10-21 Possible Headings Relative to Wind Direction

The Points of Sailing

Here is a diagram showing all the possible headings for a modern sailboat reacting to winds from different direction. Note the shaded area, a 90° arc which cannot be sailed. This unusable portion of the available headings extends 45° on either side of the *eye of the wind* — the direction from which the wind is blowing.

These are true wind directions, of course: Close-hauled, a skipper will find his wind vane seems to indicate that he is sailing to within 10° or 15° of the wind's eye, but that's only the effect of apparent wind aboard the boat.

Winds blowing from the right side of the diagram are coming over the boat's starboard side. When the wind blows from starboard, a boat is said to be sailing on the *starboard tack*. When the wind blows over a boat's port side - whether forward of or abaft the beam - the boat is on *port tack*.

Changing Direction

Sooner or later it happens that a boat will need to change from one tack to the other. There are two ways of doing this, depending on whether the boat is sailing close hauled or is running.

Tacking, or Coming About

This is the safest and most usual way of changing direction, always used when a boat's course is toward the wind's eye. Tacking successfully is a matter of practice and timing, and the whole maneuver can be divided into five steps.

10-22 Tacking: "Ready About!"

10-23 Tacking: "Hard Alee!"

1. "Ready about!" The skipper (usually the crewmember who is steering) has decided it's time to change course. "Ready about!" is his way of alerting the rest of the crew to his intentions. Normally, the crew is sitting on the windward (toward the wind) side of the boat for balance; everyone makes ready to shift sides. One crewmember unties the jib sheet and holds it, ready to release.

2. "Hard alee!" calls the skipper, pushing the tiller to leeward — away from the wind. The crew shift their weight to the middle of the boat, crouching to avoid the boom.

3. Through the wind: The bow is now passing through the wind's eye, as the boat pivots. The jib sheet is released, but the other jib sheet is not yet hauled. As the boat's bow passes through the wind, the crew complete their weight shift.

10-24 Tacking: Through the Wind

10-25   Tacking: Boom Across

10-26   Tacking: On the New Tack

Tacking along a course

It often happens that a sailboat must travel some distance to windward, in a direction which makes a direct heading to the destination impossible. In a situation like this, the sailboat skipper zig-zags in a series of tacks toward his mark, as shown in the illustration.

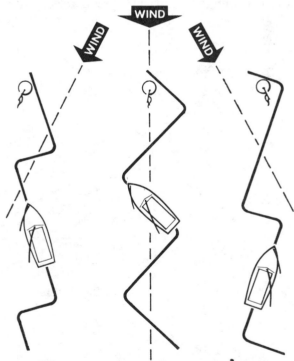

10-27   Tacking to a Windward Objective

4. Boom across: The mainsail boom swings to the opposite side of the boat, as the mainsail fills with wind from the other side. Crew takes in the leeward jib sheet until the sail stops fluttering. The mainsheet, not having been released, has allowed the boom to swing just far enough over to leeward so the mainsail fills properly.

5. Settling down on the new tack, the crew coils down the jib sheet as the boat gains speed.

It may happen that a boat is moving so slowly that it will stall out at step 3. and refuse to go through the eye of the wind. If this happens, let the jib sheets run free and wait till the boat falls back on the old tack. Then build up speed by sailing on a close reach before tacking again.

If the mark is directly upwind, the tacks will be of equal distance, except perhaps for the last one or two: Since it takes time to come about, a series of a few long tacks is faster than many short ones — yet it's sometimes much easier to keep the mark in sight with shorter tacks.

When the mark isn't directly upwind, yet cannot be reached on a single heading, the course will not be composed of equal port and starboard tacks: One or the other tack, as illustrated, will be much more advantageous.

In calculating when to tack, the skipper should take into account the leeway (or sideways slippage) of his boat. All boats make leeway when sailing close hauled, and the amount of leeway depends largely on a boat's design. Generally speaking, it's a mistake to try to sail too close to the wind: This causes the boat to stall for lack of lift, and to lose speed gradually. Keep the sails full and keep the boat moving at all times, and if a wave slows you up, head away from the wind to a close reach till you regain speed.

Jibing

Timing is also the key to changing tacks when heading downwind, which is called jibing. Note, however, the one important difference between the two maneuvers: Whereas the attached edge of the sail passes through the wind's eye when tacking, the free edge does the swinging when you jibe: The effect can be similar to what happens when the wind gets behind an open door and slams it closed.

1. "Stand by to jibe!" calls the skipper. Uncleat the mainsheet and begin to take it in quickly, coiling it so that it will be ready to run free when needed. Don't worry about the jib. Get ready to shift crew weight.

2. "Jibe-oh!" and the skipper puts the tiller over — not too hard — toward the wind (or away from the boom: it's the same thing). Crew stands by to let the mainsheet run.

3. Boom across — but it will swing fast, picking up speed as it comes. The crewman's role is vital: Do *not* snub the mainsheet up short, so the boom fetches up with a jerk. Rather, let the sheet out in a controlled run (wearing inexpensive painter's gloves is a good idea the first few times). When the boom is out at right angles to the boat, snub its sheet.

4. Off on the new tack. Now you can try to get the jib to set wing-and-wing on the opposite side, if you want.

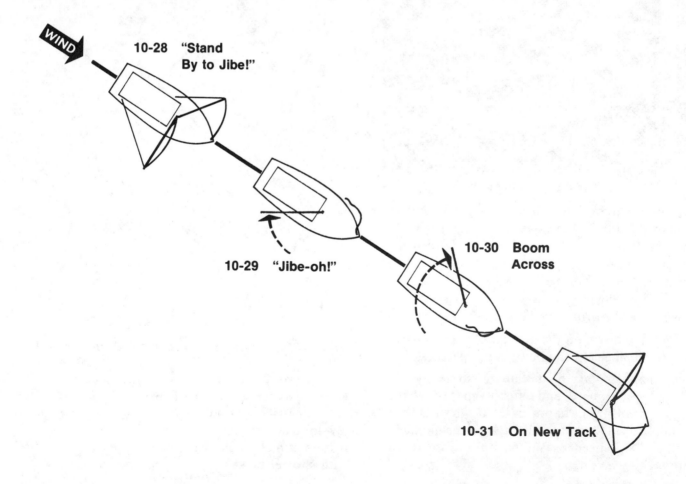

WIND

10-28 "Stand By to Jibe!"

10-29 "Jibe-oh!"

10-30 Boom Across

10-31 On New Tack

Accidental jibe

We saw earlier that a jibe is by its nature a less controlled maneuver than coming about. In high winds, or when the skipper is careless, a jibe may be quite dangerous:

10-32   Possible Result of an Uncontrolled Jibe

1. If the mainsheet is snubbed too abruptly, the boat may be jerked over and swamp or capsize.

2. If the sheet is not snubbed, the swinging boom may hit the leeward shroud, damaging the boom or shroud, or even dismasting the boat.

3. If the sheet is not controlled as the boom swings, the boom may arc upward and snag the backstay, breaking it or capsizing the boat.

Tacking downwind

When winds are gusty, the prudent skipper whose course lies downwind will frequently change direction by tacking instead of jibing, and will sail a series of broad reaches, instead of heading directly downwind on a course where a small wind shift may invite an accidental jibe.

To tack downwind, the boat must first be brought round to a close reach, then swung through the wind's eye. Trying to come about from a broad reach will seldom work, as the boat will lose its turning momentum as the wind ceases to fill the extended sail.

Rigging your boat

Many small boat skippers keep their craft at a pier or mooring all season, but an increasing number rig and launch their boats each time they go sailing. Rigging a small boat is no great problem, and every sailor should know how to set up and tune his own rigging.

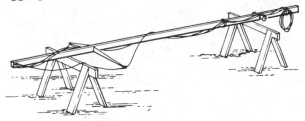

10-33   Set Mast on Supports to Check Rigging

First lay the mast on supports — a pair of carpenter's horses are ideal — and make sure the stays, shrouds, and halyards are all properly attached: Do not lose track of which is the forward side of the mast. When everything's ready, bundle the standing rigging and halyards loosely and lash them to the mast with a couple of turns of twine. Don't put these lashings on any higher than you'll be able to reach when the mast is raised, however.

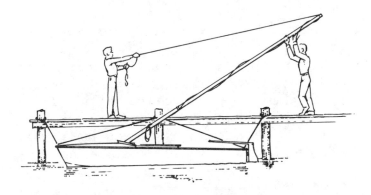

10-34   Stepping the Mast

Now have one crewmember guide the mast into its step — facing the right way — while the other walks the mast forward: Watch where you're putting your feet. If the mast is large, it may be necessary to have one crewmember take the jib halyard to help pull the mast upright (but first be sure the other end of the halyard is made fast!).

10-13

10-35 Taping a Turnbuckle

When the mast is upright and firmly stepped, attach the stays and shrouds to the proper turnbuckles or directly (in smaller boats) to the chainplates. Now wind the turnbuckles or shroud attachments with waterproof tape, to prevent the hardware ripping the sails.

Now attach the boom by its universal joint (the *gooseneck*). Insert the pintles of the rudder into the gudgeons on the transom. Lower the centerboard or daggerboard (assuming the boat's in the water). Make fast the mainsheet to its deck fitting and to the boom.

You're ready to put on the sails. Head the boat as nearly into the wind as you can. (If you're at anchor, the boat will probably head into the wind by itself.) Bend on the mainsail first: Take it from the sailbag, making sure you know which corner you have in your hand — it should be the clew. Insert this into the groove along the upper edge of the boom, feeding the foot of the sail into the groove until the

clew is as far out along the boom as it will go. Now attach the tack of the sail to the tack fitting. There's a fitting at the outer end of the boom — the outhaul — designed to set up tension on the foot of the sail, and this should be pulled reasonably tight.

Your sail may have a track on boom and mast, in which case the corresponding foot and luff of the sail will be fitted with slides that ride the track. If this is the case, you can test the tension of the outhaul by tweaking the foot of the sail: It should be taut enough, when set up, to vibrate slightly.

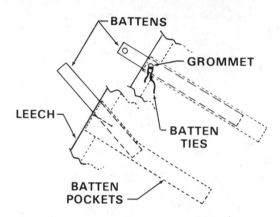

10-37 Two Types of Batten Pockets

Insert the battens in the batten pockets, as shown. Most mainsails have two or three different sizes of battens, with matching pockets. Make sure the thin end of the batten goes in the pocket first.

Make fast the halyard to the head of the sail. A bowline is a good knot to use. After checking to be sure the halyard isn't fouled on any of the rigging, and that the mainsheet is uncleated, so the boom can swing free, raise the sail, feeding its luff into the mast groove. The sail should be hoisted till there are parallel creases visible along the luff.

Now cleat and coil the halyard neatly. Exactly how you do it isn't that important, so long as the halyard is stowed so it cannot escape and at the same time is quickly releasable.

10-36 Bending the Mainsail

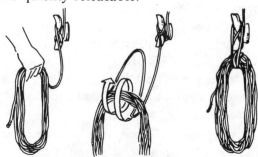

10-38 Coiling the Halyard

To raise the jib, attach its tack to the tack fitting which is usually a part of the forestay chainplate. Next, clip the snaps along the luff to the forestay. Make sure all the snaps are facing in the same direction: If they're not, you have a twist in the luff. Make fast the sheets to the clew and the halyard to the head of the jib, again using a bowline knot if special hardware snaps are not provided.

Raise the jib until the sail's luff is as taut as you can get it (but not so taut that the forestay begins to sag). Cleat and coil that halyard. As a point of interest, mainsail halyards are generally led to the starboard side of the mast, jib halyards to port. It's not a vital thing, but if you always lead the halyards the same way, you won't have to worry about which is which.

Final check

When you're learning to sail, its a good idea to make a final pre-voyage check before leaving the pier or anchorage.

1. Weather: Does the sky look as good as the forecast? If not, re-check the forecast or stay home.

2. Equipment: Is everything aboard? Accessible? Stowed so it won't fall or fly overboard?

3. Float Plan: All boatmen should leave the following information with a reliable person ashore — (1) Where you're going; (2) When you expect to return; (3) Who's aboard; (4) What the boat looks like, *in detail.* When you get back, remember to cancel out your float plan.

Setting Out

Leaving a pier, beach or mooring is the first test of your sailing skill. Before you cut loose from shore, plan ahead: Know what to expect, and what you're going to do next. Don't act until you have a good idea what nearby skippers, swimmers and fishermen are up to. And bear in mind that a boat has no brakes: The only way to stop a sailboat (short of running into something solid) is to head into the wind.

1. Start headed into the wind, with centerboard fully lowered. While you're still learning, it's not a bad idea to paddle to some quiet, deserted spot in the harbor and drop an anchor with a float, to serve as a practice mooring.

10-39 Backing the Jib

2. When all is clear around you, have your crewmember cast off the line to the mooring buoy or float. As the boat drops back, the crewmember grasps the clew of the jib and holds it out to one side of the boat or the other to catch the wind. At the same time, you put the tiller over on the opposite side the jib is extended. The boat will begin to turn in the opposite direction, as in the illustration.

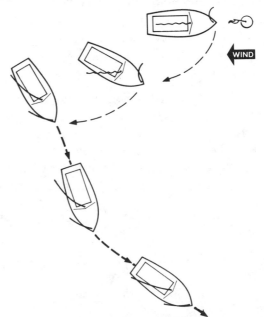

10-40 Leaving the Mooring

3. As soon as the boat is approximately at right angles to the wind, the crewmember lets go of the jib clew and pulls the lee side jib sheet taut, while the skipper takes in the mainsheet. The sails should be taken in just enough to stop fluttering.

You're on your way.

Sail Trim

Your mast should be straight on all points of sailing — if it isn't, correct the adjustment of turnbuckles until it is. Proper sail trim does *not* require that the boat be on its ear, foaming along. Most boats, remember, sail best on their bottoms. When coming to a new heading, let out or take in the sheets until the sails stop shaking — no more. If the wind changes direction, but your heading remains the same, trim the sheets accordingly.

Anchoring

There isn't space here to go into a long treatise on proper anchoring — that's another course in itself. There are many tables showing the proper size anchor for different types and sizes of boat. Your anchor should have a sound anchor line, preferably of nylon line, at least 10 times as long as the deepest spot in your harbor.

When anchoring, follow these simple steps:

1. Drop, unsnap and stow the jib as you approach your anchorage: The idea is to clear the foredeck, and to keep the sail dry and clean. Also, sails are very slippery, and one lying on deck could easily cause someone to slip overboard.

2. Head into the wind, under main alone, until the boat comes to a stop. As it begins to drift backward, lower — don't hurl — the anchor over the bow and feed the line slowly after it.

3. Once the anchor touches bottom, continue to feed out line, but keep some tension on it, to hold the boat's bow into the wind. When you've let out an amount of line equal to about seven times the depth of the water, tie off the anchor line. Check from time to time to make sure the anchor is still holding.

Landing

Whenever you come in for a landing, it seems the whole world is watching. The important thing is to avoid getting flustered: Even the best sailors have been novices in their time, and they'll understand.

1. As you approach, note how the other boats are riding. Lower your centerboard all the way. The idea is to time your turn into the wind, as shown in the illustrations, so you arrive at dock or mooring with little or no momentum.

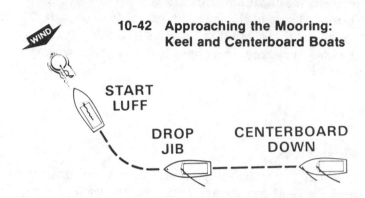

10-42 Approaching the Mooring: Keel and Centerboard Boats

2. Best final approach is usually close-hauled, if the location of other boats allows. Remember to allow for leeway!

3. At one or two boat lengths downwind of the pier or buoy, head up sharply into the wind. If you've calculated right, your boat will coast to a halt, sails shaking, right at the buoy — but have a crewmember ready to grab it. If you're approaching a dock, the crew can fend off with shod feet, but make sure they're firmly seated on the deck before they try. If you miss, follow the procedures described under *setting out,* swing round and try again.

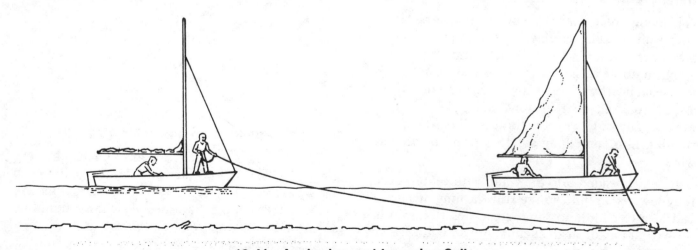

10-41 Anchoring and Lowering Sail

Unrigging

Most small boats' skippers remove the sails between voyages: Dacron sails deteriorate in direct sunlight, and in many harbors, airborn dirt may foul sails left furled on a boom for a few days.

Before bagging your sails, remove the battens and lay each sail out — if possible — on a clean surface, such as a lawn. Check for tears or worn spots. Now fold the sail as shown until it's a long, narrow strip, and then roll it up gently. Don't fold it or roll it hard — try to avoid creases.

10-43 Fold Sail . . .

10-44 . . . Into Narrow Strip

10-45 Now Roll and Bag Sail

If you do furl the mainsail on the boom, here's how:

1. Drop the sail and gather it on one side of the boom in one large fold of sail.

2. Roll it toward the boom, gathering the sail as you go. It's a good idea to remove the battens, if they're wood, as they are likely to take a permanent warp.

3. Lash the sail with elastic sail ties, just tight enough to hold it in place. The roll should have its open side facing down, so rain and spray will run off the sail and not be caught inside. If you have a sail cover, put it on over the furled sail.

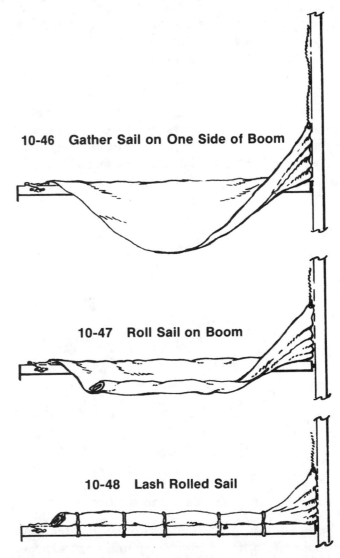

10-46 Gather Sail on One Side of Boom

10-47 Roll Sail on Boom

10-48 Lash Rolled Sail

Now remove your tiller and rudder, raise the centerboard all the way, and clean out the boat. Be sure, if you sail in salt or heavily polluted water, to wipe off all varnished wood and bright metal with a clean cloth.

In heavy weather

Sooner or later, every sailor can expect to encounter weather severe enough to make sailing difficult or even dangerous. For the beginner, a careful attention to weather forecasts and to the appearance of sea and sky should postpone an encounter with heavy weather until you and your boat are enough of a team to handle it.

If you do get caught out in a sudden squall, however, chances are you'll get through it with no great trouble, if you keep your head and follow the principles of good seamanship.

Some days, especially muggy, hazy summer afternoons, breed dangerous squalls that can creep up on you before you're aware of what's happening. If you're sailing along and suddenly find the wind increasing dramatically, or see that a thunderstorm is going to strike before you can reach harbor, the first thing to do, preferably before the gusts get too strong, is drop and furl all sail. To do this, head up into the wind, let the sheets fly, and lower the sails as quickly as you can, gathering them and furling them as you do. Lash sails to boom or deck hardware, to prevent them billowing and tearing.

10-49   Drop Sails and Anchor

Once the sails are under control, put out your anchor: Even if you haven't enough line to anchor securely, the weight of line and anchor will hold your boat's bow up into the wind — the safest attitude for any boat with difficult weather.

Have your crew put on lifejackets — and set a good example yourself. It's much easier to put on any lifesaving device in the boat than in the water. Tie down all loose gear and, if significant amounts of rain or spray get in the boat, don't wait to bail.

One good thing about sudden squalls is that they're usually over fairly quickly. In 15 minutes or so, the wind should moderate enough for you to sail home under reduced sail.

The kind of sail you set in strong winds will depend on how your boat is rigged, what sails you carry, and in what direction you want to go.

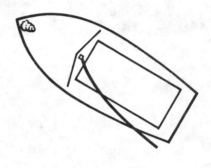

10-50   Sailing Under Main Alone

Generally speaking, most small sailboats will sail reasonably well under mainsail alone, on any heading from a broad reach up to nearly close-hauled. In a gusty wind, it's especially important to keep the boat moving, so don't try to sail as close to the wind as you normally would. Also, if you're broad reaching, be awake for sudden wind shifts: This is not the time for an unexpected jibe.

If your course is downwind, your boat may handle better under jib alone. Be sure the main is tightly furled and the boom secured. And keep the jib from unnecessary flapping, which can rip the stitching along seams.

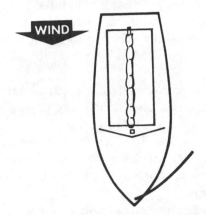

10-51　Sailing Under Jib Alone

Your boat may be equipped with reefing gear, in which case you can reduce the area of the mainsail, while still retaining some of it for a balanced sail plan. On most small boats today, reefing is accomplished by easing off the main halyard while

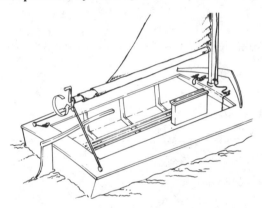

10-52　Rolling In a Reef

simultaneously rotating the boom with a built-in or attachable crank, to roll the sail around it like a window shade. If your boat has reefing gear, practice using it in harbor before you try it under way.

Emergency

It may happen that, despite your best efforts, the boat capsizes, or turns over on its side. With most modern daysailers, this is an irritation, but hardly a disaster. Know how to right your boat and the worst you'll suffer is a wetting.

1. Before righting, count heads to make sure crew are safe. Don life vests or jackets, if you haven't already done so. Gather floating gear and stuff it in a sail bag to prevent its escaping. Cast off halyards and pull sails down to the deck.

2. With centerboard extended, grasp the side of the hull, as shown, while standing on the board.

3. Chances are the boat will come upright by herself. Full of water, she will be very unstable. Swim alongside and bail until the water is six inches or so lower than the boat's sides.

4. Now a light-weight crewmember can climb in over the stern and finish bailing, after which sails can be raised again. With practice, especially in easily capsized board boats, you'll learn how to right the boat without lowering sail.

Distress

Sometimes a mast or boom is damaged to the point where the boat cannot easily be sailed. If this happens to you, or if your sail develops a sudden tear, it may be best to call for help, rather than pushing onward to incur a big repair bill. Distress signals can be carried on the smallest boat: They should be stowed in a watertight box or bag, out of the reach of small children, in a place where a capsize won't cause them to fall from the boat. Here are common ways to ask for help — never be ashamed to do so if you feel the situation is getting out of control.

10-53　Righting Capsized Boat

1. Flare or smoke signal: Hand-held orange smoke signals can be seen a long way. Be sure to follow instructions on the device, and hold the burning signal away from yourself and the boat.

2. A distress flag — usually a bright International Orange square of plastic — can be hoisted in the rigging.

3. A horn or whistle, repeatedly sounded in patterns of five blasts, is a recognized distress signal.

4. Waving the American flag upside-down is known to be a signal of distress.

5. With no signals at all, simply raising your arms over your head and lowering them level with your shoulders, over and over, is a standard distress signal.

When making any distress signal, be sure you do it vigorously: You may know you're in need of help, but the other fellow may think you're just waving or tooting to be friendly.

Conclusion

There's nothing difficult or mysterious about sailing, once you have the hang of it, but don't think that you'll ever know it all. That's one of the fascinations of the sport: There's always something new to learn, some way to improve your sailing skills.

Now that you've completed this introduction to sailing, there are two complementary things to do next. First, practice what you've learned: Use it till you can come about, jibe, enter and leave tight corners with real confidence. As noted earlier, a good way to learn more quickly is to crew for an experienced sailor.

Second, take another sailing course. One you may want to consider is the Coast Guard Auxiliary's own Principles of Sailing, a seven-lesson course that explains in depth what you've learned here in outline, and which will teach you more about fine points of sailing than we've had room to touch on in this short space. Cost of the Auxiliary's course is very slight - often no more than the price of the textbook - and it will expose you to the kind of information you must acquire to be a complete skipper.

10-54 A Modern High Performance Sloop

CHAPTER 11

Weather

Weather is one of the greatest influences on the sport of boating. It determines when you shall go, what your course will be, the time required to arrive at your ultimate destination and in many cases, the degree of your enjoyment in the passage.

As a boatman, you must realize the speed with which weather can change. You must learn to recognize those weather signs that warn of impending bad weather. You must know where to obtain the latest weather information and be able to relate this information to your own situation and capabilities.

The importance of weather to boatmen was tragically emphasized in an incident that took place in September 1967 on Lake Michigan. Seven people were drowned and many others injured by seas that were apparently too high for the boats used. The tragic part is that forecasters had given warnings of the bad weather and these forecasts were available to the boatmen, in sufficient time for the ensuing tragedies to have been avoided.

Weather forecasts the morning of the incident had warned of winds increasing to 20 to 30 knots in the afternoon and Small Craft Warnings were posted. By late morning the forecasts included a warning of thundershowers. Many boatmen either did not obtain the weather reports or did not heed their warnings.

The following report is quoted from the Coast Guard Board of Investigation convened to examine the disaster.

"On 23 September 1967 approximately five hundred motorboats, mainly outboards of 16 feet or less, were underway in eastern Lake Michigan between Empire and Manistee, Michigan engaged in salmon fishing. A large number of these craft had been launched from ramps at these and intermediate communities. A number of boats also launched directly into Lake Michigan from the nearby beaches. Many of the boats proceeded to Platte Bay, the area of reportedly good fishing. The weather began to deteriorate at about 8:00 AM. Progressively from late morning through the afternoon boatmen in the Platte Bay area discontinued fishing and beached their craft in the immediate vicinity or attempted to return in departing sheltered Platte Bay, exposed themselves to the more severe sea conditions along the coastline. About 200 boats attempting this open lake passage found it difficult and headed for the nearest beach area, and attempted to land through a heavy surf. Seven persons lost their lives, and all were occupants of boats which had capsized in or near the surf. At least 16 boats were damaged in making beach landings and a number of other boats swamped and/or capsized and were damaged but removed from the beaches before count could be made. Most occupants of the boats involved did not wear lifesaving devices although they were available to them. Fifteen persons were taken to hospitals suffering from exposure and water inhalation. None of those hospitalized were incapacitated for more than 72 hours. At least 150 persons and 75 boats were assisted from conditions of peril or distress by rescue forces."

The Board considered all available facts and concluded, in part,

"1. That the evidence indicates the damage to boats, swampings and/or capsizings, and endangering of or loss of life, which occurred in the Frankfort to Empire, Michigan area on the eastern shore of Lake Michigan on 23 September 1967, were primarily caused by the operation of boats of limited capability for the existing weather conditions by persons not experienced in open lake operations while:

a. attempting hazardous open water passages in trying to return to their launch sites,

b. proceeding within, or too close to, heavy surf,

c. attempting beach landings through heavy surf.

2. That recognizing the limited experience and boating knowledge of many boat operators, and the sea conditions prevailing during most of 23 September 1967, the general type of boat in use—less than 16 feet in length and of open construction—did not afford the desired level of safety. It is emphasized that this assessment does not reflect on the adequacy and safety of any particular size or design boat per se, but rather is made in relation to the general operator capability and operating conditions existent.

3. That the evidence indicates that a contributing cause to the casualties and endangerment to life and property which occurred on 23 September 1967 was a general lack of knowledge of boating safety by an appreciable number of boatmen in one or more of the following respects:

a. failure to obtain weather forecasts,

b. failure to recognize or heed the small craft warning signal displayed at the Frankfort Coast Guard Station,

c. disregard of the recommendations of Coast Guard and other law enforcement personnel to not proceed into Lake Michigan because of unfavorable weather conditions,

d. proceeding into the open lake at the same time other boatmen, experienced in open lake operation, aborted their cruises because of observed sea conditions,

e. failure to recognize or heed indications of deteriorating weather,

f. failure to attempt to land at the nearest available shore upon first observing the increasing winds and seas,

g. failure to wear available life saving devices while operating in heavy sea or surf.

4. That the evidence indicates that the weather conditions predicted by the National Weather Service for 23 September 1967 materialized as forecast. The wind and seas conditions progressively worsened from about 8:00 A.M. to 3:00 P.M.; it was not a sudden storm which endangered the boats and their occupants.

5. That because of the apparent general lack of knowledge of weather on the part of many operators of small boats it is probable that many boatmen do not realize that:

a. the weather forecast can change within a few hours,

b. the absence of any language in a forecast expressly stating a small craft warning does not remove that possibility for succeeding periods,

c. the wind force and direction must be evaluated in relation to the particular shore,

d. small craft warnings are simply precautionary and indicate that further information is available and should be obtained."

Although other factors were involved the fundamental one was the failure of the boatmen to obtain and heed weather information. Coast Guard and Sheriff patrol boats had warned boatmen to remain in harbors because of the weather but many ignored the warning.

The important lesson to be learned from this incident is that weather should be taken seriously. Get the latest report before you depart, and keep informed while you are out.

Movement of Air Over the Earth

For us to understand why weather varies from day to day it is necessary to learn something about our Earth's atmosphere. The lower atmosphere consists of air, which is a mixture of oxygen, nitrogen, and other gases, plus water vapor. You are familiar with the temperature of air on the surface; however, the temperature drops as we climb to higher altitudes and is about—50° F at 50,000 ft. Air in the lower atmosphere is heated by

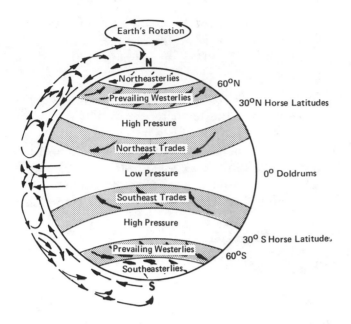

11-1　Ideal Atmospheric Circulation

The sun's rays are transmitted more directly and intensely to the lower latitudes near the equator, causing the air there to be heated more than in the higher latitudes. The rotation of the earth around the sun and topographical features also help to make the true circulation very complicated.

This warm air rises and is replaced by cooler air from regions closer to the poles. With this in mind, you can envision a circulation pattern such as depicted here.

Air does indeed circulate about the earth, but it is not as simple as this. The earth rotates on its axis. Just as you would have trouble making a straight line across a moving record turntable so air set in motion does not follow a straight line across the moving surface of the Earth. As the Earth rotates under the moving air, its path relative to the Earth bends to the right in the Northern Hemisphere. This is called the coriolis effect.

Upper air flowing north in the Northern Hemisphere will bend at an increasing rate until it "bunches" up near 30° N latitude. This causes an increase in atmospheric pressure and East-West winds. Since the pressure and wind are different,

incoming solar radiation and heat radiation from the Earth's surface. The temperature is dependent on the season and latitude.

11-2　Thunderhead

the weather is different here than in other areas to the north or south. So you can see the illustrated circulation pattern is oversimplified. The important fact, however, is that air masses do move about the earth. As we will see, different types of weather are associated with air masses and these also move about the Earth.

Clouds

We have stated that the atmosphere contains water vapor. Hotter air is capable of holding more vapor than colder air. When a weatherman says the *relative humidity* is now 70%, he means that at the current temperature, the air is holding 70% of the vapor it is capable of holding.

We know that air, if warmed, will rise. We also know that the temperature usually gradually drops as altitude increases. One cause of this is the drop in pressure. Rising humid air will also cool and will continue until it is cooled to the point where it can no longer hold its moisture and reaches 100% relative humidity. Here the moisture will condense

11-3   Altocumulus Clouds

11-4   Rain Clouds

into very small droplets and clouds will form. If enough moisture is formed into a cloud, the droplets will combine and become larger until they are too heavy to remain in the cloud. Precipitation will then occur, usually in the form of rain or snow.

There are many different types of clouds. Meteorologists can identify over 70 of them but we will not attempt to describe them.

One method weathermen use to classify clouds is according to whether they are layered (flat looking) or built up (clouds with great vertical development). Layered clouds are stable and built-up clouds are unstable. We saw that warmed air will rise and, if humid enough, will form clouds. Often clouds can form if air is cooled by some other means. Clouds can be located at many altitudes such as low rain clouds, high "mares tails", or thick thunder clouds extending from low to high altitudes. Often on a warm sunny day puffs of cumulus clouds will float by you.

Atmospheric Stability

If the surface temperature is much higher than temperatures aloft, an unstable pattern of rising air and cloud formation will occur. If the surface temperature is equal or nearly so, to that aloft, a stable situation exists and cloud formations will be minimal. The line of demarcation between stable and unstable conditions is dependent on the relationship between both temperature changes and changes in altitude. As we will see later, an unstable condition can cause various kinds of bad weather.

Weather Instruments

There are several devices used to describe the weather by measuring physical properties of the atmosphere. Unless you are planning to formulate your own forecast, having a lot of weather instruments will not be of much benefit to you. There are so few that would be of great use to you. However, you may wish to purchase an inexpensive barometer. These instruments will give a rough indication of approaching fronts and low pressure systems. Leave the reading and interpreting of the highly technical instruments to the professionals.

The following definitions are intended for your general information only. An *Anemometer*, measures wind speed. A *Barometer* measures atmospheric pressure in either inches of mercury or millibars. A *Thermometer* measures degree of temperature. A *Hygrometer* measures relative humidity. A *Psychrometer* measures wet and dry bulb air

11-5 Altocumulus of a Chaotic Sky

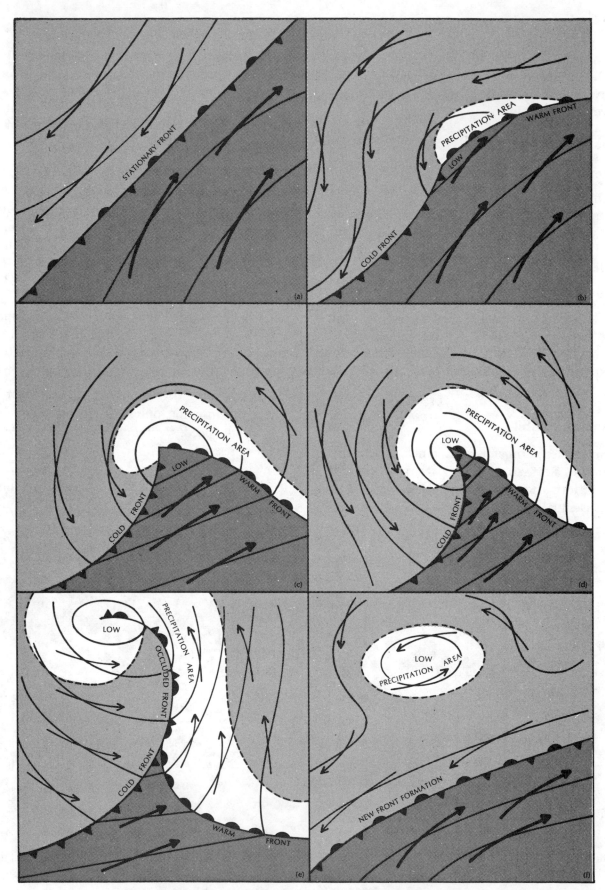

11-6 Formation of a Low Pressure System Along a Front

temperatures. With either of these, one can use psychrometric charts to determine relative humidity and dewpoint.

Further explanation here might be helpful. Relative humidity is the ratio of water vapor in the air to the amount the air could hold at that temperature. The dewpoint is the temperature below which moisture will condense out of the air to form droplets as fog or cloud. A psychrometer is a set of two thermometers with the bulb of one enclosed in a wet gauze. The "wet bulb" thermometer will read lower because of the cooling effect of evaporation. The amount of evaporation depends on the relative humidity of the air. If the air is humid, there will be little evaporation and the "wet bulb" thermometer will not read very much lower than the "dry bulb" thermometer. In other words, the difference between the two thermometer readings varies with the relative humidity.

Air Masses

The United States is swept by air masses of great contrasts. Cold, dry air masses continually form in the Arctic regions and move southward. These are referred to as Polar Air Masses, and noted on weather charts as P. Hot, moist air masses form in the tropics and move northward. These are noted by T. When a hot, moist mass meets a cold, dry mass, a weather front usually develops.

Meteorologists further classify air masses as to the surfaces over which they are formed. So we now have continental (c) and oceanic or maritime (m). This gives us the four major types of air masses which affect the United States as shown below.

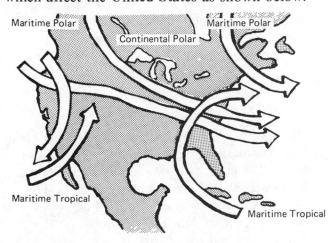

11-7 Air Masses

Fronts

Where air masses of different types meet, fronts exist. Fronts are significant because it is along these borders that most severe weather occurs.

An example might clarify this somewhat. A mass of cold air from Canada has invaded the United States. On its border there exists a cold front. The cold air is heavy and stays low to the ground. There is warm air, probably humid, ahead of the front. Somewhere along the edge of cold air, a weak spot in the front might develop. It could be caused by a mountain in its path. Here the warm air will be surrounded by cooler air. It will rise, clouds will form, and precipitation will probably follow.

The rising pattern of the warm air will cause a drop in barometric pressure and a clearly defined low pressure area or a "low" can soon be located. Around the low, there is a wide area of clouds and precipitation.

As more warm air is undercut by the cool air, more clouds form and the area of precipitation increases. Winds tend to head into the low; but the coriolis effect veers them to the right (Northern Hemisphere) so that a circular counter clockwise pattern develops. The warm air will be surrounded on the three sides by the cool air as it circulates around the low.

Ultimately the low will be completely surrounded by cold air. The supply of warm air able to rise and form clouds is reduced to nothing. With the rising air pattern which originally caused the low pressure area now stopped, the low will become less vigorous and will eventually dissipate.

The entire process from formation to dissipation may take 3 to 10 days or more.

Different air mass types will form various kinds of weather. Weathermen compare the type of air invading an area with the air already there. If there are great differences in temperature and moisture content, a great deal of activity along the front can be expected.

Squall Lines

Squall lines may precede fast-moving cold fronts. They are an unbroken line of black, ominous clouds, towering 40,000 feet or more into the sky, including thunderstorms of almost incredible violence and occasional tornadoes. Such squall lines are extremely turbulent, sometimes more so than a typical hurricane. From the water, a squall line looks like a wall of rolling, boiling black fog. Winds shift and sharpen suddenly with the approach of the squall line, and downward-pouring rain may carry the cloud clear to the water in sharp, vertical bands. Torrential rains fall behind the leading edge of the squall line.

Squall lines occur when winds above a cold front, moving in the same direction as the front's advance, prevent the lifting of a warm air mass. This is why little bad weather occurs right at the surface front. But 100 to 150 miles ahead of the front the strong winds force up the warm air with almost explosive violence, producing the squall line.

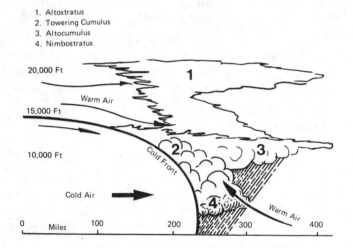

1. Altostratus
2. Towering Cumulus
3. Altocumulus
4. Nimbostratus

11-8 Squall Line is a Fast Moving Cold Front that is Usually Fierce, Turbulent and of Short Duration. They are Very Dangerous to Small Boats.

Weather Information

The National Weather Service formulates forecasts for the U.S. and adjoining waters. The process demands the input of a great deal of surface and upper air data from stations around the world.

Each weather station observes the following:

1. temperature
2. wind speed and direction
3. cloud type and amount of coverage
4. barometric pressure and change in last three hours
5. weather in last 6 hours and present weather
6. visibility
7. dewpoint
8. precipitation amount

The observation data from many stations are collected at a center and plotted on a weather map. Using this information, an analyst then tries to locate different air masses and the fronts that separate them. He does this by comparing temperature, barometric pressure, dew point, and wind velocity. This allows the analyst to "see" masses of cold dry air or warm moist air. By examining the various stations' reports, he can tell which way the air masses are moving and what kind of fronts he is observing, he can then locate the well defined high, or low pressure areas. Next he draws in isobars (lines that identify places of equal barometric pressure).

With all this information on the map, the forecaster can then attempt to estimate what conditions will prevail in the future. Using wind speeds and direction he can predict in what direction the high and low pressure areas will travel in a given time and what can be expected of their associated weather.

Fog

One weather feature that is of particular concern to boatmen is fog. Fog is formed when air is cooled to the point (the dewpoint) where its moisture condenses into very small droplets. This is similar to the way a cloud forms. Fog is really a cloud that is on, or near the ground.

To understand more about fog, let's review some facts we discussed earlier. Cool air cannot hold as much moisture as warm. Thus if air that is already moist is made cooler, fog will form. This occurs in several ways.

On land, if the air is very humid at sunset, the land, and the air close to it, will cool off and fog may form. This is known as *radiation* fog.

When the sun rises the following morning, it will warm the air a few degrees. The condensed moisture will disappear and the fog will dissipate ("burn off").

The fog most common to boatmen is caused by moist air moving over a cool surface. An example of this is warm moist air from land blowing over cold coastal waters. This is called *advection* fog because the temperature change is brought on by air moving to a cooler location. It is a particular hazard to boatmen because it commonly occurs on coastal waters especially in cold seasons, and it moves in a "bank" that can overtake and surprise the unwary boatman. The fog will usually be concentrated close to the water's surface and may be absent at a height of 50 feet. This is because the water is the cooling agent.

Fog is likely wherever an area of cold water exists; as for example, on the Pacific coast, where upwelling brings cold water to the surface. For this same reason, fog can form on rivers where cold water flows through areas with very moist air. The cold river will cool air near the surface causing fog. Sometimes this situation occurs below dams because water becomes cold in the deep pool behind.

Fortunately, weathermen, by carefully predicting temperature change and measuring dew point (the temperature at which moisture condenses), can predict fog with high reliability. Marine weather forecasts include information about any anticipated fog. Inasmuch as the normal weather forecasts often don't give this information, wise boatmen always get the marine forecast before departing.

Weather Information

The best source for weather information is the one that is easiest for you to obtain and most up to date. Several sources are noted here.

Your instructor will have information on the availability of each one in your area. RECORDED TELEPHONE MARINE WEATHER REPORTS are available in many large cities. If there is one in your area, it is a very convenient means of finding the forecast. Call while you are planning your boat trip, for instance, the day before, and again just before you leave to get the latest report.

V H F-FM CONTINUOUS MARINE WEATHER BROADCASTS are another excellent source. These National Weather Service radio weather transmissions repeat taped messages about every five minutes. Tapes are updated every 3-6 hours and include weather and radar summaries, wind observations, visibility, sea and detailed lake conditions including reports from Coast Guard units, and detailed local and area forecasts. When severe weather warnings are in order, routine transmissions are interrupted and the broadcast is devoted to emergency warnings. A sample detailed local marine weather forecast that might be included in a National Weather Service Broadcast is given below:

> "The marine forecast for the Chesapeake Bay north of Point Lookout and for the lower Potomac. Easterly winds 10 to 15 knots this afternoon, tonight, and Tuesday. Weather cloudy with rain this afternoon and tonight and chance of some rain or drizzle Tuesday. Visibility 3 to 5 miles, but variable to 1 mile or less in fog tonight."

National Weather Service radio weather transmissions can usually be received up to 30 miles from the antenna site, depending on terrain and type of receiver. The frequencies used, 162.55 MHz and 162.40 MHz lie just above the marine band; therefore, special tuners or receivers are required. An increasing variety of these are becoming available ranging in price from $20.00 to $200.00 or more. It's a good idea to equip your boat with one.

SCHEDULED WEATHER SERVICE MARINE BROADCASTS ON COMMERCIAL AM STATIONS are also available in a great many areas. Typical schedule times are early morning, noon, early evening, and midnight. Some of these broadcasts come directly from the Weather Service offices and contain all the necessary information. Details for your area will be covered by your instructor.

MARINE INFORMATION BROADCASTS by the Coast Guard provide the public with weather information, Notices to Mariners, and hydrographic information. The public is alerted on Channel 16 and asked to shift to Channel 22 for the regularly scheduled broadcasts.

Scheduled weather broadcasts are normally twice daily, but in high boating density areas are scheduled more frequently.

Special storm warnings are initiated by Coast Guard broadcasting stations on receipt of National Weather Service warnings or observed conditions.

Your radio telephone is also valuable when special storm warnings are issued by the Weather Service. Special broadcasts are made over the usual marine radiotelephone stations. These broadcasts are also announced in most cases over Channel 16. If you have your set tuned to this frequency, which should normally be the case when underway, you will hear the announcement and instructions to tune to the correct frequency.

SMALL CRAFT

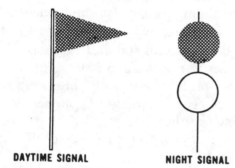

DAYTIME SIGNAL   NIGHT SIGNAL

One RED pennant displayed by day and a RED light over a WHITE light at night to indicate winds as high as 33 knots (38 m.p.h.) and/or sea conditions considered dangerous to small craft operations are forecast for the area.

STORM

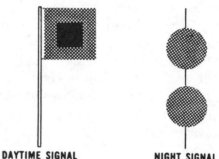

DAYTIME SIGNAL   NIGHT SIGNAL

A single square RED flag with a BLACK center displayed during daytime and two RED lights at night to indicate that winds 48 knots (55 m.p.h.) and above are forecast for the area. If the winds are associated with a tropical cyclone (hurricane), the "Storm Warning" display indicates winds 48 to 63 knots (55 to 73 m.p.h.) are forecast.

GALE

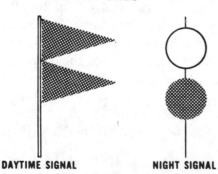

DAYTIME SIGNAL   NIGHT SIGNAL

Two RED pennants displayed by day and a WHITE light above a RED light at night to indicate winds within the range 34 to 47 knots (39 to 54 m.p.h.) are forecast for the area.

HURRICANE

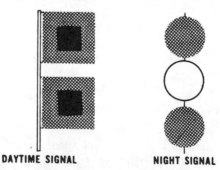

DAYTIME SIGNAL   NIGHT SIGNAL

Displayed only in connection with a tropical cyclone (hurricane). Two square RED flags with BLACK centers displayed by day and a WHITE light between two RED lights at night to indicate that winds 64 knots (74 m.p.h.) and above are forecast for the area.

11-9 Warning Display Signals

TELEVISION WEATHER REPORTS are presented by almost all TV stations on a scheduled basis. Some reports include boating forecasts.

NEWSPAPERS in most cities contain weather forecasts and usually a simple weather map. Beware of old information. Hunt through the forecast and you will see that it is usually more than 12 hours old. More information can be obtained from radio (AM, FM, or VHF-FM) and TV. It is suggested that these sources be consulted.

WARNING DISPLAY SIGNALS are posted in many boating areas when directed by the Weather Service. Most display sites use only the daytime warning signal and do not post nighttime signals.

Pennants and Lights

Visual warning displays are shown by yacht clubs, marinas and many Coast Guard facilities. The most common signal seen by boatmen is the small craft advisory. The term "small craft" includes boats of many designs and sizes, and the advisory covers a wide range of wind speed and sea condition. It forecasts possible hazardous conditions to small boats, such as 30 knot winds or scattered afternoon thundershowers. You may see it displayed on what appears to be a beautiful day for boating and be tempted to ignore it. Do not do this. Instead, regard the small craft advisory as an alert that wind and/or sea conditions potentially dangerous to "small craft" exist or are forecast.

The more severe gale and storm warnings should be given more respect. If these warnings are displayed it is unlikely that you would want to go out.

You may note from Fig. 11-7 that the Storm Warning can have two meanings. If no hurricane is around, it means winds over 48 knots and often of much greater velocity, are forecast. When the winds are part of a hurricane system the meaning changes to 48-63 knots and a special Hurricane Warning is used for winds 64 knots and above.

Watch the Weather

We hope that before you depart on a boating trip, you take time to get the latest weather information. However, your need for weather information does not stop there. While you are out,

have a radio of some kind aboard and check the weather broadcasts periodically. If you hear static on your AM radio, it may be an indication of thunderstorm activity nearby. Keep your weather eye "peeled" for the approach of dark, threatening clouds that often form part of a squall or thunderstorm. You may see lightning but hear no thunder if the storm is too far away.

Try to note any increase in wind speed, increase in sea conditions, or shift in wind direction that may be occurring. If you are enjoying yourself in a protected anchorage this will often not be readily apparent. A judicious weather eye may save you an uncomfortable ride home.

Local Weather Conditions

You may have noticed that during the warm season an afternoon breeze will very often come up to cool you and provide good sailing weather. You have probably wondered what the reason for this is.

The sun heats the land and sometime during the late morning or afternoon, a "sea" breeze forms. The heating of the land, if excessive, can cause an unstable condition which was discussed earlier. As warm air rises clouds will form. If the warm air is plentiful and moisture laden, conditions may be right for the formation of a thunderstorm. With sundown the flow halts.

At night, the pattern will be reversed. Water temperature does not vary at all. The air overlying water is relatively warm. It rises a little and cooler air from land areas moves in to fill the space.

Thunderstorms

This weather is of particular concern to boatmen because of the rain and lightning and also because of squalls or sudden violent winds that often accompany it. Individual storms cannot be predicted with great accuracy and are capable of forming in hours. We will describe a typical storm and see how it forms.

It is a hot summer day. The weather forecast warns of "widely scattered afternoon thundershowers." As you depart on your boat at noon it is a beautiful day with light breezes and a few puffs of cumulus clouds floating by.

11-11

During the day the land has been heated and the sea air has been blown landward. The moist air becomes warm and rises forming clouds. With a continuing supply of this air, clouds will grow larger and rise higher.

From aboard your boat you notice larger clouds forming nearby. One cloud in particular has great upward development growing higher and larger and giving the appearance of a misshapen cauliflower.

This cloud has found a supply of hot, moisture laden air and is growing at a rapid rate. Near the top, which may be 25,000 ft., moisture is condensing and forming ice crystals. When a certain amount of moisture has condensed it falls towards the earth as rain or even hail and snow. The falling precipitation causes a "chute" to form in the center of the cloud. The wind velocity in this area is high because of the coolness of the air and the weight of its moisture. When these high winds strike the surface of the water they produce squalls accompanied by heavy pelting precipitation.

Your observation indicates that the cloud has continued to grow. It rises to an altitude where the winds are stronger and begins to assume an "anvil" shape as the top of the cloud flattens out. The higher the cloud, the more severe its storm will be. The storm cloud moves in the same direction as other clouds. The direction is indicated by the point of the anvil. A dark area of rain is visible under the middle of the cloud. You see the flash of lightning and hear the clap of thunder off in the distance. Incidentally, the distance between you and the storm, can be estimated by multiplying the seconds that elapse between a flash of lightning and a clap of thunder by 0.2. A five second delay would mean that the storm is about 1 mile away.

As the storm approaches you, a low threatening black cloud rolls toward you. As this cloud approaches you notice that white objects such as sails and boat hulls appear to have a bright, almost fluorescent appearance. Suddenly the wind dies completely and you think perhaps the storm has passed over. Suddenly, you are hit with a gust of wind and a driving rain. The rain is so heavy that visibility is reduced to near zero and even your windshield wipers are inadequate. This continues for a few minutes and then the rain and wind gradually stop. Soon the storm passes and the sky clears.

A sudden storm is very exciting but it can also be very dangerous. Squalls can have winds of 30-40 or more knots and will stir up very steep, choppy seas.

Be weather prudent. Keep your eyes open—particularly if the weather forecast contains a word of warning. Watch for clouds that are building rapidly in height. Listen for static on your radio. If you think there's a good chance of thunderstorms, do not venture too far from protected waters.

If it appears you are going to be caught in the approaching storm, make your way to the nearest safe anchorage and ride it out at anchor. Button up any covers you may have, to keep out some of the rain. Stay away from any objects that may provide a path for lightning. Turn on your anchor light so other people can see you. The storm will probably last only a few minutes; but it may give you a rough ride and a severe drenching while it does.

Weather Signs to Notice

There are a number of general weather signs to help the boater recognize the possibility of approaching bad weather. You should be aware that these signs are not absolutely reliable, but they do give an indication of upcoming weather when used in conjunction with other reports.

In the northern hemisphere, with the wind in your face, low pressure will always be on your right hand side.

Weather will generally remain fair when:

a. The winds blow gently from west or northwest.

b. Cumulus clouds dot the summer sky in the afternoon.

Rainy weather or snow may come when:

a. Cirrus clouds thicken and are followed by lower clouds, especially if barometer is dropping.

b. Puffy cumulus clouds begin to develop vertically.

c. The wind, especially a north wind, shifts in a counterclockwise direction, from north to west to south.

d. Southerly winds increase in speed with clouds moving from west.

e. If pressure is falling, a ring around the moon may mean rain within 18 to 48 hours.

CHAPTER 12

Radiotelephone

General

This chapter is addressed to owners and operators of vessels voluntarily equipped for radiotelephone communication. For practical purposes, recreational boats are not required by Federal law to carry radiotelephone equipment. If you do decide to equip your boat, there are certain regulations of the Federal Communications Commission that you must observe. These regulations are reflected in the text of this chapter, and are set forth in Volume IV, Part 83, of the FCC Rules and Regulations available from the Superintendent of Documents, U. S. Government Printing Office, Washington, D. C. 20402.

Boats carrying more than six passengers for hire, as well as many other commercial craft, are required to carry radio equipment. If you operate any type of commercial vessel, consult your nearest FCC office to determine the requirements which may apply to you and your boat.

Communications Purposes

With the distress, safety and calling frequencies — Channel 16 (156.8 MHz) VHF-FM and the 2182 kHz AM — as the keystones, the marine radiotelephone system is designed to accomplish all the following communications functions:

1. Provide monitored distress and safety frequencies. By designating the distress frequencies as calling frequencies, the radio regulations ensure that a maximum number of stations will be listening at any given time. *The success of this arrangement depends on cooperation,* both in maintaining a listening watch on 2182 kHz or Channel 16 (156.8 MHz) and in keeping those frequencies clear of all unnecessary communication.

2. Allow for communication between your vessel and local and Federal agencies.

3. Provide frequencies for the exchange of information pertaining to navigation, movement or management of vessels.

4. Provide special frequencies for stations and vessels engaged in commerce.

5. Provide noncommercial frequencies for the special needs of recreational boating people.

6. Provide separate frequencies for vessels to communicate with shore telephones.

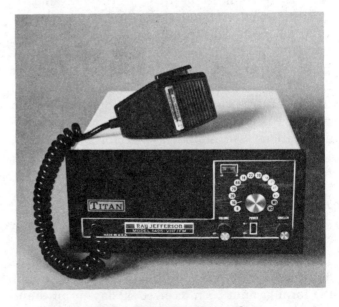

12-1   Radiotelephone Set

How To Get Ship Station and Operator Licenses

Ship Station Licenses

All radio stations aboard vessels must be licensed by the Federal Communications Commission. Ship stations are licensed primarily for the safety of life and property; therefore, distress and safety communications must have absolute priority. The licensee is responsible at all times for the lawful and proper operation of his station.

Application for a ship station license including radionavigation (radar) and EPIRB (see a later section for special information concerning EPIRBs) is made on FCC Form 502. This form may be obtained from any FCC Field Office. The completed application, signed and with the $4.00 application fee enclosed is then sent to the Federal Communications Commission, P. O. Box 1040, Gettysburg, PA 17325. Application processing time is approximately 6 to 8 weeks. The regular term of a ship station license is 5 years.

Interim Station License

The Commission realizes that some individuals may want to start operating their radiotelephones immediately and not wait the 6 to 8 week processing time. To meet this need, the applicant may obtain an interim ship station license. This may be done by the applicant or his representative appearing in person at the nearest FCC Field Office, filing a properly completed application (FCC Form 502) and requesting an interim ship station license. This license, valid for six months from the date of issuance, permits the applicant to operate his ship radiotelephone station while awaiting receipt of the regular term license. The regular term license will be mailed to the licensee prior to the expiration of the interim permit. An interim license does not apply to renewal applications. The application fee for a ship station license is $10.00 when accompanied with a request for an interim station license.

Renewal of Ship Station License

An application for renewal of a ship radiotelephone station license is made on FCC Form 405-B. This form is ordinarily mailed to the station licensee 60 days prior to the expiration date of his license. If the form has not been received 30 days prior to the expiration of current license, FCC Form 405-B may be obtained upon request from any FCC office. Application for renewal must be received by the Commission prior to the expiration date of the station license. A $4.00 fee is required.

Discontinuing Ship Station Operation

If you permanently discontinue the operation of the ship radio station, as for example, if you sell your boat, you are required to promptly return the station license to the Secretary, Federal Communications Commission, Washington, D. C. 20554. In the event that the license is not available for this purpose, a letter or telegram must be sent to the Secretary stating the reason why the license is not available and requesting that the license be cancelled. Otherwise, any violations committed in the operation of the station may be your responsibility.

Modification of Ship Station License

An application for modification of the station license must be filed when any transmitting equipment is added that does not operate in a frequency band or bands authorized in the ship station license. This application should be filed on FCC Form 502. A $4.00 application fee is required.

No application for modification is required for additions and/or replacement of FCC type accepted radiotelephone transmitters that operate in the same frequency band(s) as specified in the station license.

The licensee must promptly notify the Commission when the name of the licensee is changed, when the mailing address of the licensee is changed, or in the event that the vessel's name is changed. This notice, which may be in letter form, should be sent to the Federal Communications Commission, P. O. Box 1040, Gettysburg, PA 17325, or to the Secretary, Federal Communications Commission, Washington, D. C. 20554. A copy of the letter should be posted with the station license until a new license is issued. No formal application or fee is required in these cases.

VHF Equipment

All ship stations employing frequencies in the 2 MHz band must also be equipped to operate in the 156-162 MHz band. Licensees authorized by their existing licenses to operate in the 2 MHz band may install and operate VHF equipment under authority of their existing licenses.

Operator Permit or License

The radiotelephone transmitter in a ship station may be operated only by a person holding a permit or operator license. The authorized operator may permit others to speak over the microphone if he starts, supervises, and ends the operation, makes the necessary log entries, and gives the necessary identification. The authorization usually held by radio operators aboard small vessels is the Restricted Radiotelephone Operator Permit.

The Restricted Radiotelephone Operator Permit is the minimum authorization required for the operation of a ship station. Neither the Restricted Radiotelephone Operator Permit nor the Third Class Radiotelephone Operator Permit allow the operator to make any transmitter adjustment that may affect the proper operation of the station. Any such adjustments must be made by only the holder of a First- or Second-Class Radiotelegraph or Radiotelephone License. The Restricted Radiotelephone Operator Permit or verification card of a higher class license must be posted or kept on the operator's person.

An application for a Restricted Radiotelephone Operator Permit is made on FCC Form 753. The completed form is sent to the Federal Communications Commission, P. O. Box 1050, Gettysburg, PA 17325, along with the $4.00 application fee. No oral or written examination is required. Applicants must be at least 14 years of age. Field offices will accept applications if the applicant makes a satisfactory showing of immediate need for the permit and if the application (Form 753) is presented in person by the applicant. The Restricted Radiotelephone Operator Permit is issued for the lifetime of the licensee.

Special Provisions for Aliens

Except for foreign governments and representatives of foreign governments, aliens may be granted ship station licenses and Restricted Radiotelephone Operator Permits. The operator permit granted to an alien is valid only for operating the ship station licensed in his name. Special forms and provisions are applicable to aliens and, therefore, an alien should contact an FCC Field Office for information before applying for his license and permit.

Radiotelephone Equipment

FCC Type Acceptance

All radiotelephone transmitters used in a ship station must be type accepted under Part 83 of the FCC Regulations. A list of all equipment acceptable for licensing in the marine service is included in the Commission's Radio Equipment List. Any FCC Field Office can advise you whether the radiotelephone you propose to use is type accepted under Part 83, if you furnish them with the manufacturer's name and the model or type number of the transmitter.

Adjustments of Transmitting Equipment

The station licensee is responsible for the proper technical operation of his equipment. All transmitter measurements, adjustments, or repairs that may affect the proper operation of the transmitter must be made by or under the immediate supervision and responsibility of a person holding a valid First- or Second-Class Radiotelegraph or Radiotelephone Operator License. A special license endorsement is required to service a radar set.

Selecting a VHF Radiotelephone

Before purchasing a VHF-FM radiotelephone, you should carefully consider your requirements and select a unit that will meet these needs. You should remember that VHF communications are essentially "line of sight." The average ship-to-ship

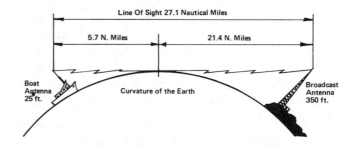

12-2 Line of Sight Distances for Radio

range is about 10 to 15 miles, while the normally expected ship-to-shore range is 20 to 30 miles. These figures vary depending upon transmitter power, antenna height, and terrain.

The FCC limits the transmitter power for VHF-FM to 25 watts for vessels and also requires the capability to reduce transmitter power to not more than one watt for short range communication. No matter how powerful your transmitter is, if you can't hear the other station — you can't communicate. The receiver performance of your radiotelephone is therefore an important aspect of your communication capability.

Two of the most important receiver specifications are sensitivity and adjacent channel rejection. These two factors are usually a good indication of how a particular receiver will perform.

In a VHF-FM receiver, the sensitivity is usually given as the number of microvolts required to produce 20 decibels (dB) of quieting. The lower or smaller the number of microvolts for the same amount of quieting, the better the sensitivity of the receiver; for example, 0.5 microvolt is better than 2.0 microvolts. (Note: Some manufacturers specify the sensitivity at other than 20 dB, so you should be sure you are comparing receivers based on the same criteria.)

The adjacent channel rejection is one of several different specifications that indicate the receiver's ability to reject unwanted signals and accept only the desired signal. It is usually given as a negative number of dB. The larger the absolute number of dB, the better the adjacent channel rejection of the receiver. For example, a receiver with an adjacent channel rejection of –70 dB would normally perform much better than one with an adjacent channel rejection of –50 dB.

Although many manufacturers do not include these figures on their data sheets, they are a highly reliable indication of the performance of a receiver; and the prospective buyer would be well advised to contact the manufacturer to obtain this information. It is also strongly recommended that the buyer seek the advice of a competent communications technician before making a final choice on a particular radiotelephone.

Installation of a VHF Radiotelephone

The licensee of a ship station may install a *pretested* VHF marine radiotelephone transmitter in his ship station. No operator license is required to perform this kind of installation. This permission does NOT authorize the ship station licensee to add or substitute channels or to make any modifications to the transmitter, with the exception that where the FCC has type accepted a transmitter in which factory sealed pretested "plug-in" modules are used for the addition or substitution of channels in the transmitter, the licensee may add or substitute channels using these "plug-in" modules. Unless the individual is working with coaxial cable, he should have a technician attach the coaxial cable plug to the antenna cable.

Required Frequencies and Equipment Channelization

All ship radiotelephone stations in the 156 to 162 MHz band must be equipped to operate on:

1. Ch. 16 (156.8 MHz) International Distress, Safety and Calling frequency for VHF.

2. Ch. 6 (156.3 MHz) Intership Safety Channel.

3. At least one working frequency.

The number of channels installed in your set will depend largely on how the set will be used, where the vessel will be operated, and what coast stations are operating in your area. While fewer than twelve channels may be satisfactory for some vessels, installation of a radiotelephone with less than twelve channel capability is not recommended.

The marine VHF band in the United States consists of 47 channels including two weather channels.

12-3 Thunderstorm

The following tables include a listing of the noncommercial frequencies available, an explanation of the use of the various channels and some suggestions on the selection of channels for recreational (noncommercial) vessels.

The more channels you have in your set, the better your communication capability will be. Caution must be exercised, however, in selecting and using channels in accordance with their authorized purposes as set out in Table II.

The following table can be used as an aid in selecting the proper channels to install in your VHF radio. The suggested number of channels to be selected from each group is given for recreational vessels equipped with radiotelephones having six and twelve channel capability. An explanation of the use of each channel is given in Table II.

TABLE I

Channel Numbers	Type of Communication	Suggested Channel Selection for Recreational Vessels 6 Ch.	12 Ch.
16	**DISTRESS, SAFETY & CALLING** Intership & ship to coast	*	*
6	**INTERSHIP SAFETY** Intership. NOT to be used for non-safety intership communications	*	*
22	Communications with U. S. Coast Guard ship, coast, or aircraft stations.	1	1
65, 66, 12, 73, 14, 74, 20	**PORT OPERATIONS** Intership & ship to coast		1
13	**NAVIGATIONAL**		1
68, 9	**NON-COMMERCIAL** Intership & ship to coast	1	2
69, 71, 78	**NON-COMMERCIAL** Ship to coast		1
70, 72	**NON-COMMERCIAL** Intership		2
24, 84, 25, 85, 26, 86, 27, 87, 28	**PUBLIC CORRESPONDENCE** Ship to public coast	2	2
162.40 & 162.55 MHz	**NOAA WEATHER SERVICE** Ship receive only	**	**

* These stations are required to be installed in every ship station equipped with a VHF radio.

**The weather receive channels are half-channels (receive only) one or both of which are recommended to be installed in each ship station. Many manufacturers include one or both of these channels in their sets in addition to the normal six or twelve channel capacity.

TABLE II

CHANNEL USAGE

Channel Number	Ship Transmit	Ship Receive	Intended Use
6	156.300	156.300	INTERSHIP SAFETY. Required for all VHF-FM equipped vessels for intership safety purposes and search and rescue (SAR) communications with ships and aircraft of the U. S. Coast Guard. Must not be used for non-safety communications.
9	156.450	156.450	COMMERCIAL AND NON-COMMERCIAL (INTERSHIP AND SHIP-TO-COAST). Some examples of use are communications with commercial marinas and public docks to obtain supplies to schedule repairs and contacting commercial vessels about matters of common concern.
12	156.600	156.600	PORT OPERATIONS (INTERSHIP AND SHIP-TO-COAST). Available to all vessels. This is a traffic advisory channel for use by agencies directing the movement of vessels in or near ports, locks, or waterways. Messages are restricted to the operational handling, movement and safety to ships and, in emergency, to the safety of persons. It should be noted, however, in the Ports of New York and New Orleans channels 11, 12 and 14 are to be used exclusively for the Vessel Traffic System being developed by the United States Coast Guard.
13	156.650	156.650	NAVIGATIONAL — (SHIP'S) BRIDGE TO (SHIP'S) BRIDGE. This channel is available to all vessels and is required on large passenger and commercial vessels (including many tugs). Use is limited to navigational communications such as in meeting and passing situations. Abbreviated short

operating procedures and 1 watt maximum power (except in certain special instances) are used on this channel for both calling and working. For recreational vessels, this channel should be used for *listening* to determine the intentions of large vessels. This is also the primary channel used at locks and bridges operated by the U. S. Army Corps of Engineers.

14	156.700	156.700	PORT OPERATIONS (INTERSHIP AND SHIP-TO-COAST). Same as channel 12.
15	156.750	156.750	ENVIRONMENTAL (RECEIVE ONLY). A receive only channel used to broadcast environmental information to ships such as weather, sea conditions, time signals for navigation, notices to mariners, etc. Most of this information is also broadcast on the weather (WX) channels.
16	156.800	156.800	DISTRESS, SAFETY AND CALLING (INTERSHIP AND SHIP-TO-COAST). Required channel for all VHF-FM equipped vessels. Must be monitored at all times station is in operation (except when actually communicating on another channel). This channel is monitored also by the Coast Guard, public coast stations and many limited coast stations. Calls to other vessels are normally initiated on this channel. Then, except in an emergency, you must switch to a working channel. For additional information see the sections on operating procedures.
17	156.850	156.850	STATE CONTROL. Available to all vessels to communicate with ships and coast stations operated by state or local governments. Messages are restricted to regulation and control, or rendering assistance. Use of low power (1 watt) setting is required by international treaty.
20	157.000	161.600	PORT OPERATIONS (SHIP-TO-COAST). Available to all vessels. This is a traffic advisory channel for use by agencies directing the movement of vessels in or near ports, locks, or waterways. Messages are restricted to the operational handling, movement and safety of ships and, in emergency, to the safety of persons.
21A	157.050	157.050	U. S. GOVERNMENT ONLY.
22A	157.100	157.100	COAST GUARD LIAISON. This channel is used for communications with U. S. Coast Guard ship, coast and aircraft stations after first establishing communications on channel 16. *It is strongly recommended that every VHF radiotelephone include this channel.*
23A	157.150	157.150	U. S. GOVERNMENT ONLY
24	157.200	161.800	PUBLIC CORRESPONDENCE (SHIP-TO-COAST). Available to all vessels to communicate with public coast stations operated by telephone companies. Channels 26 and 28 are the primary public correspondence channels and therefore become the first choice for the cruising vessel having limited channel capacity.
25	157.250	161.850	PUBLIC CORRESPONDENCE (SHIP-TO-COAST). Same as channel 24.
26	157.300	161.900	PUBLIC CORRESPONDENCE (SHIP-TO-COAST). Same as channel 24.
27	157.350	161.950	PUBLIC CORRESPONDENCE (SHIP-TO-COAST). Same as channel 24.

28	157.400	162.000	PUBLIC CORRESPONDENCE (SHIP-TO-COAST). Same as channel 24.
65A	156.275	156.275	PORT OPERATIONS (INTERSHIP AND SHIP-TO-COAST). Same as channel 12.
66A	156.325	156.325	PORT OPERATIONS (INTERSHIP AND SHIP-TO-COAST). Same as channel 12.
68	156.425	156.425	NON-COMMERCIAL (INTERSHIP AND SHIP-TO-COAST). A working channel for non-commercial vessels. May be used for obtaining supplies, scheduling repairs, berthing and accommodations, etc. from yacht clubs or marinas, and intership operational communications such as piloting or arranging for rendezvous with other vessels. It should be noted that channel 68 (and channel 70 for intership only) is the most popular non-commercial channel and therefore is the first choice for vessels having limited channel capacity.
69	156.475	156.475	NON-COMMERCIAL (SHIP-TO-COAST). Same as channel 68, except limited to ship to shore communications.
70	156.525	156.525	NON-COMMERCIAL (INTERSHIP). Same as channel 68, except limited to intership communications.
71	156.575	156.575	NON-COMMERCIAL (SHIP-TO-COAST). Same as channel 68, except limited to ship to shore communications.
72	156.625	156.625	NON-COMMERCIAL (INTERSHIP). Same as channel 68 except limited to intership communications.
73	156.675	156.675	PORT OPERATIONS (INTERSHIP AND SHIP-TO-COAST). Same as channel 20.
74	156.725	156.725	PORT OPERATIONS (INTERSHIP AND SHIP-TO-COAST). Same as channel 20.
78A	156.925	156.925	NON-COMMERCIAL (SHIP-TO-COAST). Same as channel 68, except limited to ship to shore communications.
81A	157.075	157.075	U. S. GOVERNMENT ONLY.
82A	157.125	157.125	U. S. GOVERNMENT ONLY.
83A	157.175	157.175	U. S. GOVERNMENT ONLY.
84	157.225	161.825	PUBLIC CORRESPONDENCE (SHIP-TO-COAST). Same as channel 24.
85	157.275	161.875	PUBLIC CORRESPONDENCE (SHIP-TO-COAST). Same as channel 24.
86	157.325	161.925	PUBLIC CORRESPONDENCE (SHIP-TO-COAST). Same as channel 24.
87	157.375	161.975	PUBLIC CORRESPONDENCE (SHIP-TO-COAST). Same as channel 24.
WX1		162.550	WEATHER (RECEIVE ONLY). To receive weather broadcasts of the Department of Commerce, National Oceanic and Atmospheric Administration (NOAA).
WX2		162.400	WEATHER (RECEIVE ONLY). Same as WX1.

NOTE: The addition of the letter "A" to the channel number indicates that the ship receive channel used in the United States is different from the one used by vessels and coast stations of other countries. Vessels equipped for U. S. operations only, will experience difficulty communicating with foreign ships and coast stations on these channels.

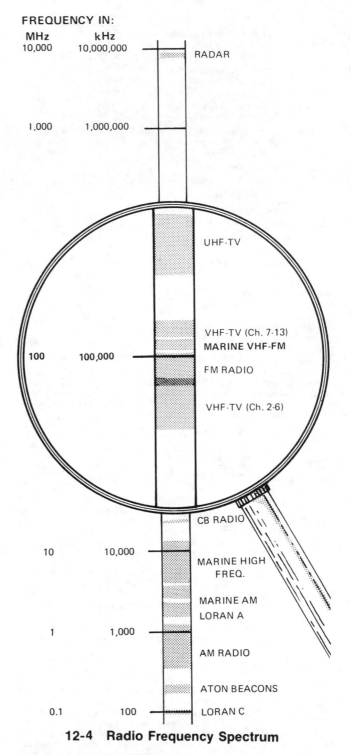

FREQUENCY IN:

MHz	kHz	
10,000	10,000,000	RADAR
1,000	1,000,000	
		UHF-TV
		VHF-TV (Ch. 7-13)
100	100,000	MARINE VHF-FM
		FM RADIO
		VHF-TV (Ch. 2-6)
		CB RADIO
10	10,000	MARINE HIGH FREQ.
		MARINE AM
		LORAN A
1	1,000	
		AM RADIO
		ATON BEACONS
0.1	100	LORAN C

12-4 Radio Frequency Spectrum

Medium and High Frequency Radiotelephone Equipment

Previously, most marine radiotelephones operated in the 2-3 MHz medium frequency (MF) band. This equipment, which is now obsolete, employed double sideband (DSB) full carrier type of amplitude modulation (AM). These DSB radiotelephones have been superseded by single sideband (SSB) equipment. The FCC requires that all new installations in the medium frequency (MF) band employ the SSB mode. Further, all DSB transmitters must cease operation by January 1, 1977.

Single sideband provides a number of advantages over DSB equipment. Most important, the occupied bandwidth is narrower. Therefore, more stations can be accommodated in the marine bands. The SSB mode is more efficient than DSB. This permits longer range communications with less battery consumption than for DSB radiotelephones.

SSB medium and high frequency radiotelephones are primarily for offshore and high-seas service. For that reason, information on SSB technique is beyond the scope of this chapter.

Emergency Position Indicating
Radio Beacon (EPIRB)

The EPIRB is basically a small VHF transmitter that operates on 121.5 and 243 MHz, and sends out a distinctive signal on these two frequencies. These frequencies are aeronautical emergency frequencies and are monitored by commercial, private (121.5 MHz), and military (243 MHz) aircraft.

There are two different EPIRBS available. There is the Class A EPIRB which is capable of floating free of a sinking vessel and activating automatically, and there is a Class B EPIRB which must be activated manually. Either one must be FCC licensed.

In making application for FCC license, use FCC Form 502, whether the EPIRB is to be a part of the complement of transmitting equipment aboard or even if an EPIRB only is to be authorized. If no transmitters other than the EPIRB are to be authorized, however, no fee is required.

27 MHz Citizens Radio Band (CB)

Operations in the Citizens Radio Service is intended primarily to provide an individual means of conducting personal or business communications over a typical range of 5 to 15 miles. You may operate CB equipment aboard your boat on any of the 23 channels that have been made available in the 27 MHz Class D service on a shared basis.

FCC regulations limit the maximum power output from the transmitter to 4 watts peak envelope power (PEP) for amplitude modulation (AM) equipment, and 12 watts PEP for single sideband transmitters, with a maximum antenna height of 20 feet above the highest point of the vessel.

Channel 9 in the Citizens Band has been designated as an emergency channel for emergency communications involving the safety of life of individuals, protection or private property, or for rendering assistance to a motorist. Channel 11 is designated for calling and is limited to that use only.

No operator permit or operator license is required; however, a station license is required prior to operation of a CB radio. The application should be filed with the FCC using Form 505. The filing fee is $4.00. Mail the application to the Federal Communications Commission, P. O. Box 1010, Gettysburg, PA 17325.

Citizens Radio Service is NOT a substitute for the marine distress system, as the Coast Guard does not monitor any of the Citizens Band channels and is not equipped with radios to operate on any CB frequency.

Operating Procedures (Other than Distress, Urgency and Safety)

Maintain a Watch

Whenever your radio is turned on, keep the receiver tuned to the appropriate distress and calling frequency, 156.8 MHz or 2182 kHz. This listening watch must be maintained at all times the station is in operation and you are not actually communicating.

Since this watch is required for safety and to facilitate communications by providing a common calling channel, it is not permissible for one vessel in a fleet of vessels traveling together to maintain this watch while the other vessels guard another channel, such as common intership channel. You may maintain a watch on a working channel, however, and may establish communications directly on that channel provided you simultaneously maintain your watch on the distress and calling channel.

Don't forget to record the times you maintain this watch in your Radio Log.

Choose the Correct Channel or Frequency

Each of the marine frequencies and channels is authorized for a specific type of communication. It is therefore required that you choose the correct channel for the type of communications you wish to engage in. For example, certain channels are set aside exclusively for intership use and may not be used for ship to coast communications. Channels are further classified according to the subject matter or content of the communications. For example, Commercial communications are limited to commercial operations and may be used only to discuss matters pertaining to the commercial enterprise the vessel is engaged in.

The authorized use of each of the VHF channels is given in Table II. For recreational boats, most of the communications will be limited to what is known as Non-commercial (Operational in the MF band) communications and Public Correspondence.

Public Correspondence

By using the channels set aside for Public Correspondence and establishing communications through the facilities of the public coast stations, you are able to make and receive calls from any telephone on shore. There is no restriction on the content of your communication and you do not have to limit your messages strictly to ship's business. Except for distress calls, public coast stations will charge for this service.

Non-Commercial or Operational

These channels have been set aside to fulfill the wide scope of needs of the recreational (non-commercial) vessel. Frequencies are available for both intership and ship to shore (with limited coast stations) communications. Permissible communications on these channels are those concerning the movement of vessels, obtaining supplies and service and, in general, anything else that pertains to the needs and normal operation of the vessel. "Chit-chat" is not permitted.

Coast Guard

The government frequencies 157.1 MHz (Channel 22) and 2670 kHz are widely used by recreational boating operators for communicating with U. S. Coast Guard shore stations and ship stations, and with USCG Auxiliary vessels when these vessels are operating under orders. When using these channels, you must first establish communications on the appropriate calling frequency (Channel 16 or 2182 kHz).

12-5 Coast Guard Communication Station

Calling Intership

Turn your radiotelephone on and listen on the appropriate distress and calling frequency, Channel 16 or 2182 kHz, to make sure it is not being used. If it is clear, put your transmitter on the air. This is usually done by depressing the "push to talk" button on the microphone. (To hear a reply, you must release this button.)

Speak directly into the microphone in a normal tone of voice. Speak clearly and distinctly. Call the vessel with which you wish to communicate by using its name; then identify your vessel with its name and FCC assigned call sign. Do not add unnecessary words and phrases such as "come in, Bob" or "Do you read me?" Limit the use of phonetics to poor transmission conditions.

This preliminary call must not exceed 30 seconds. If contact is not made, wait at least 2 minutes before repeating the call. After this time interval, make the call in the same manner. This procedure may be repeated no more than three times. If contact is not made during this period, you must wait at least 15 minutes before making your next attempt.

Once contact is established on Channel 16 or 2182 kHz, you must switch to an appropriate frequency for further communication. You may only use Channel 16 and 2182 kHz for calling and in emergency situations.

Since switching to a "working" frequency is required to carry out the actual communications, it is often helpful to monitor the "working" frequency you wish to use, briefly, before initiating the call on Channel 16 or 2182 kHz. This will help prevent you from interrupting other users of the channel.

All communications should be kept as brief as possible and at the end of the communication each vessel is required to give its call sign, after which, both vessels switch back to the distress and calling channel in order to reestablish the watch.

Two examples of acceptable forms for establishing communication with another vessel follow:

EXAMPLE I

Vessel	Voice Transmission
BLUE DUCK (on Channel 16)	"MARY JANE THIS IS BLUE DUCK WHISKEY ALFA 1234" (The name of the vessel being called may be said two or three times if conditions demand).
MARY JANE (on Channel 16)	"BLUE DUCK THIS IS MARY JANE WHISKEY ALFA 5678 REPLY 68" (Or some other proper working channel.)
BLUE DUCK (on Channel 16)	"68 or "ROGER" (If unable to reply on the channel selected, an appropriate alternate should be selected.)
BLUE DUCK (on working channel)	"BLUE DUCK"
MARY JANE (on working channel)	"MARY JANE"
BLUE DUCK (on working channel)	(Continues with message and terminates communication within 3 minutes. At the end of the communication, each vessel gives its call sign.)

EXAMPLE II   A short form most useful when both parties are familiar with it.

BLUE DUCK (on Channel 16)	"MARY JANE BLUE DUCK WHISKEY ALFA 1234 REPLY 68"
MARY JANE (on Channel 68)	"MARY JANE WHISKEY ALFA 5678"
BLUE DUCK (on Channel 68)	"BLUE DUCK" (Continues message and terminates communications as indicated in EXAMPLE I.)

Calling Ship to Coast (Other than U. S. Coast Guard)

The procedures for calling coast stations are similar to those used in making intership calls with the exception that you normally initiate the call on the assigned frequency of the coast station.

Routine Radio Check

Radio checks may be made on 156.8 MHz (Channel 16) but should be completed by immediately shifting to a working channel.

Listen to make sure that the Distress and Calling frequency is not busy. If it is free, put your transmitter on the air and call a specific station or vessel and include the phrase "request a radio check" in your initial call. For example, "MARY JANE - THIS IS BLUE DUCK - WHISKEY ALFA 1234 - REQUEST RADIO CHECK CHANNEL _____ (names working channel) - OVER." After the reply by Mary Jane, Blue Duck would then say "HOW DO YOU HEAR ME? - OVER." The proper response by Mary Jane, depending on the respective conditions, would be:

"I HEAR YOU LOUD AND CLEAR," or

"I HEAR YOU WEAK BUT CLEAR," or

"YOU ARE LOUD BUT DISTORTED," etc.

Do not respond to a request for a radio check with such phrases as:

"I HEAR YOU FIVE BY FIVE," or

"I *READ* YOU LOUD AND CLEAR."

Figures are not a clear response as to the character of the transmission and the word *"read"* implies a radio check by a meter.

It is illegal to call a Coast Guard Station on 2182 kHz for a radio check. This prohibition does not apply to tests conducted during investigations by FCC representatives or when qualified radio technicians are installing equipment or correcting deficiencies in the station radiotelephone equipment.

Radiotelephone Station Log

A radio log is required; each page must (1) be numbered; (2) bear the name of the vessel and call sign; and (3) be signed by the operator. Entries must show the time each watch begins and ends. All distress and alarm signals must be recorded as completely as possible. This requirement applies to all related communications transmitted or intercepted, and to all urgency and safety signals and communications transmitted. A record of all installations, services, or maintenance work performed that may affect the proper operation of the station must also be entered by the licensed operator doing the work, including his address and the class, serial number, and expiration date of his license.

The 24-hour system is used in a radio log for recording time; that is, 8:45 a.m. is written as 0845 and 1:00 p.m. as 1300. Local time is normally used, but Eastern Standard Time (EST) or Greenwich Mean Time (GMT) must be used throughout the Great Lakes. Vessels on international voyages use GMT exclusively. Whichever time is used, the appropriate abbreviation for the time zone must be entered at the head of the time column.

Radio logs must be retained for at least a year, and for 3 years if they contain entries concerning distress, and for longer periods if they concern communications being investigated by the FCC or against which claims or complaints have been filed.

Station logs must be made available for inspection at the request of an FCC representative, who may remove them from the licensee's possession. On request, the licensee shall mail them to the FCC by either registered or certified mail, return receipt requested.

A sample "Ship Radio Station Log Sheet" and a "Ship Radio Station Maintenance Log Sheet" are shown.

SAMPLE

SHIP RADIO STATION LOG SHEET

(Recreational Vessels)

Page No. _____ Name of Vessel _____ Radio Call _____

DATE /1	DISTRESS LISTENING WATCH TIME /2 /3 (EST, GMT, ETC.) Start Stop	Channel or Freq. /4	Priority MESSAGE TIME /2	MESSAGE /5	OPERATOR'S SIGNATURE

1 Log: Day, Month, Year

2 Use GMT or Local Time. Show which used. Use 24-hour system; that is, 8:45 a.m. is entered as 0845, and 2:15 p.m. as 1415.

3 Log time when radiotelephone is turned on and when turned off.

4 Log VHF Channel 16 (156.800 MHz) or 2182 kHz, as appropriate.

5 Record as completely as possible all distress communications transmitted or intercepted and all urgency and safety communications transmitted. Retain logs for at least one year; for 3 years if they include entries related to distress; longer if they concern communications being investigated by the FCC or against which claims or complaints have been filed.

SAMPLE

SHIP RADIO STATION MAINTENANCE LOG

(Recreational Vessels)

Page No. _____ Name of Vessel _____ Radio Call _____

DATE	SERVICE RECORD	TECHNICIAN'S LICENSE DATA
		Class _____ Number _____ Expiration Date _____ Signature _____ Address _____
		Class _____ Number _____ Expiration Date _____ Signature _____ Address _____

Include record of installations, repairs, adjustments and service performed by FCC licensed Radiotelegraph or Radiotelephone 1st or 2nd Class Radio Operator. Special endorsement required for Radar installation and repair.

Secrecy of Communications

The Communications Act prohibits divulging interstate or foreign communications transmitted, received, or intercepted by wire or radio to anyone other than the addressee or his agent or attorney, or to persons necessarily involved in the handling of the communications, unless the sender authorizes the divulgence of the contents of the communication. Persons intercepting such communications or becoming acquainted with them are also prohibited from divulging the contents or using the contents for the benefit of themselves or others.

Obviously, this requirement of secrecy does not apply to radio communications relating to ships in distress, nor to radio communications transmitted by amateurs or broadcasts by others for use of the general public. It does apply, however, to all other communications. These statutory secrecy provisions cover messages addressed to a specific ship station or coast station or to a person via such station.

Obscenity, Indecency and Profanity

When two or more ship stations are communicating with each other, they are talking over an extensive party line. Users should always bear this fact in mind and assume that many persons are listening. All users therefore have a compelling moral obligation to avoid offensive remarks. They also have a strict legal obligation inasmuch as it is a criminal offense for any person to transmit communications containing obscene, indecent, or profane words, language, or meaning. Whoever utters any obscene, indecent or profane language by means of radio communication may be fined not more than $10,000 or imprisoned not more than 2 years, or both.

Procedure Words

One way of cutting down the length of radio transmissions without loss of meaning is by the use of Procedure Words. These are individual words and short phrases which express complex thoughts in abbreviated form. They are employed in transmitting situations which frequently recur — the most obvious example, perhaps, is the word "OUT," which (when spoken at the end of a message) signifies: "THIS IS THE END OF MY TRANSMISSION TO YOU AND NO ANSWER IS REQUIRED OR EXPECTED."

Procedure words can only be successful in shortening message sending when (1) their meaning is fully understood by sender and listener and (2) they are properly used. The phrase over and out, for instance, is improper, since the two terms are contradictory.

Following is a list of procedure words and their meanings. It will take time for the novice operator to become used to this form of verbal shorthand, but effort spent in learning these few phrases will be repaid in clearer, shorter messages.

PROCEDURE WORD	MEANING
OUT	This is the end of my transmission to you and no answer is required or expected.
OVER	This is the end of my transmission to you and a response is necessary. Go ahead and transmit.
	(Note: Observe the considerable difference between "Over," used during a message exchange, and "Out," employed at the end of an exchange. "Over" should be omitted when the context of a transmission makes it clear that it is unnecessary.)
ROGER	I have received your last transmission satisfactorily.
WILCO	Your last message has been received, understood, and will be complied with.
THIS IS	This transmission is from the station whose name or call sign immediately follows.
	(Note: Normally used at the beginning of a transmission: "BLUE DUCK — THIS IS — GIMLET — WHISKEY ZULU ECHO 3488." Sometimes omitted in transmissions between experienced operators familiar with each other's boat names.)
FIGURES	Figures or numbers follow.
	(Used when numbers occur in the middle of a message: "Vessel length is figures two three feet.")
SPEAK SLOWER	Your transmission is at too fast a speed, speak more slowly.
SAY AGAIN	Repeat.
WORDS TWICE	Communication is difficult — give every phrase twice.

I SPELL	I shall spell the next word phonetically.	
	(Note: Often used where a proper name or unusual word is important to a message: "Boat name is *Martha*. I spell Mike; Alfa; Romeo; Tango; Hotel; Alfa." See phonetic alphabet.)	
MESSAGE FOLLOWS	A message that requires recording is about to follow.	
BREAK	I separate the text from other portions of the message; or one message from one immediately following.	
WAIT	I must pause for a few seconds; stand by for further transmission.	
	(Note: This is normally used when a message must be interrupted by the *sender*. If, for instance, one station is asked for information not instantly available, its operator might send "WAIT" while looking up the required data. In addition, WAIT may also be used to suspend the transmission of an on-the-air test. If a station announces its intention of making such a test, another station using the channel may transmit the word "WAIT;" the test shall then be suspended.	
AFFIRMATIVE	You are correct, or what you have transmitted is correct.	
NEGATIVE	No.	
SILENCE (said three times)	Cease all transmissions immediately. Silence will be maintained until lifted.	
	(Note: Used to clear routine business from a channel when an emergency is in progress. In this meaning *Silence* is correctly pronounced SEE LONSS.)	
SILENCE FINI	Silence is lifted.	
	(Note: Signifies the end of the emergency and the resumption of normal traffic. Correctly pronounced SEE LONSS FEE NEE.)	

Letter	Phonetic Equivalent	Pronunciation
A	ALFA	*AL* FAH
B	BRAVO	*BRAH* VOH
C	CHARLIE	*CHAR* LEE
D	DELTA	*DELL* TAH
E	ECHO	*ECK* OH
F	FOXTROT	*FOKS* TROT
G	GOLF	GOLF
H	HOTEL	HO *TELL*
I	INDIA	*IN* DEE AH
J	JULIETT	JEW LEE *ETT*
K	KILO	*KEY* LOH
L	LIMA	*LEE* MAH
M	MIKE	MIKE
N	NOVEMBER	NO *VEM* BER
O	OSCAR	*OSS* CAH
P	PAPA	PAH *PAH*
Q	QUEBEC	KEH *BECK*
R	ROMEO	*ROW* ME OH
S	SIERRA	SEE *AIR* RAH
T	TANGO	*TANG* GO
U	UNIFORM	*YOU* NEE FORM
V	VICTOR	*VIK* TAH
W	WHISKEY	*WISS* KEY
X	XRAY	*ECKS* RAY
Y	YANKEE	*YANG* KEY
Z	ZULU	*ZOO* LOO
0	ZERO	ZERO
1	ONE	WUN
2	TWO	TOO
3	THREE	THUH REE
4	FOUR	FO WER
5	FIVE	FI YIV
6	SIX	SIX
7	SEVEN	SEVEN
8	EIGHT	ATE
9	NINE	NINER

Operating Procedures (Distress, Urgency and Safety)

General

If you are in distress, you may use any means at your disposal to attract attention and obtain assistance. You are by no means limited to the use of your marine radiotelephone. Often, visual signals, including flags, flares, lights, smoke, etc., or audible signals such as your boat's horn or siren, or a whistle, or megaphone will get the attention and help you need.

For boats equipped with a marine radiotelephone, help is just a radio signal away. Two marine radiotelephone channels have been set aside for use in emergencies. Channel 16 (156.8 MHz), the VHF-FM Distress, Safety and Calling frequency is the primary emergency channel in the VHF marine band. For those who have medium frequency (MF) radiotelephone also, 2182 kHz is the emergency frequency for use in that band. You are not limited to the use of these channels; you may use any other frequency channel available to you. The working frequency of the local marine operator (public telephone coast station) is a good example of a channel that is monitored.

There are other types of marine stations located ashore that are listening to Channel 16 and 2182 kHz along with the marine radio equipped vessels operating in the area. Because of this coverage, almost any kind of a call for assistance on Channel 16 (or 2182 kHz) will probably get a response. There are times, however, when the situation demands immediate attention; when you just can't tolerate delay. These are the times when you need to know how to use (or respond to) the Distress and Urgency signals and how to respond to the Safety signal.

Spoken Emergency Signals

There are three spoken emergency signals:

1. *Distress Signal: MAYDAY*
   The distress signal MAYDAY is used to indicate that a mobile station is threatened by grave and imminent danger and requests immediate assistance. MAYDAY has priority over all other communications.

2. *Urgency Signal: PAN (Properly pronounced PAHN)*
   Used when the safety of the vessel or person is in jeopardy. "Man overboard" messages are sent with the Urgency signal. PAN has priority over all other communications with the exception of distress traffic.

3. *Safety Signal: SECURITY (Pronounced SAY-CURITAY)*
   Used for messages concerning the safety of navigation or giving important meteorological warnings.

Any message headed by one of the emergency signals (MAYDAY, PAN, or SECURITY), must be given precedence over routine communications. This means listen. Don't transmit. Be prepared to help if you can. The decision of which of these emergency signals to use is the responsibility of the person in charge of the vessel.

Radiotelephone Alarm Signal

This signal consists of two audio frequency tones transmitted alternately. This signal is similar in sound to a two-tone siren used by some ambulances. When generated by automatic means, it shall be sent as continuously as practicable over a period of not less than 30 seconds nor more than 1 minute. The purpose of the signal is to attract attention of the person on watch or to actuate automatic devices giving the alarm. The radiotelephone alarm signal shall be used only with the distress signal except in two situations dealing with the Urgency Signal.

Sending Distress Call and Message

First end the Radiotelephone Alarm Signal, if available.

1. Distress signal MAYDAY (spoken three times)
2. The words THIS IS (spoken once)
3. Name of vessel in distress (spoken three times) and call sign (spoken once)

The Distress Message immediately follows the Distress Call and consists of:

4. Distress signal MAYDAY (spoken once)
5. Name of vessel (spoken once)

6. Position of vessel in distress by latitude and longitude or by bearing (true or magnetic, state which) and distance to a well-known landmark such as a navigational aid or small island, or in any terms which will assist a responding station in locating the vessel in distress

7. Nature of distress (sinking, fire, etc.)

8. Kind of assistance desired

9. Any other information which might facilitate rescue, such as:
   length or tonnage of vessel
   number of persons on board and number needing medical attention
   color of hull, decks, cabin, masts, etc.

10. The word OVER

EXAMPLE: Distress Call and Message

(Send Radiotelephone Alarm Signal, if available, for at least 30 seconds but not more than 1 minute.)

"MAYDAY - MAYDAY - MAYDAY
THIS IS — BLUE DUCK — BLUE DUCK —
BLUE DUCK — WHISKEY ALFA 1234
MAYDAY — BLUE DUCK
DUNGENESS LIGHT BEARS 185
DEGREES MAGNETIC — DISTANCE 2
MILES
STRUCK SUBMERGED OBJECT
NEED PUMPS — MEDICAL ASSISTANCE
AND TOW
THREE ADULTS — TWO CHILDREN
ABOARD
ONE PERSON COMPOUND FRACTURE
OF ARM
ESTIMATE CAN REMAIN AFLOAT TWO
HOURS
BLUE DUCK IS THIRTY-TWO FOOT
CABIN CRUISER — BLUE HULL —
WHITE DECK HOUSE
OVER"

NOTE: Repeat at intervals until answer is received. If no answer is received on the Distress frequency, repeat using any other available channel on which attention might be attracted.

Acknowledgement of Distress Message

If you hear a Distress Message from a vessel and it is not answered, then YOU must answer. If you are reasonably sure that the distressed vessel is not in your vicinity, you should wait a short time for others to acknowledge. In any event, you must log all pertinent details of the Distress Call and Message.

Offer of Assistance

After you acknowledge receipt of the distress message, allow a short interval of time for other stations to acknowledge receipt, if there are any in a position to assist. When you are sure of not interfering with other distress-related communications, contact the vessel in distress and advise them what assistance you can render. Make every effort to notify the Coast Guard. The offer-of assistance message shall be sent only with permission of the person in charge of your vessel.

Urgency Call and Message Procedures

The emergency signal PAN (pronounced PAHN), spoken three times, begins the Urgency Call. The Urgency Call and Message is transmitted on Channel 16 (or on 2182 kHz) in the same way as the Distress Call and Distress Message. The Urgency signal PAN indicates that the calling person has a message concerning the safety of the vessel, or a person in jeopardy. The Urgency signal is authorized for situations like the following:

—Transmission of an urgent storm warning by an authorized shore station.

—Loss of person overboard but only when the assistance of other vessels is required.

—No steering or power in shipping lane.

Sending Urgency Call and Message

The Urgency Call and Message usually includes the following:

1. The Urgency signal PAN (spoken three times)

2. Addressee ALL STATIONS (or a particular station)

3. The words THIS IS

4. Name of calling vessel (spoken three times) and call sign (spoken once)

5. The Urgency Message (state the urgent problem)

6. Position of vessel and any other information that will assist responding vessels. Include description of your vessel, etc.

7. The words THIS IS

DISTRESS COMMUNICATIONS FORM

Instructions: Complete this form now (except for items 6 through 9) and post near your radiotelephone.

Speak SLOWLY — CLEARLY — CALMLY

1. Make sure your radiotelephone is on.

2. Select either *VHF Channel 16* (156.8 MHz) or *2182* kHz.

3. Press microphone button and say: "MAYDAY — MAYDAY — MAYDAY."

4. Now say: "THIS IS _____ , _____ ,
   <u>your boat name</u>   <u>your boat name</u>

   _____ , _____ .
   <u>your boat name</u>   <u>your call letters</u>

5. MAYDAY _____
   <u>your boat name</u>

6. Now TELL WHERE YOU ARE (What navigational aids or landmarks are near?).

7. STATE THE NATURE OF YOUR DISTRESS.

8. GIVE NUMBER OF ADULTS AND CHILDREN ABOARD, AND CONDITIONS OF ANY INJURED.

9. ESTIMATE PRESENT SEAWORTHINESS OF YOUR BOAT.

10. BRIEFLY DESCRIBE YOUR BOAT:

    _____ _____ FEET; _____ FEET;
    State Registration No.   Length   Draft

    _____ ; _____ HULL;
    Type   Color

    _____ TRIM; _____ MASTS;
    Color   Number

    POWER;
    _____
    Type; Horsepower   Construction Material

    _____
    Anything else you think will help rescuers to find you.

11. Say: "I WILL BE LISTENING ON CHANNEL 16 / 2182." Cross out one which does not apply.

12. End Message by saying: "THIS IS _____
    your boat name
    _____ . OVER,"
    and call sign

13. Release microphone button and listen: Someone should answer. IF THEY DO NOT, REPEAT CALL, BEGINNING AT ITEM 3 ABOVE. If there is still no answer, switch to another channel and begin again.

VESSEL INFORMATION DATA SHEET

When requesting assistance from the Coast Guard, you may be asked to furnish the following details. This list should, therefore, be filled out as completely as possible and posted alongside your transmitter with the *Distress Communications Form*.

1. *Description of Vessel Requiring Assistance.*

Hull markings _____

Home port _____

Draft _____

Sails: Color _____

Markings _____

Bowsprit ? _____

Outriggers ? _____

Flying Bridge ? _____

Other prominent features _____

2. *Survival Gear Aboard (Circle Yes or No)*

Personal Flotation Devices	Yes	No
Flares	Yes	No
Flashlight	Yes	No
Raft	Yes	No
Dinghy or Tender	Yes	No
Anchor	Yes	No
Spotlight	Yes	No
Auxiliary power	Yes	No
Horn	Yes	No

3. *Electronic Equipment*

	VHF	MF	HF
Radiotelephone(s)			
Channels/Frequencies available	22 / 2670 kHz	Yes / Yes	No; / No
Radar		Yes	No
Depth Finder		Yes	No
Loran		Yes	No
Direction Finder		Yes	No
EPIRB		Yes	No

4. *Vessel Owner/Operator*

Owner name _____

Address _____

_____

Telephone number _____

Operator's name _____

Address _____

_____

Telephone number _____

Is owner/operator an experienced sailor?   Yes   No

5. *Miscellaneous*

Be prepared to describe local weather conditions.

8. Name of calling vessel and radio call sign (spoken once)
9. The word OVER

EXAMPLE: Urgency Call and Message

(Not involving possible use of radiotelephone alarm)

"PAN — PAN — PAN — ALL STATIONS (or a particular station)
THIS IS — BLUE DUCK — BLUE DUCK — BLUE DUCK — WHISKEY ALFA 1234
THREE MILES EAST OFF BARNEGAT LIGHT
HAVE LOST MY RUDDER
AM DRIFTING TOWARD SHORE AND REQUIRE TOW
SEVEN PERSONS ON BOARD
BLUE DUCK IS THIRTY-TWO FOOT CABIN CRUISER — BLUE HULL — WHITE DECK HOUSE
THIS IS — BLUE DUCK — WHISKEY ALFA 1234
OVER"

Safety Call and Message Procedures

The Safety Call, headed with the word SECURITY (Say-curitay, spoken three times), is transmitted on the Distress and Calling frequency (Channel 16 or 2182 kHz), together with a request to shift to a working frequency where the Safety Message will be given. The Safety Message may be given on any available working frequency.

United States Coast Guard stations routinely use the Safety Call SECURITY to alert boating operators that they are preparing to broadcast a message concerning safety of navigation. The call also precedes an important meteorological warning. The Safety Message itself usually is broadcast on Coast Guard Channel 22 (157.1 MHz) and 2670 kHz. Although recreational boating operators may use the Safety Signal and Message, in many cases they would get better results and perhaps suffer less criticism by giving the information to the Coast Guard without making a formal Safety Call. The Coast Guard usually has better broadcast coverage from its shore stations and will rebroadcast the information if it is appropriate.

Sending the Safety Call and Message

The Safety Call usually includes the following: (On Channel 16 or 2182 kHz.)
1. The Safety Signal SECURITY (spoken three times)
2. Addressee - ALL STATIONS (or a particular station)
3. The words THIS IS (spoken once)
4. Name of vessel calling and radio call sign
5. Announcement of the working channel (frequency) where the Safety Message will be given
6. Radio Call Sign
7. The word OUT

The Safety Message usually includes the following:
1. Select working channel (frequency) announced in step 5 above
2. The Safety Signal SECURITY (spoken three times)
3. The words ALL STATIONS (spoken once)
4. The words THIS IS (spoken once)
5. Name of vessel calling and radio call sign
6. Give the Safety Message
7. Repeat the Radio Call Sign
8. The word OUT

EXAMPLES: Safety Call and Message

on Channel 16

"SECURITY — SECURITY — SECURITY — ALL STATIONS
THIS IS — BLUE DUCK — WHISKEY ALFA 1234
LISTEN CHANNEL 68
WHISKEY ALFA 1234 — OUT

on Channel 68

"SECURITY — SECURITY — SECURITY — ALL STATIONS
THIS IS — BLUE DUCK — WHISKEY ALFA 1234
A LOG APPROXIMATELY TWENTY FEET LONG TWO FEET IN DIAMETER ADRIFT OFF HAINS POINT POTOMAC RIVER
WHISKEY ALFA 1234 — OUT"

Public Coast Stations

General

By utilizing the services of Public Coast Stations, ships may make and receive telephone calls to and from any telephone with access to the nationwide telephone network, including telephones overseas and on other ships and aircraft. In effect, these coast stations extend the talking range of ship telephones almost without limit.

Description of Public Coast Stations

Three categories of Public Coast Stations operate in different frequency bands to provide for telephone service over a wide range of situations. The following brief descriptions of these services are of interest in selecting a service appropriate for your requirements. This information is followed by some suggestions for operating ship stations on public correspondence channels.

VHF-FM Service

VHF-FM service offers reliable operation with good transmission quality over relatively short distances up to 20-50 miles, using channels in the 157-162 MHz range. Channels 24, 25, 26, 27, 28, 84, 85, 86 and 87 are available for assignment to public coast stations in the United States. Channels 26 and 28 are used in more areas than any others. To obtain information on VHF-FM ship-to-shore telephone coverage in your area, call your local Marine Operator, according to instructions in your telephone directory.

In addition, in some localities not yet served by VHF-FM coast stations, ships are permitted to make telephone calls through local VHF-FM base stations operating in the land mobile radio telephone service. In these instances, a different license authorization as well as different transmitting equipment is required.

Medium Frequency Service

The Medium Frequency Service operates over considerably greater distance ranges than VHF-FM, but ranges vary widely with time of day and a variety of other circumstances. Distances in excess of 1,000 miles are possible at certain times, but may be limited to less than 100 miles at other times.

Medium Frequency Coast Stations operate on frequencies in the 2 MHz band along the sea coasts and Gulf of Mexico. Stations serving the Great Lakes and the Mississippi River valley also operate on frequencies in the high-frequency bands.

High Frequency

A High Seas Service using high frequencies provides long-range radiotelephone communications with suitably equipped vessels throughout the world. Service is provided via four coast stations within the United States coastal areas plus one station in the state of Hawaii. These stations operate on various radio channels in the 4 through 23 MHz bands and are equipped for single sideband operation.

Registration With Your Public Coast Station

It is important for the vessel owner who plans on using the public radiotelephone service to register with the telephone company in the location where you wish to be billed.

This registration provides all coast stations with the name and address to be used in billing for ship-originated calls. Public coast stations are supported by charges made in accordance with tariffs filed with regulatory authorities. If a ship is not registered, billing information must be passed to the coast station operator each time a call is made, with consequent expenditure of time and effort. Registration may also serve to establish the procedures under which a coast station will call the ship in completing land-originated calls. Should you encounter any problems, contact your local telephone company business office and request assistance in registering your vessel.

Making Ship-To-Shore Calls

Use the VHF-FM Service (up to 20 to 40 miles) in preference to the Medium Frequency or High Frequency Services, if within range.

1. Select the public correspondence channel assigned to the desired shore station. Do not call on Channel 16 or on 2182 kHz except in an emergency.

2. Listen to determine if the working channel of the desired coast station is busy. A busy condition is evidenced by hearing speech, signalling tones, or a busy signal.

3. If the channel is busy, wait until it clears or switch to an alternate channel if available.

4. If the channel is not busy, press the push-to-talk button and say: (Name of the coast station) — THIS IS — (your call sign once). Do not call for more than a few seconds.

5. Listen for a reply. If none is received, repeat call after an interval of two minutes.

When the coast station operator answers, say:

THIS IS — Name of vessel, call sign, and ship's telephone or billing number (if assigned), CALLING (city, telephone number desired).

If your vessel is not registered or if the coast station operator does not have the listing, the operator will ask for additional information for billing purposes. At completion of call say:

Name of vessel — Call sign — OUT.

Receiving Shore-to-Ship Calls

Obviously, to receive public coast station calls, a receiver must be in operation on the proper channel. When calling on VHF-FM frequencies, coast stations will call on Channel 16 unless you have selective signalling, in which case the shore station will dial your number on a working channel. When calling on SSB medium frequencies, the preferred channel is the working channel of the coast station. Bell System coast stations operating on channels in the 2 MHz band routinely call on a working channel, but will call on 2182 kHz when requested to do so by the calling party. If you are expecting calls on medium frequencies and are not planning to monitor the working channel, you should tell prospective calling parties to so advise the Marine Operator. Note: A guard must be maintained on the distress, safety and calling channel; therefore a second channel receiver capability is essential if a guard is to be maintained on a coast station working channel.

Selective signalling, of course, requires a second receiver, since monitoring of the working channel would be essential. It is illegal to send dial pulses over Channel 16 or 2182 kHz.

Making Ship-to-Ship Calls Through a Coast Station

Although contacts between ships are normally made directly, ship-to-ship calls can be made by going through your coast station, using the same procedure as you do for the ship-to-shore calls.

How to Place a Shore-to-Ship Call

The basic procedure that the telephone subscriber should follow in placing a telephone call to a ship station from his home or office is found in the first few pages of most Telephone Directories. These instructions generally consist of dialing "0" (Zero) for the Operator, and asking for the "Marine Operator."

It is further necessary to know the name of the vessel being called (not the owner's name) and the approximate location so that the Marine Operator may judge which coast station to place the call through.

More specific information about the vessel is often useful. For instance, the channel generally monitored for receiving calls, a selective signalling number (if applicable), and the coast station through which calls can generally be received.

Remember that the ship station generally operates using push-to-talk techniques, so that it is impossible for you to break in while the ship station is being received.

Limited Coast Stations

The term *limited coast stations* includes coast stations which are there to serve the operational and business needs of vessels, but are not open to public correspondence. Many, such as those operated by a harbor master coordinating the movement of vessels within a confined area, or a station at a highway bridge, serve a safety function as well. Shore stations operated by the United States Coast Guard provide a safety communications service rather than business or operational. They are classified as Government stations rather than as limited coast stations although they also are not open to public correspondence.

While limited coast stations are not new to the Marine Service, most small vessel operators are finding this service available for the first time on VHF-FM. Thus, tug companies may have a limited coast station for the purpose of dispatching their own tugs. A fleet of fishing vessels may be directed from a limited coast station operated by a fish cannery.

Yacht clubs having docking facilities, marina operators, ship chandlers, boatels, harbor masters, dock-side restaurants, marine police, and marine radio service shops are among those who maintain and operate limited coast stations as a part of their regular operations. No charge is made for the communications service, which is incidental to their business.

How to Use the Services of Limited Coast Stations

Vessels should call limited coast stations on the limited coast station's working channel. All limited coast stations have Channel 16 plus one or more working channels. Limited coast stations, on the other hand, will call boats on Channel 16; therefore you do not need to monitor his working channel even if you are expecting a call.

As a general rule, limited coast stations operate only during their normal working hours. The calling procedure to use is the same as you would use to call another vessel except that you should initiate the call on the coast station's working channel. Be sure to give them plenty of time to answer your call as operating the radio is secondary to the operator's normal tasks. Many of these stations monitor Channel 16 as well as their working channels. If you don't know their assigned working channel, or if they don't appear to be watching their working channel, call on Channel 16.

CHAPTER 13

Locks and Dams

River Boating

Some of the finest boating this country offers can be found on the inland waterways of interconnected rivers and lakes. Throughout the United States there are nearly 30,000 miles of inland waterways. The Mississippi River system alone covers more than 12,000 miles. Rivers as a rule seldom offer large open expanses, but they do require unique piloting skills. On the river local knowledge often outweighs many of the fundamental piloting skills. Changing conditions on the rivers put a premium on local knowledge and raise river navigation to an art. Piloting the riverways can be both exciting and interesting. Although the rivers hold no dark secrets, they do have peculiarities which are unique and offer new challenges to the coastal and lake boater.

13-1   River Roads

While the coastal boater keeps close watch on the tides and water depth, the river boater watches overhead clearance, buoys, channels, dikes, wing-dams, and low water dams in back channels. Except for flooding conditions which occur following a heavy rain, the only fluctuation in river level is seasonal. In some of the navigable streams, sudden rains may raise the level several feet in a very few hours.

In the spring, freshets flood down from the headwaters carrying much debris in the strong currents resulting in dangerous conditions. Boaters should use extreme caution, especially in the upper reaches of the river and during periods of reduced visibility. Although dams can hold slight rises in water levels, extreme high water levels must be released from upper pools. At St. Louis, the fluctuation in river level from flood conditions in the early spring to normal levels in the late summer and fall may be from 35 to 40 feet.

Silt and flocculation are responsible for many river problems. Flocculation is a jellied mass of muck which is deposited on the river bed to a depth of several feet. Larger craft can plow through it without much problem and smaller craft are not seriously affected by it. However both silt and flocculation have clogged water strainers and have worn out strut bearings and shafts. Currents, especially during the spring, stir up this silt and additional silt is washed into the river from the banks. It is then carried in suspension by the current until deposited, building up a sand bar or mud bank. This occurs on the inside of bends or where the current is slowed, as at a river mouth or at an entrance to a wide lake or bay.

Indeed, currents are the greatest concern to the river boater. And, until he becomes acquainted with them, they can be both surprising and frustrating. Surface currents, for instance, which affect small craft may run opposite those which pull at large, deep keeled craft. Currents can also change at the junction of rivers, at bends, or where a river widens or narrows. Currents also differ at different points between banks. The friction between water and the river bed tends to slow the current velocity. Hence, you can expect a faster current in the channel, which usually tends toward the outside of bends. A boater who runs downstream in the faster current and upstream in the slower current at the edge of channels can expect to save both time and fuel by letting the current work for him and not fighting it. A boater proceeding upstream along the edge of a channel should be extra cautious and observe his wake closely. A wake will become sharply peaked or broken as it enters shallow water or contacts an under water obstruction, such as a "wing dam". After some experience, the boater will be able to read the surface and get a fair estimate of the conditions below.

Commercial Tows

Most of the inland waterways handle a great deal of commercial traffic. Recreational boaters should give commercial tows a wide berth. It is wise to give such traffic as wide a berth as safety, with respect to channel widths, permits.

Large barges lashed together in one enormous tow may cover many acres. The pleasure boater should appreciate the problems of handling such enormous floats and never jeopardize their activities, regardless of any considerations of right of way. Integrated tows generally are made up of a bowpiece, a group of square ended barges, and a towboat at the stern lashed together in one unit. These tows can be 1,000 feet or more in length. In a narrow channel a big tow or tanker requires the better part of the channel.

As a commercial tow approaches, you will see a sizeable bow wave built up, running almost the level of her, and the water drawn away by suction to lower the water level at both sides. The wake put out by a commercial tow creates a powerful turbulence extending several hundreds of feet astern of the tow.

Particularly, stay away from the front of tows underway. If you were to stall in such a spot, it may be impossible for the tow to stop or steer clear.

With the weight a commercial tow carries, it may travel half a mile or more before it can come to a full stop. In addition, there is a "blind spot" ahead of the tow that extends for a considerable distance. A good rule of thumb to use is to always keep the pilot house in view.

The swinging effect of a tow must be taken into account at bends in the channel, so it is generally wise to pass on the inside of the bends. Most of the "towing" is accomplished by pushing scows and barges ahead of the tug. This will keep the tow under better control as a single unit. Tugs with tows astern present a real problem to approaching small craft, due to additional swinging.

Special caution is required when running lighted on the rivers at night. At night, to an observer in a small boat, the towboat's lights may be more conspicious than those on the tow far out ahead. Lights on the shore add to the difficulty because of the reflections on the water. When the tows are using powerful searchlights their blinding beams make it impossible to see anything at all.

A TOWBOAT OPERATOR'S VISION IS BLOCKED AHEAD FOR SEVERAL HUNDRED FEET...STAY CLEAR

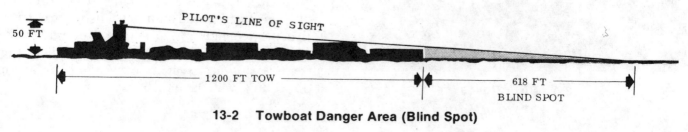

13-2 Towboat Danger Area (Blind Spot)

13-2

13-3 **View from Towboat Pilothouse**

Locks and Dams

Before the development of our present-day system of locks and dams, some rivers were not much more than rapids, with rushing water and many dangerous obstacles. When dams were built at carefully planned locations along the rivers the water filled behind them, creating a series of pools. Since rivers flow "down hill", each downstream pool was somewhat lower in elevation than the preceding one. These dams, of themselves, could have effectively controlled the river but would just as effectively have blocked all river navigation. Consequently, a system of locks was devised to allow vessels to pass from one pool to another. The term "pool stage" indicates the height of water in a pool with reference to the datum *for that pool.* Pool stages are posted on bulletin boards along the river so as to be easily read from a passing vessel. Locations of the bulletin boards and the normal pool gauges are given on the river charts. A normal pool reading on the gauge indicates a minimum channel depth of 9 feet will be available through the area.

The locks and dams were constructed to provide a navigable channel for river traffic. The impounded water in the pool above the dams is released as necessary to maintain a navigable channel of sufficient depth to insure uninterrupted movement of river traffic during the navigation season. These locks and dams present a safety problem equally shared by the owners of small boats, the commercial barge lines, the Coast Guard and the U.S. Army

Corps of Engineers whose function it is to build, maintain and operate them. A knowledge of these locks and dams, their types and locations, how to approach, enter and leave them, and a realization of the hazards that are incident to their navigation is essential if the boatman is to use them with confidence and safety.

Construction and Operation of Dams

The average individual's conception of a dam is a solid wall of concrete or earth extending from bank to bank across a stream, with a spillway or overflow section to permit excess impounded waters to escape downstream. The navigation dams on the Mississippi, Illinois and Ohio rivers are quite different. On the Mississippi two types of gates are in common use, the Tainter gate and the Roller gate. Refer to the sketch showing a cross section of a typical dam tainter gate. You can see by the locations of the arrows the manner in which strong currents are created as the water passes through the gates of a dam. Should a boat get too close to the lower or down-stream side of a dam it would be drawn into the dam by the powerful surface current, which actually flows in an upstream direction, and smashed to bits against the steel gate.

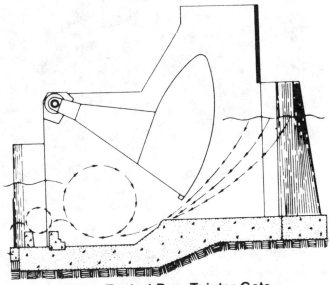

13-4 **Typical Dam Tainter Gate**

On the upper side of a dam of this type there is a strong suction created by the rush of water underneath. A boat drifting into the dam on the upper side would be in no danger of being drawn under the gate if its occupants would sit still and not become panicky and try to climb out on the gate or jump into the water. The latter course would mean almost certain death. If the occupants would keep calm and make an effort to cushion the impact of hitting the dam by fending off the boat with a pike pole, boathook or fender, or all three if available, then "sit tight" until help arrives, their chances of survival are fairly good. If this situation should ever happen to you, the thing to remember is to do everything possible to keep the boat afloat, and stay with it as long as possible.

Dams are sometimes controlled remotely. In Illustration 13-5 an operator presses a button (insert). Sixty miles away at Markland Dam the tainter gates rise, sending tons of turbulent water down stream. The boater should be constantly aware of the possibility of such remote control and stay clear of danger areas at all times.

13-5   Tainter Gate Dam

Although tainter gates can be lowered so as to permit water to flow over them, they are normally operated in the partially open position so that the water flows underneath. This is done to permit the mud and silt to pass the dam with the water, thereby precluding the possibility of the river filling up with mud and blocking navigation. The logic in this type of construction can easily be understood by anyone who is familiar with the muddy Mississippi and Missouri rivers.

Another type of dam, the Chanoine Wicket Navigable Pass Dam, is found on the Illinois, Ohio, and Ouachita rivers. It consists of a series of framed timber wickets individually supported so that each wicket can be raised and lowered separately. The wickets are made of oak, reinforced by steel and have a rubber seal attached to the downstream lower edge. They are 3'9" wide and spaced 4'0" on centers with a three inch space between wickets.

13-6   Raising a Typical Wicket

During times of low flow these spaces are filled with 5″ x 5″ wooden timbers, called needles. At a point slightly below center, the wicket is hinge connected to a structural and forged steel frame called a horse, and a forged steel strut called a prop. The horse in turn is pivot connected to the concrete foundation of the dam through a series of steel castings called horse boxes. The lower end of the prop rests in an iron casting called a hurter, embedded in the concrete foundation of the dam. In the raised position, the lower end of the wicket rests against a steel sill casting bolted to the foundation of the dam, and the lower end of the prop is seated in an offset or "seat" in the hurter. The foundation of the dam is supported on steel and wood piling.

A wicket is lowered by pulling it forward using a small derrickboat. The attached prop is guided in its forward movement by a warped surface on the side face of the hurter. This surface guides the lower end of the prop into a groove which by-passes the hurter seat. The wicket is then released, the prop slides freely back in the groove and the wicket falls flat on the sill. As the prop slides freely back in this groove an additional warped surface on that face of the hurter guides it back into an additional groove directly behind the hurter seat. In raising the wicket, the prop follows forward again as the wicket is raised, drops over the seat, and again rests against it as the lower end of the wicket is released and bears against the sill.

When a dam is being raised or lowered all passing craft must use the lock until signaled that the pass is clear. Vessels desiring to wait to use the pass must remain outside the lock area.

When dams are up all vessels in the upper pools not intending to enter the lock are forbidden to approach nearer to the dams than a line extending across the river from the head of the upper guide wall unless authorized to do so by the lockmaster.

On locks at all fixed dams, and at all movable dams *when the dams are up so that there is no navigable pass through the dam,* the following navigation lights will be displayed during hours of darkness:

(1) Three green lights visible through an arc of 360 degrees arranged in a vertical line on the upstream end of the river (guard) wall unless the intermediate wall extends farther upstream. In the later case, the lights will be placed on the upstream end of the intermediate wall.

(2) Two green lights visible through an arc of 360 degrees arranged in a vertical line on the downstream end of the river (guard) wall unless the intermediate wall extends farther downstream. In the later case, the lights will be placed on the downstream end of the intermediate wall.

(3) A single red light visible through an arc of 360 degrees on each end (upstream and downstream) of the land (guide) wall.

If one or more beartraps or weirs are open or partially open, which may cause a "set" in current conditions at the upper approach to the locks, this fact will be indicated by displaying a circular disc five feet in diameter, on or near the light support on the upstream end of the land guide wall during hours of daylight, and will be indicated during hours of darkness by displaying a white light vertically under and five feet below the red light on the upstream end of the land (guide) wall.

At *movable* dams when the dam has been lowered or partly lowered so that there is an *unobstructed navigable pass through the dam* the navigation lights indicated below will be displayed during hours of darkness until lock walls and weir piers are awash.

(1) Three red lights visible through an arc of 360 degrees arranged in a vertical line on the upstream end of the river (guard) wall.

(2) Two red lights visible through an arc of 360 degrees arranged in a vertical line on the downstream end of the river (guard) wall.

(3) A single red light visible through an arc of 360 degrees on each end (upstream and downstream) of the land (guide) wall.

S tay clear of danger zones - 600 feet above and 100 feet below dams.

A pproach dams, at reduced speed, along the shore at the lock.

F or a safe cruise obtain navigation charts from the U.S. Corps of Engineers.

E very boat should carry approved PFD's and a good anchor and line.

T ake precautions to know your position with reference to each lock and dam.

Y ou endanger your life, as well as that of others, when you disregard safety.

Be "Dam" Conscious

During the filling process, it is dangerous to approach near the intake ports in the lock walls above the upstream lock gates because of the powerful suction created by the water as it rushes into the culverts. Small boats must stay clear of the locks until signaled to enter.

During the emptying process a strong under-current and suction is created in the lock chamber, adjacent to the lock walls, due to the water rushing into the filling and emptying ports at the bottom of the lock. Occupants of small boats should take care that they do not fall overboard in the lock, for it is very doubtful if anyone could survive a rushing trip through the lock culvert to the river below.

The wearing of a personal flotation device would be no guarantee of safety under these circumstances.

Operation of Locks

While locks come in all shapes and sizes, they all operate on the same principle, that water tends to seek its own level. Basically, a lock is an enclosure with accomodations at both ends (generally called gates) to allow vessels to enter and exit the lock. By a system of culverts and valves, the water level in the lock can be made to align with the pool level of the upstream or downstream side of the lock.

The accompanying sketches show a general plan of a typical lock and the vital parts of the filling and emptying system. These culverts are 10 feet to 12 feet in diameter, with the sections near the valves being square or rectangular in shape.

When the upstream valves are opened and the downstream valves and all miter gates are closed, water will flow from the upper pool through the culverts into the lock chamber filling it to the level of the upper pool. The lock chamber may be emptied to the lower level by opening the downstream valves while keeping the upstream valves and all miter gates closed. The miter gates are operated only when the water level on either side is at the same elevation.

The actual time required to fill or empty the lock depends upon the difference between the upper and lower pool. Under normal river conditions, the lock can be filled or emptied in 7 to 10 minutes.

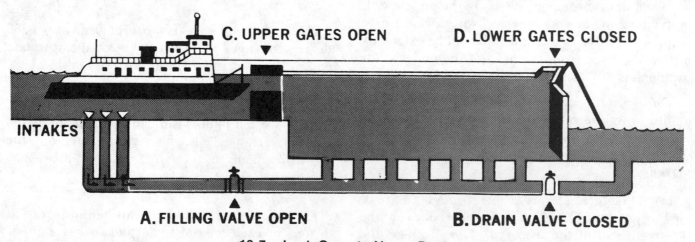

13-7   Lock Open to Upper Pool

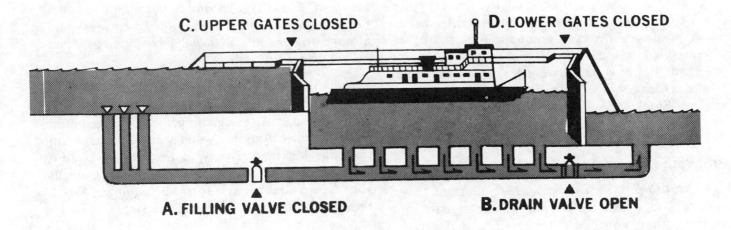

C. UPPER GATES CLOSED **D. LOWER GATES CLOSED**

A. FILLING VALVE CLOSED **B. DRAIN VALVE OPEN**

13-8　　Water Level Lowering

A vessel traveling downstream will enter the lock when the water is at the upper pool level.

The upstream gates are then closed and the water in the lock is allowed to escape through valves and culverts. When the water level in the lock is the same as that of the lower pool, the water will cease to flow out of the lock.

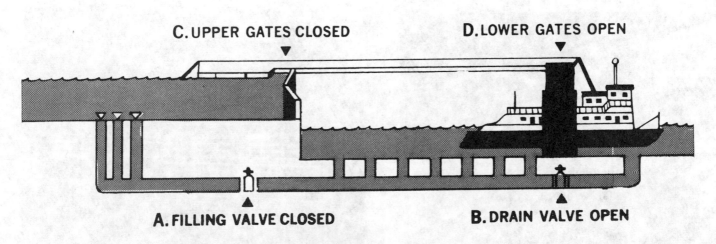

C. UPPER GATES CLOSED **D. LOWER GATES OPEN**

A. FILLING VALVE CLOSED **B. DRAIN VALVE OPEN**

13-9　　Lock Open to Lower Pool

The downstream gates are then opened and the vessel leaves the lock to continue on its downstream voyage.

A vessel traveling upstream may then enter the lock. After the vessel is secured in the lock the downstream gates are closed and the water from the upper pool is allowed to enter the lock until the water level in the lock is the same as that of the upper pool. The upper stream gates are then opened and the vessel leaves the lock to continue its upstream voyage. Single vessels are sometimes locked, but more often many vessels of varying sizes are raised or lowered in a single lockage.

Procedure for Lockage

As you approach a lock, local regulations may require you to sound certain whistle signals indicating that you wish to be locked though. Regulations may prohibit you from approaching closer than several hundred feet from the lock while waiting. Additionally, you may be required to maintain your position close to the bank to allow exiting vessels to use the center of the channel as they come out of the lock.

Since the signals used on locks may be lights, whistles, or other devices, we will attempt to briefly describe them. If you normally cruise on a certain section of a particular waterway, you should obtain a copy of the local regulations in force in your waters. Your course instructor will tell you which set

of regulations apply and where you will be able to get them. These regulations contain, among other things, signals displayed and utilized by locks and also the proper signals you will be required to sound on your boat's whistle.

At locks where "small craft signals" are installed, the boat operator may signal the lockman that he desires passage. After signaling, the operator should stand clear with his boat and wait for instruction from the lockman. Many of the locks are radio equipped and can be signaled via radio. Consult your navigational charts for radio equipped locks, the operational frequency and call sign.

Let us assume that you are coming downstream in a boat and desire to pass through a single lock, or landward lock, in case of double locks. When the boat arrives within one-half mile of the lock, you give the proper signal for lockage. The signals vary from one area to another; your course instructor will tell you what signals are used in your area. Do not approach closer than 400 to 600 feet of the upper extremity from the lock wall until you see that the lock gates are open and the lockman signals you to enter. The signal will be from an air horn, or traffic signals, or both. One long blast of the air horn means "Enter landward lock", two long blasts

13-10   Dam and Lock Details

13-11   Typical Lock Wall

means "Enter the riverward lock". The traffic signal lights look like automobile traffic lights. A flashing red light means, "Stand Clear Do Not Enter". A flashing amber means, "Approach Lock But Under Full Control". A flashing green means, "Enter Lock".

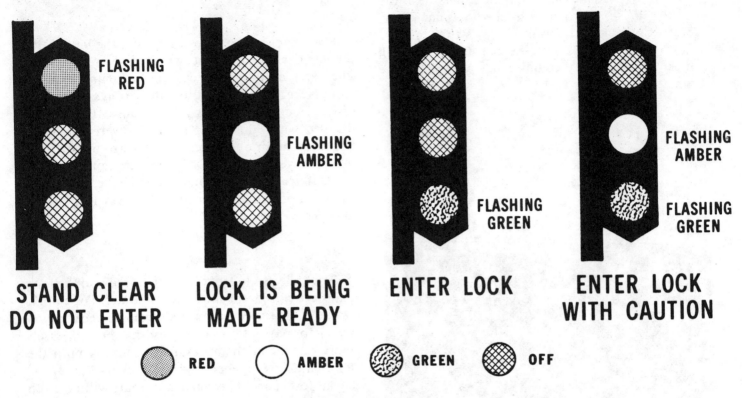

13-12   Traffic Signal Lights

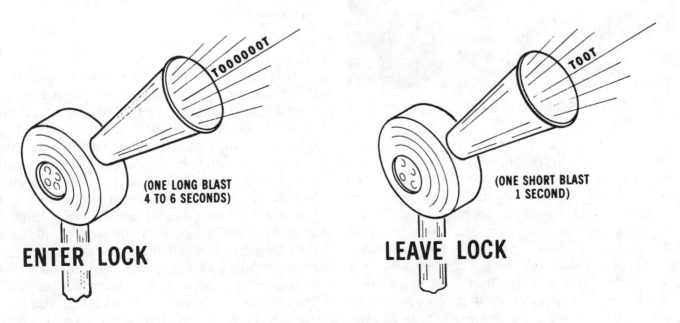

13-13   Air Horn Signals

After receiving the signal to enter, proceed into the lock. Once inside the lock chamber the boat should proceed to the vicinity of the lockman on the lock wall and be prepared to pass or receive a mooring line. In some areas mooring lines are provided by the lockman and in other areas the mooring lines are provided by the boatman. These mooring lines should be sufficiently strong to serve as a bow line. They should be at least 50 feet long (longer if locking through some locks on the Tennessee Lakes system).

13-14   Securing to a Fixed Bollard

They must reach from the top of the lock wall and have sufficient line to make fast to a ring or bitt on deck. The end of the line that is passed to the lockman should have a 12-inch eye-splice for dropping over the checkpost, the operator should always wear USCG approved personal flotation devices. Mooring lines should not be tied to the boat. They must be carefully tended at all times. Extra care must be exercised during a downbound lockage that the mooring lines are not fouled when the water level in the lock is being lowered. A fouled line may result in a boat hanging up on the line and could cause serious damage or even capsize the boat. Be prepared to cast off lines in an emergency. Use plenty of fenders to protect the hull from damage from rough or dirty lock walls.

Some locks have mooring pins in the lock walls. Others have floating bitts which raise or lower with the water level. In either case the lockman will direct you. Never moor a boat to ladder rungs embedded in the lock walls. This might cause the boat to capsize when the water level is lowered. Do not stand up in an open boat or walk around on deck without wearing a PFD. Vessels are not permitted to drift around within the lock while the water level is being raised or lowered. All vessels must be moored.

After all vessels are securely moored and the lock gates are closed, the lock is allowed to fill or empty. While being raised or lowered it will be necessary to take in or pay out line as the case may be. All vessels must remain in their assigned positions until the lock gates are opened and the lockman gives the signal to depart. The signal to depart will be given from the air horn, one short blast means, "Leave landward lock", two short blasts means, "Leave riverward lock".

After the signal is given, boats shall depart from the lock in the same order as they entered, except when directed otherwise by the lockman. In the case of a small pleasure boat making a lockage simultaneously with a commercial tow, the small boat will usually be directed verbally to depart ahead of the tow. This is done as a precaution against accident or damage to the more fragile pleasure boat and can be accomplished without delay if properly executed. In no event should small craft attempt to depart from the lock before lock gates are fully recessed, as the wake can do serious damage to the gates. As the small boat leaves the lock, he should head for the channel, keeping a sharp lookout for craft approaching from the other direction.

Certain priorities have been established by the Secretary of the Army (under authority of Section 7 of the River and Harbor Act of August 8, 1917) for safe and efficient passage of various types of craft which use the inland waterways. The priorities thus established are as follows:

1st - U. S. Military Craft
2nd - Vessels Carrying U.S. Mail
3rd - Commercial Passenger Craft
4th - Commercial Tows
5th - Commercial Fishermen
6th - Pleasure Boats

Under certain conditions small craft (pleasure boats) may be locked through with other craft having a higher priority, but only when no delay is occasioned thereby and the safety of either craft is not jeopardized.

The lockmen have been given the same authority over your boat in the lock as traffic policemen have over your car at intersections. For your safety you must obey their instructions.

Every boat should have aboard a copy of the regulations governing navigation on the rivers in their area. Small boat operators should study and refer to these "Regulations" whenever in doubt as to the proper procedure in making a lockage. Your course instructor has prepared handouts for this purpose and you should study them closely.

It's only natural to have feelings of apprehension, but if you will put to practice what you have learned in this lesson, you will have unlimited pleasure in river boating. Have a safe and pleasant journey.

Index

AIDS TO NAVIGATION ON NAVIGABLE WATERS
except Western Rivers and Intracoastal Waterway

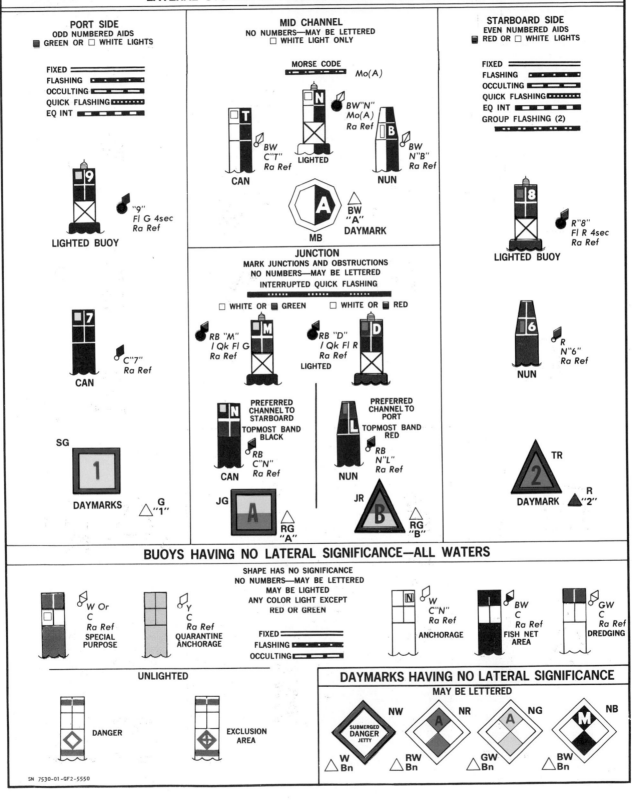

SN 7530-01-GF2-5550

AIDS TO NAVIGATION ON THE INTRACOASTAL WATERWAY

AS SEEN ENTERING FROM NORTH AND EAST—PROCEEDING TO SOUTH AND WEST

PORT SIDE
ODD NUMBERED AIDS
■ GREEN OR □ WHITE LIGHTS

FIXED ══════ OCCULTING ▭▬▭▬▭
FLASHING ▬▭▬▭ QUICK FLASHING ▪▪▪▪▪▪▪
EQ INT ▬▭▬▭▬

"3"
Fl G 4sec
Ra Ref
LIGHTED BUOY

"9"
C"9"
Ra Ref
CAN

SG-I
1
△G "1"
DAYMARKS

JUNCTION
MARK JUNCTIONS AND OBSTRUCTIONS
NO NUMBERS—MAY BE LETTERED
INTERRUPTED QUICK FLASHING
▪▪▪▪▪▪ ▪▪▪▪▪▪ ▪▪▪▪▪▪

□ WHITE OR ■ GREEN LIGHTS   □ WHITE OR ■ RED LIGHTS

RB "J"   RB "N"
J I Qk Fl G   N I Qk Fl R
Ra Ref   Ra Ref

PREFERRED CHANNEL
TO STARBOARD   TO PORT
TOPMOST BAND   TOPMOST BAND
BLACK   RED

A   S
RB   RB
C"A"   N"S"
Ra Ref   Ra Ref
CAN   **NUN**

A   △RG "A"
B   △RG "B"
           JR-I

MID CHANNEL MORSE CODE NO NUMBERS—MAY BE LETTERED
▬▭▭▬▭ □ WHITE LIGHT ONLY

B   △BW "B"
MB-I   DAYMARK

T   N   B
C"T"   BW   BW
Ra Ref   Mo(A)   N"B"
           "N"   Ra Ref
           Ra Ref
CAN   LIGHTED   NUN

STARBOARD SIDE
EVEN NUMBERED AIDS
■ RED OR □ WHITE LIGHTS

FIXED ══════ OCCULTING ▭▬▭▬▭
FLASHING ▬▭▬▭ QUICK FLASHING ▪▪▪▪▪▪▪
EQ INT ▬▭▬▭▬
GROUP FLASHING (2) ▪▪▬▭▪▪▬▭

"8"
R"8"
Fl R 4sec
Ra Ref
LIGHTED BUOY

"6"
R
N"6"
Ra Ref
NUN

TR-I
2
△R "2"
DAYMARK

DUAL PURPOSE MARKING USED WHERE THE ICW AND OTHER WATERWAYS COINCIDE

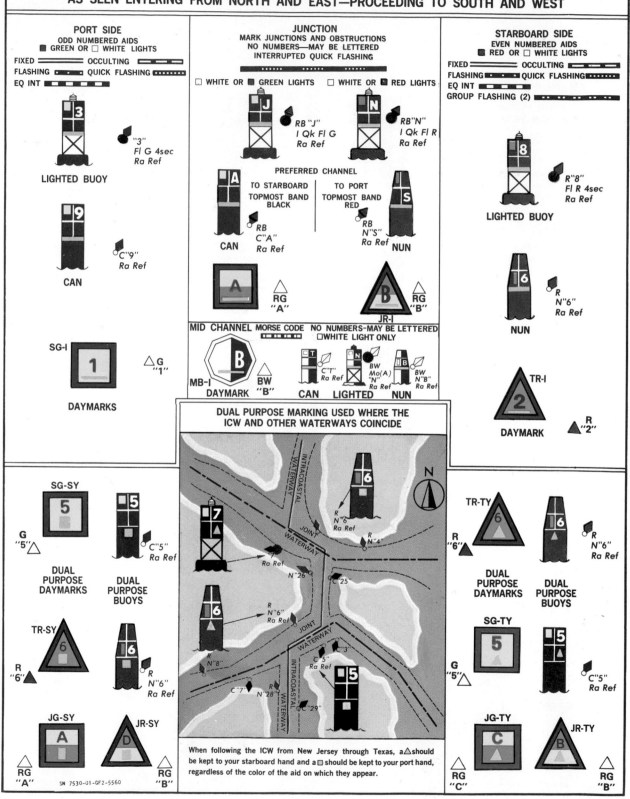

When following the ICW from New Jersey through Texas, a △ should be kept to your starboard hand and a ▣ should be kept to your port hand, regardless of the color of the aid on which they appear.

SG-SY
5
G "5" △
DUAL PURPOSE DAYMARKS

5
C"5"
Ra Ref
DUAL PURPOSE BUOYS

TR-SY
6
R "6" △

6
R
N"6"
Ra Ref

JG-SY
A
△RG "A"

JR-SY
D
△RG "B"

TR-TY
6
R "6" △
DUAL PURPOSE DAYMARKS

6
R
N"6"
Ra Ref
DUAL PURPOSE BUOYS

SG-TY
5
G "5" △

5
C"5"
Ra Ref

JG-TY
C
△RG "C"

JR-TY
B
△RG "B"

AIDS TO NAVIGATION ON WESTERN RIVERS

AS SEEN ENTERING FROM SEAWARD

PORT SIDE	JUNCTION	STARBOARD SIDE
■ GREEN OR □ WHITE LIGHTS FLASHING	MARK JUNCTIONS AND OBSTRUCTIONS INTERRUPTED QUICK FLASHING	■ RED OR □ WHITE LIGHTS GROUP FLASHING (2)

JUNCTION

PREFERRED CHANNEL TO STARBOARD — TOPMOST BAND BLACK

PREFERRED CHANNEL TO PORT — TOPMOST BAND RED

LIGHTED BUOY

□ WHITE OR ■ GREEN LIGHTS   □ WHITE OR ■ RED LIGHTS

LIGHTED

CAN   NUN

SG — PASSING DAYMARK

TR — PASSING DAYMARK

CAN   NUN

CG — CROSSING DAYMARK

CR — CROSSING DAYMARK

JG   JR

176.9 MILE BOARD

123.5 MILE BOARD

RANGE DAYMARKS AS FOUND ON

NAVIGABLE WATERS EXCEPT — ICW — MAY BE LETTERED

KWB	KWR	KRW	KRB	KBW	KBR	KGB	KBG	KGR	KRG

INTRACOASTAL WATERWAY — MAY BE LETTERED

KWB-I	KWR-I	KRW-I	KRB-I	KBW-I	KBR-I	KGB-I	KBG-I	KGR-I	KRG-I

SN 7530-01-GF2-5530

UNIFORM STATE WATERWAY MARKING SYSTEM

STATE WATERS AND DESIGNATED STATE WATERS FOR PRIVATE AIDS TO NAVIGATION

REGULATORY MARKERS

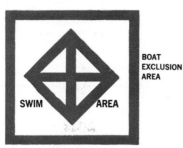

BOAT EXCLUSION AREA

SWIM AREA

EXPLANATION MAY BE PLACED OUTSIDE THE CROSSED DIAMOND SHAPE, SUCH AS DAM, RAPIDS, SWIM AREA, ETC.

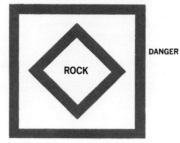

DANGER

ROCK

THE NATURE OF DANGER MAY BE INDICATED INSIDE THE DIAMOND SHAPE, SUCH AS ROCK, WRECK, SHOAL, DAM, ETC.

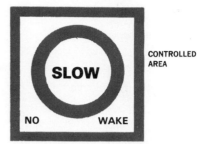

CONTROLLED AREA

SLOW
NO   WAKE

TYPE OF CONTROL IS INDICATED IN THE CIRCLE, SUCH AS SLOW, NO WAKE, ANCHORING, ETC.

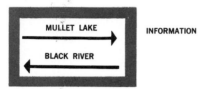

MULLET LAKE
BLACK RIVER

INFORMATION

FOR DISPLAYING INFORMATION SUCH AS DIRECTIONS, DISTANCES, LOCATIONS, ETC.

BUOY USED TO DISPLAY REGULATORY MARKERS

MAY SHOW WHITE LIGHT
MAY BE LETTERED

5 MPH

AIDS TO NAVIGATION

MAY SHOW WHITE REFLECTOR OR LIGHT

MOORING BUOY

WHITE WITH BLUE BAND

MAY SHOW WHITE REFLECTOR OR LIGHT

RED-STRIPED WHITE BUOY

MAY BE LETTERED
DO NOT PASS BETWEEN BUOY AND NEAREST SHORE

BLACK-TOPPED WHITE BUOY

MAY BE NUMBERED

PASS TO NORTH OR EAST OF BUOY

RED-TOPPED WHITE BUOY

PASS TO SOUTH OR WEST OF BUOY

CARDINAL SYSTEM

MAY SHOW GREEN REFLECTOR OR LIGHT   MAY SHOW RED REFLECTOR OR LIGHT

SOLID RED AND SOLID BLACK BUOYS

USUALLY FOUND IN PAIRS
PASS BETWEEN THESE BUOYS

3

PORT SIDE ———— LOOKING UPSTREAM ———— STARBOARD SIDE

4

LATERAL SYSTEM

SN 7530-01-GF2-5540